Alexander Mackenzie

History of the Chisholms

With genealogies of the principal families of the name

Alexander Mackenzie

History of the Chisholms
With genealogies of the principal families of the name

ISBN/EAN: 9783337322106

Printed in Europe, USA, Canada, Australia, Japan

Cover: Foto ©ninafisch / pixelio.de

More available books at **www.hansebooks.com**

OF THE

CHISHOLMS

WITH

GENEALOGIES OF THE PRINCIPAL
FAMILIES OF THE NAME,

BY

ALEXANDER MACKENZIE, F.S.A. Scot.,

AUTHOR OF "THE HISTORY AND GENEALOGIES OF THE CLAN MACKENZIE;" "THE
HISTORY OF THE MACDONALDS AND LORDS OF THE ISLES;" "THE HISTORY
OF THE CAMERONS;" "THE HISTORY OF THE MACLEODS;" THE HISTORY
OF THE MATHESONS;" "THE PROPHECIES OF THE BRAHAN
SEER;" "THE HISTORICAL TALES AND LEGENDS OF THE
HIGHLANDS "THE HISTORY OF THE HIGHLAND
CLEAI " "THE SOCIAL STATE OF
YE;" ETC., ETC.

INVERNESS: A. & W. MACKENZIE.

MDCCCXCI.

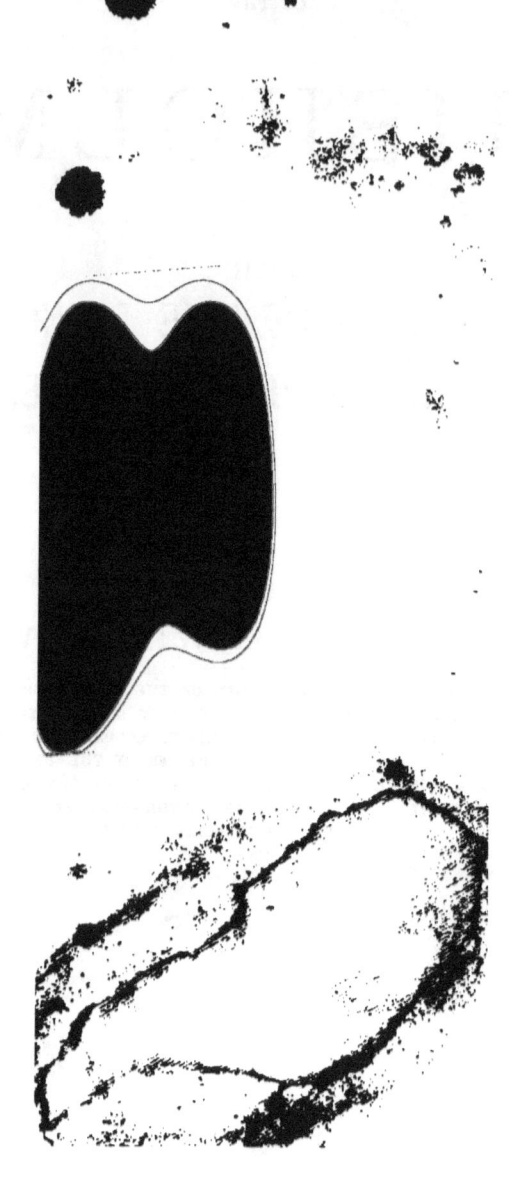

INSCRIBED

TO

THE MEMORY

OF

MARY CHISHOLM OF CHISHOLM

(AFTERWARDS MRS. JAMES GOODEN, LONDON),

A noble-souled woman, whose warm-hearted and patriotic
conduct towards her father's and, subsequently, her
mother's tenants in Strathglass, under the most
trying circumstances, first attracted the
author's attention to her clan, and
without whose inspiration this
book would never have
been written.

PREFACE.

——:o:——

THE HISTORY OF THE CHISHOLMS, as given in this volume, is not an ambitious work. The materials are not extensive, and those available are not of an important or stirring character.

I claim to have disposed of the absurd and groundless contention, so long maintained by the Northern clan, that they sprang originally from the Earls of Caithness and Orkney, and to have established, on the contrary, that they first came to the Highlands from the Scottish Borders, and that all the families of the name, north and south, can trace their descent to one common ancestor, heard of for the first time in Scotland in the county of Roxburgh towards the end of the thirteenth century.

I am indebted to various friends for assistance, but above all others to Mr. Colin Chisholm, Namur Cottage, Inverness, whose interesting *Traditions of Strathglass* and genealogical storehouse I have freely and profitably drawn upon.

A. M.

INVERNESS,
CHRISTMAS DAY, 1890.

CONTENTS.

——:o:——

LIST OF SUBSCRIBERS.

——:o:——

Aitken, Dr., District Asylum, Inverness.

Balderston, W. H., Esq., Inverness.
Batten, Major J. Chisholm, Sheffield.
Biscoe, T. R., Esq. of Newton.
Bisset, Duncan J., Esq., Boston, U.S.A.
Blair, Sheriff, Inverness.
Brown, William, Esq., Edinburgh (2 Copies and 1 Large Paper).
Buccleuch, His Grace the Duke of (Large Paper).
Bunsen, Von, Madame Charles, Germany (Large Paper).
Burgess, Peter, Esq., banker, Glenurquhart.
Burns, William, Esq., solicitor, Inverness.
Byrne, Mrs. W. Pitt, London (Large Paper).

Cameron, Donald, Esq., Moniack Castle.
Cameron, D. M., Esq., merchant, Inverness.
Cameron, John, Esq., Inverness.
Cameron, J. A., Esq., M.D., Edinburgh.
Campbell, J. L. Esq., Broughty Ferry.
Chisholm, Alex., Esq., Glasgow (Large Paper).
Chisholm, Alexander, Esq., The Castle, Inverness.
Chisholm, Alexander A., Esq., Marydale, Nova Scotia.
Chisholm, A., Esq., Liverpool (Large Paper).
Chisholm, Allan, Esq., Mid Crochail, Strathglass.
Chisholm, Æneas, Esq., Invercannich.
Chisholm, Archibald A., Esq., Lochmaddy.
Chisholm, Archibald M., Esq., Ely, Minn, U.S.A.
Chisholm, Captain Macra, Glassburn, Strathglass.

Chisholm, Chisholm Gooden, Esq., Assiniboia, Canada (Large Paper).

Chisholm, Christoper, Esq., San Rafael, California.

Chisholm, Christopher P., Esq., Antigonish, Nova Scotia.

Chisholm, Colin, Esq., Namur Cottage, Inverness (Large Paper).

Chisholm, Colin, Esq., London.

Chisholm, Colin, Esq., Holm Mills, Inverness.

Chisholm, Colin, Esq., Marydale, Nova Scotia.

Chisholm, Colin, Esq., Antigonish, Nova Scotia.

Chisholm, Colin, Esq., Glasgow.

Chisholm, Colin A., Esq., Denver, Colorado, U.S.A.

Chisholm, Colin R., Esq., Montreal, Canada.

Chisholm, Colonel W., Cheltenham (Large Paper).

Chisholm, David, Esq., Edinburgh.

Chisholm, D. H., Esq., Inverness (2 Copies).

Chisholm, Donald, Esq., Glasgow.

Chisholm, Donald, Esq., Greenhead, Glasgow.

Chisholm, Duncan, Esq., Inverness.

Chisholm, Duncan, Esq., Colorado, U.S.A.

Chisholm, Duncan D., Esq., St. Andrews, Nova Scotia.

Chisholm, Duncan G., Esq,, St. Andrews, Nova Scotia.

Chisholm, Emilie M., Miss, Namur Cottage, Inverness (Large Paper.)

Chisholm, Georgina M., Miss, Inverness.

Chisholm, Helena, Miss, Namur Cottage, Inverness.

Chisholm, Henry James, Esq., Liverpool (Large Paper).

Chisholm, James, Esq., M.A., Hamilton, Canada.

Chisholm, James, Esq., London (Large Paper).

Chisholm, John, Esq., Edinburgh (Large Paper).

Chisholm, John, Esq., Glasgow.

Chisholm, John, Esq., Glasgow.

Chisholm, John Keith, Esq., Edinburgh.

Chisholm, Joseph A., Esq., Halifax, Nova Scotia.

Chisholm, Rev. Alexander, Antigonish, Nova Scotia.

Chisholm, Rev. Angus, D.D., D' Escousse, Nova Scotia.

Chisholm, Rev. Archibald, Nairn.

Chisholm, Rev. Colin, Port Hood, Nova Scotia.

Chisholm, Rev. Donald, P.P., Nova Scotia.

Chisholm, Rev. Finlay, Little Glace Bay, Nova Scotia.

Chisholm, Rev. James, Barra.

Chisholm, Rev. John J., Heatherton, Nova Scotia (4 Copies).

Chisholm, Roderick, Esq., Antigonish, Nova Scotia.

Chisholm, Roderick Gooden, Esq., London (Large Paper).
Chisholm, Samuel, Esq., Glasgow,
Chisholm, The, (1 Copy and 1 Large Paper).
Chisholm, The Very Rev. Hugh Canon, Paisley.
Chisholm, Theodore, Esq., Inverness.
Chisholm, Walter, Esq., Hawick (Large Paper).
Chisholm, William, Esq., Muirtown (2 Copies and 1 Large Paper).
Chisholm, William, Esq., Inverlochy Castle.
Chisholm, William, Esq., Caledonian Bank, Inverness.
Chisholme, Mrs. Scott, Brighton (Large Paper).
Chisholme, The Misses Scott, Edinburgh.
Clark, D., Esq., *Courier* Office, Inverness.
Cook, James, Esq., merchant, Inverness.
Cran, John, Esq., Kirkton, Bunchrew.

Douglas & Foulis, Messrs, Edinburgh (4 Copies).
Duncan, Colonel P., Brighton (Large Paper).

Elliott, Andrew, Esq., Edinburgh (2 Copies).

Fergusson, Sir James, baronet, Kent (Large Paper).
Fraser, Alexander, Esq., solicitor, Inverness.
Fraser, Duncan, Esq., Ballifeary, Inverness.
Fraser, Ex-Provost, Inverness.
Fraser, Robert, Esq., Brackla.

Gray, Mrs. Dwyer, Dublin (2 Copies).

Hall, P. W., Esq., Lanarkshire.
Hilton, James, Esq., F.S.A., London (Large Paper).

Jenkins, Rev. Canon, Kent (Large Paper).
Jenkins, R. P., Esq., solicitor, Inverness.

Kegan Paul, French, Trübner & Co., Messrs., London.

Lambert, F., Esq., Junr., Surrey (Large Paper).
Lambert, Miss, London.

Macandrew, Sir H. C., Inverness.
Macbain, Alexander, Esq., M.A., Inverness.
Macdonald, Alexander, Esq., Stratherrick.
Macdonald, Alexander, Esq., Millerton.

Macdonald, Andrew, Esq., solicitor, Inverness.

Macdonald, Donald, Esq., Park, Nairn.

Macdonald, Ewen, Esq., Water Manager, Inverness.

Macdonald, Kenneth, Esq., Town Clerk, Inverness (Large Paper).

Macdonald, Lachlan, Esq. of Skeabost (1 Copy and 1 Large Paper).

Macgillivray, Alex., Esq., London.

Macgillivray, Angus, Esq., Barrister, Antigonish.

Mackay, John, Esq., C.E., J.P., Hereford (Large Paper).

Mackay, William, Esq., solicitor, Inverness.

Mackenzie, Donald, Esq., Fasnakyle.

Mackenzie, Dr. F. M., Inverness.

Mackenzie, Dr. M. T., Scolpeg, North Uist.

Mackenzie, H. Rose, Esq., solicitor, Inverness.

Mackenzie, John A., Esq., burgh surveyor, Inverness.

Mackenzie, Mrs. James H., Inverness (2 Copies).

Mackenzie, W. Dalziel, Esq. of Farr (Large Paper).

Mackenzie, William, Esq., Ardgowan, Inverness.

Mackenzie, William, Esq., Caberfeidh House, Inverness.

Mackintosh, Charles Fraser, Esq. of Drummond, M.P. (Large Paper).

Mackintosh, Duncan, Esq., Inverness.

Maclean, Major Roderick, Inverness.

Macleod, John, Esq., H.M.I. of Schools, Elgin.

Macnee, Dr., Inverness.

Macrae, Rev. Angus, South Uist.

Macritchie, Andrew J., Esq., solicitor, Inverness.

Malcolm, George, Esq., Invergarry.

Matheson, Dr. F., London.

Middleton, R. M., Esq., London (Large Paper).

Mitchell Library, The, Glasgow.

Munro, David, Bailie, Inverness.

Napier and Ettrick, Right Hon. Lord, K.T.

Noble, John, Esq., Inverness (2 Copies and 1 Large Paper).

North, C. N. Macintyre, Esq., London.

Ross, Alexander, Esq., Inverness.

Ross, James, Esq., solicitor, Inverness.

Ross, Provost, Inverness.

Skues, Brigade Surgeon William Mackenzie, London.

Stewart, James, Esq., Dalkeith House.
Stuart, John, Esq. of Kishorn (Large Paper).
Stuart, Mrs., of Dalness (Large Paper).
Sutherland, George Miller, Esq., Wick.

Thin, James, Esq., Edinburgh (3 Copies).
Thomson, James, Esq., Gas Manager, Inverness.
Trinder, Mrs. Arnold, Surrey (Large Paper).

Wilson, Mrs. A. Chisholm, Edinburgh.
Wyllie & Son, Messrs., Aberdeen.

THE HISTORY OF THE CHISHOLMS

—◆◇◆◇◆—

O R I G I N.

THERE has been much controversy between members of the Clan and among antiquarians regarding the origin of the Chisholms. Some have maintained that they were of native Celtic descent, and that the Strathglass Chisholms originally migrated from Caithness, though those who uphold this theory differ among themselves as to how they came to that county, and how the name first originated. Others have maintained, with greater reason and historical accuracy, that the progenitors of the northern Chisholms came from the south of Scotland, and are the direct representatives of the Roxburgh family, which can be traced without much difficulty, first to England, and thence back to a Norman source ; while the Caithness theory can be shown to be purely fabulous. The family can be traced back for more than six centuries and a half through an unbroken descent in Scotland, although the records of the northern families have hitherto been much clouded and confused by the fictitious origin and early annals which the native chroniclers have invented for them. These and the genealogists of the seventeenth century—following the example of the Earl of Cromarty in the case of the Mackenzies, and of the other inventors who, from similar unpatriotic motives, drew on their imaginations for a foreign ancestry for most of the Highland clans — fabricated an impossible Norwegian origin for the Chisholms, a family which will be proved to have possessed, for nearly six hundred years, extensive landed estates not only in Inverness-shire, but in the counties of Perth, Moray, Nairn, Ross, Sutherland and Caithness. What these lands were, how they were first procured, and in what manner the greater portion of them were finally lost, will be seen in the sequel. It will also be shown, from official documents preserved in the public records, from family charters and other deeds, that the theory of a Caithness origin is pure fable, and that the heads of the Strathglass family can be deduced without a break as the chiefs of all the Chisholms, north and south, from the first appearance of the name in the thirteenth century on the Scottish Borders to the present day.

Of the alleged Caithness origin no trace is found in any authentic document known to exist. Towards the end of the fourteenth century the Chisholms of Strath-glass certainly did become connected with, and acquired lands in both the counties of Sutherland and Caithness through marriage, and it is probably in that connection that the confusion about their northern origin afterwards arose. What that connection was will appear as the real history of the family proceeds, and the actual facts are brought into view. In the meantime, however, the Caith-ness fable must be given, so that the reader may judge of its character for himself. The best, and most ingeniously stated version, though the author himself expresses dis-satisfaction with it, is set forth in a manuscript by the late James Logan, author of the *Scottish Gael.* In the course of the narrative, which is printed in his own words, Logan quotes Sir Robert Gordon's *Earldom of Sutherland ;* but Sir Robert, as everyone who knows him admits, is no guide where he is not supported by others, and no independent contemporary authority makes any mention of Chisholm as a clan name in connection with the events described by him. Mr Logan's version is in the following terms :—

"The antiquity of the Clan Chisholm in the Highlands

of Scotland has been, by some late writers, very unaccountably disputed, to them the name appearing to justify a Norman descent, an origin of which many families are justly proud. In this case it seems to me a mere conjecture ; for those who hold that opinion cannot prove to us where the Chisholms first settled in Scotland, and the Roll of Battle Abbey, which contains the names of all who came over with the Conqueror does not exhibit any one under this appellation. In the history of Scotland and Orkney, Harald, the reputed founder of the Clan, is stated to have been a branch from the Royal stock of Norway, and certainly 'Gall-thaobh,' the appropriate name of Caithness, meaning the side or Country of the Strangers in contradistinction to 'Cat-thaobh,' the original appellation given to Sutherland, would favour a supposition that the Chisholms appearing there must have been of foreign extraction ; but can it be shown that Harald brought a clan or a sufficient following with him who bore the name when they arrived on those shores, assumed, or received it, on their arrival ? As the northern invaders who remained in the country necessarily incorporated themselves with the natives, adopting their names and manners, it is much more probable that the Scandinavian leader, by force or by fear—perhaps by means of both—obtained the lands and leadership of the people of the county, and became distinguished by their appellation as a surname.*

"In a question of this nature, etymology often affords valuable assistance, and its application effects the solution of many difficulties otherwise insurmountable. Its application here may not serve so usefully as could be desired ; the real derivation of the name eludes our researches ; the uncertainty respecting remote origins is great. The true appellation of the Thane of Caithness is not settled, for it is indifferently given as Harald and Guthred. The

---

* This idea assumes that "the people of the county"—of Caithness—were already known as Chisholms, a proposition for which no foundation whatever exists.

Chisholms of the north were never known in their verna-
cular tongue by any other designation than "An Siosalach,"
i.e., 'The Chisholm,' emphatically as the Chief. Siosalach
Straghlais (Chisholm of Strathglass) never being called
'Siosalach nan Siosalach' (Chisholm of Chisholm), which
is now the customary translation. This is not only incon-
sistent with the idiom of the Gaelic, but is, besides, improper,
there being no place called Chisholm in this country, *
and the name being unknown, whereas on the border of
the Kingdom there is a property so designated by a
Saxon word, imposed perhaps a thousand years ago by
the people whose language was altogether foreign to the
Highlanders, and has hardly yet approached the country
of the Chisholms.

"The Norman 'de' was at first applied to proper
names with exact propriety, for some individual, the founder
of a family, must have imparted a designation to his relatives
and followers. Personal appearances, or qualification, and
local position were the obvious reasons for individual
distinctions—in the latter case 'de' was the fitting article,
and in the former "le" was required. Chiefs who hold
no territorial possessions are now discriminated by the
use of the distinctive article 'the' and a repetition of their
names, as Mackinnon of Mackinnon, Macnab of Macnab,
etc., and a similar mode of address has also fallen into
use where its necessity does not exist, as Macleod of
Macleod, Mackintosh of Mackintosh, and others. This
is, however, a practice unknown among the proper Gael,
and arose from the Scottish manner of designating proprietors by their holdings, as Arnot of Arnot, Balmanno
of Balmanno, or *Scotice*, that Ilk, an easy and effective
mode of particularising individuals where so many are
found bearing the same name. When the Chiefs and

* The designation would, however, be quite correct so long as the
family remained the Chisholms of Chisholm in Roxburghshire, and is
so now of the representative of the family who owned that original possession of the Clan, but not of the Chisholms of the north, the proper
designation for them being undoubtedly the Chisholms of Strathglass.

'ceanntigh,' or gentlemen, employed 'Writers,' in Edinburgh and elsewhere to manage their affairs by process
of law, these persons, ignorant of Highland usage, adhered
to the same style and gave a sanction to the mistake.

" Chesholme is a Saxon word, descriptive of a locality,
and many such names are found in England, as Chese-
ham, Chesbury, Chesworth, Cheswick, Chesnut, Cheshurst,
and others. Chesholme, or Chisholme, then is unknown
in Gaelic, and is supposed to be the English translation of
Siosal (Cecil, Seisylt). Whence then did this name arise,
and what is its import ? Conjecture may be made where
the subject is so obscure, and an attempt permitted at a
solution without the confidence of having made a successful guess. The final syllable 'al' found in so many Gaelic
words signifies young, or progeny of any kind, and hence
a race or generation ; thus we have Con-all which, with
the plural termination 'ach,' makes the race of Con. If
the latter syllable is disposed of the prefix requires ex-
planation, and it is not certainly so apparent. ' Sios ' is
lower, beneath, or east, and may not the Chisholms have been
called Sios-al, the lower or eastern race, by their countrymen who occupied the higher or more westerly districts ?
If the etymology given to Argyle (Aira-Gael), which
makes it imply the Western Gael, be correct, we have a
notable example of such a method of local distinction.*

" A Gaelic etymology for the designation of a Gaelic
tribe, powerful at the earliest epoch of historical record,
is surely more reasonable than to adopt a Saxon or
Norman deduction. It is submitted that such a derivation is entitled to equal or better credit than many of
the fabulous origins assigned to families by monkish
chroniclers and the degenerate bards of later ages. It
must at least appear from what has been said, and from

---

* Logan does not seem to have been aware that while the Gaelic-
speaking inhabitants of the East Coast speak of the *east*, the direction in
which their rivers flow, as " sios," the Highlanders of the West Coast
reverse the process and call the *west*, " sios," down or downwards. Argyle,
according to our author's argument, would thus be " sios " also.

the history which follows, that the original seat of the Chisholms was not so 'probably in Roxburghshire.'*

" The Chisholms of the south had indeed some notion that they were of the same race with those of the north, and it would appear there did exist a certain connection ; but this, no doubt, arose in consequence of finding a considerable clan bearing a name which, given through the English language, was the same as their own. The conjecture amongst families or similar approximate names, that they are all descended from, or once were of, an identic stock is so natural that it is found, even now that the age of clanship is gone, almost invariably to prevail. This much is to be observed : all the well-informed Chisholms of the south acknowledge the Chisholm of Strathglass as their undoubted chief."

In that acknowledgment the " well-informed Chisholms of the south " are certainly correct. Logan proceeds—

" Leaving the less important subject of etymology, which may appear more curious than satisfactory, we shall proceed to the history of the ' race and name ' of Chisholm, as preserved among themselves and illustrated by details of the national transactions in which the clan bore a share. In this pursuit the narrative must necessarily be supplied chiefly from the family records of the Chisholms, who as successive chiefs held the patriarchal rule when a body of followers who, if not so numerous as some neighbouring tribes, were firmly knit by kindred ties—resolute and independent—happy and devoted as ever clan who owned the sway of their natural lords, and rendered to them the cheerful homage of affectionate kinsmen.

" Harald or Guthred, Earl or Thane of Caithness, Orkney and Shetland, appears to be the first of this family on record, and however he may have acquired the addition of Chisholm, he possessed great influence in the

---

* In this, as in other respects, Logan will be shown to be altogether wrong.

north. His power was much increased by marriage with the daughter of Mached or Madach, Earl of Athol, the last male descendant of Donald Bàn, sometime King of Scotland. Holding Orkney and Shetland from the King of Norway, and being vassal to the Scottish monarch for the distant Thanedom of Caithness, living also in times when feudal rights were loosely observed, and with difficulty enforced, collision with either superior was scarcely to be avoided. He began therefore to raise serious disturbances, and in the year 1196, instigated by his wife, whose descent would foster a restless spirit of rebellion, he broke out in open insurrection, committing many atrocities. William the Lion, then King of Scotland, found it necessary to lead an army against him, when he succeeded in dispersing the insurgents, but their spirit of disaffection was not easy to be subdued. Next year (1197), they again took up arms under Torfin the son of Harald, and one Roderick, when the Royal forces once more encountered them near Inverness, where they were routed with great slaughter, and Roderick was among the slain. William thus victorious, marched northwards in pursuit of Harald, who, being captured, was imprisoned in the castle of Roxburgh, where he remained until his son Torfin surrendered himself as a hostage for his father's future obedience.

"Freskin, the progenitor of the Earls of Sutherland at that time Sheriff of Inverness-shire, was of much service in apprehending Harald and his adherents, for which he was rewarded by the southern division of the county of Caithness, from that time said to have acquired the Saxon name of Southern or Southerland. Harald was no sooner at liberty than, smarting under the severity of his imprisonment and greatly irritated at the dismemberment of his territories, he again rebelled, and his unhappy son paid a heavy penalty for the father's offence —his eyes were put out, and he was left to perish miserably in his dungeon ! The ferocious chief ravaged the country, and, highly incensed with John, Bishop of

Caithness, whose only crime appears to have been a
strenuous defence of the liberties of the Church, and
a strict exaction of his Episcopal dues, he assailed him
in his house at Halkirk, and burned or slew him with
circumstances of great cruelty. For these outrages he
was again pursued by King William, and falling into his
hands, received final retribution for his multiplied offences
by undergoing an ignominious punishment and excruciat-
ing death; a fate which the leading men among his followers
likewise underwent.

" The details of those proceedings are given by Sir
Robert Gordon in his *History of the Earls of Sutherland,*
with characteristic minuteness and simplicity. ' Herald
Chisholm, or Herald Guthred, Thane of Catteyness (he
says), accompanied with a number of scapethrifts and
rebells (so the Historie calleth them), began to exercise
all kynd of misdemeaners and outrages; which uncivil
people, incensed with want and hatred do not usuallie omitt,
by invading the poor and simple with cruell spoillings;
these rebells having ravaged abroad in Catteyness, and
not being satisfied with what they had done there, they
turn their course towards Sutherland. Earl Hugh speedilie
conveined some of the inhabitants of Southerland and defended that countrie from their furie. Whereupon Harald
returned agane into Catteynes, and being offended at
John, Bishop of Catteynes, for defending the liberties of
his Church, and staying him from obtaining what he had
desired from the King in prejudice of his Bishoprick, he
apprehended Bishop John—pulled out his tung and both
eyes, then killed him most cruellie. King William coming
out of England, the yeir of God one thousand one hundred,
thrie score and eighteen, wher he had been for that tyme,
and hearing of this cruell and barbarous fact, he pursued
Herald with most of his complices, even unto Dunsby in
Catteynes, and apprehended them. He commanded exact
justice to be done, *lege talionis.* Herald had first his eyes
pulled out, then he was gelded, and lastlie he was
publiclie hanged. All his whole linage and familie were

in lyke manner used, and their blood utterlie extinguished, leist any succession should spring from so detestable a seid." He then quotes Boece XIII. and adds, 'the rest of the offenders, his followers, were all diversely punished to the terror of others: all of them, both chieftain and servants, had a competent and ignominious death deservedlie drawn on by demerite.'

This terrible visitation, continues Logan, was a shock from which the race of Harald seem never to have recovered. It was apparently the cause of dispersing a great portion of the inhabitants, the forfeiture of whose Chief and proscription of his posterity as Thanes of Caithness, left them in that country without a natural head, the estates being conferred on Magnus, son of the Earl of Angus, a stranger. It is not at all probable, he correctly enough adds, that so complete an extermination took place, as Sir Robert Gordon relates. "'There is,' says the learned and acute Lord Hailes, 'an obscurity in our historians concerning the Earls of Caithness which I am unable to dispel. It is the opinion generally received, that Alexander II. granted the Earldom of Caithness to Magnus, second son of Gillebreid, Earl of Angus, in 1222. This is scarcely consistent with the story I have just recited; the only solution of the difficulty which occurs to me is this: that Harald, Earl of Caithness, had been forfeited in the reign of William the Lion—that the Crown had divided the estates and given Southerland to Freskin, Sheriff of Inverness, 1204, but that the old family retained possession, whereby the grants remained for a season ineffectual.'"

"This certainly appears the only conclusion," continues Logan, "and it may serve to account for the relation of peerage writers, that Adam, who succeeded Bishop John, was put to death by John who possessed the Earldom in 1222. It seems incredible that two successive prelates should be slain by nobles, one of whom acquired his possessions by the forfeiture of the other, and that one's deepest crime being the sacrilegious slaughter of the first Bishop.

"It is very probable that the settlement of the Clan Siosal in the county of Inverness, is to be dated from the period of the rigorous persecution to which they were subjected, and, as was the case with the Macpherson branch of the Clan Chattan and some others, they retreated from the scene of their misfortunes and resolved to maintain their independence within the fastnesses of Strathglass.*

"There is a traditional legend of their having first received their lands in Inverness-shire by a Royal Grant, as a reward for having saved the life of one of the Scottish Kings, who was attacked while hunting by a furious boar. This savours much of genealogical fable. [And so it is.] A similar tale is given to account for the deer's head which is the heraldic bearing of the Mackenzies, and the Forbeses acquired the bear's head, which is their cognisance, from a successful grapple with one of those unsightly animals. The armorial devices borne by families are not always to be received as genealogical proof of origin or descent. The popular tradition is that two brothers determined to destroy a ferocious boar which kept the whole Strath in constant terror, and having discovered his den, one of the men, as the animal was about to attack him, thrust his hand down its throat, and dragging out the tongue and stomach, his companion exclaimed "Si salaich," meaning that he had made a filthy grasp. From this comes Si'sal, and the brothers became the armorial supporters.†

"That the Clan Siosal was powerful at an early period is evinced by their alliance being sought by Sir Robert Lauder of Quarrelwood, an influential nobleman in the north, who gave his daughter and heiress in marriage to the Chief, anno 1334. Lauder was constable of the im-

---

* This " probable " retreat from Caithness, and the settlement in Strathglass, described by Logan, will be shown by charters and other documents to be absolutely groundless.

† Tradition still points out the place in Glenconvinth where this combat is said to have taken place.

portant fortress on the north bank of Loch-ness, called the Castle of Urquhart, from the valley in which it is situated, and he resolutely defended it against the faction of Baliol.

"This is," Logan admits, "the first well authenticated intimation of the Chisholms being established in the locality which they have retained until this day (1840), a period of more than 500 years. The names indeed of ' Richard de Cheschelm del Count de Roxburgh' and 'John de Cheshome ' in the county of Berwick are in the bond of fealty to Edward I. of England, more familiarly known as ' Ragman's Roll,' but if the reasoning in a foregoing page is just, these individuals could not have been of the Gaelic Siosals. Some of the clan in the north might have been induced to attach their signatures to this deed, did not their distance and mountain security protect them from the degradation ; for, as it was the policy of Edward, and an object of great anxiety, to swell the list of those who appeared willing to acknowledge him as their liege lord, the signatures of a great many appeared in this remarkable deed who were of incomparably less importance than the Laird of Chisholm must have been at the close of the 13th century."

Thus far the Logan manuscript has been closely followed. That its author was wrong in adopting the Caithness theory of the origin of the clan will be conclusively proved. It is indeed quite clear from several incidental remarks of his own that even Logan himself was conscious of its impossibility and absurdity. But the necessary documents by which to establish the continuous connection of the Chisholms of the north with those who had in the eleventh century settled on the Scottish borders, and which show how they gradually acquired and ultimately lost the greater portion of their Highland possessions, were not so accessible when Logan wrote his brief and imperfect memoir * as they are now. His historical

* *The History of the Clan Chisholm, being Genealogical and Historical Memoirs of the Chiefs and Cadets of this Ancient Highland Family,* drawn up by James Logan, F.S.A. Sc., Cor. mem., S.A. Normandy, etc., etc., 1840.

account of the principal family is scrappy and meagre,
and his genealogy is, in many particulars—several generations being altogether omitted—incomplete and inaccurate.
It is, however, in many respects suggestive, and contains
a number of useful facts and dates mixed up with not a
few more calculated to lead astray than guide the unwary.

The late John Scott Chisholme of Stirches, writing to Mr.
Augustus C. Mackenzie of Findon, ridicules the Caithness
origin of the family, and effectually disposes of it in the
following terms.   Referring to a writer who maintained
that origin for all the Chisholms, Mr. Scott Chisholme
says :—" Had he left to me the Border barons, and the
bishops, I would have made him welcome to prove, if he
could, that the Comar family are descended from Harald,
Thane of Caithness, Orkney, and Shetland, who married
the daughter of Mudac or Machead, Earl of Athol, the
last male descendent of Donald Bàn, King of Scotland,
but I decline the honour of having such Royal ancestry
thrust upon me, either by him or the reveries of Sir
Robert Gordon, specially because Boece and other historians affirm that William the Lion hanged Harald, put
out the eyes of his only son, Torphin, after causing him
to be cruelly mutilated, and emasculating every male of
his race, a procedure on the part of that monarch so
inimical to my existence from such a source that I prefer
the more humble Norman origin in which I have been
taught to believe, substantiated as it is by indisputable
written evidence."   This argument, all rational people will,
it is believed, accept as absolutely conclusive.

Skene, discussing the same subject and specially referring
to the Chisholms of Strathglass, says :—" Few families have
asserted their claim to be considered as a Gaelic clan with
greater vehemence than the Chisholms, notwithstanding
that there are few whose Lowland origin is less doubtful.
Hitherto no one has investigated their history, but their
early charters suffice to establish the real origin of the
family with great clearness.   The name Chisholme does
not occur in Battle Abbey Roll, so there is no distinct

authority to prove that the name is actually Norman, but their documents distinctly show that the name was introduced from the Low Country into the Highlands. Their original seat is in Roxburghshire, as we find the only person of the name who signed Ragman's Rolls is Richard de Chisholme del Counte de Rokesburgh, and in that county the family of Chisholme still remains. Therefore their situation, with the character of the name itself, seems with sufficient clearness to indicate a Norman origin."

We shall now proceed to trace the Chisholms, step by step from their first recorded appearance in Scotland to the present day.

The first of the name of whom any record is found in Scotland had his seat in the western district of the county of Roxburgh, formerly included in the Old Deanery of Teviotdale and Diocese of Glasgow. Malcolm, the historian, says that the Chisholms "came soon after the Conquest, A.D. 1066, from Tindale in England. The original name," he proceeds, "is said to have been 'De Chesé,' to which the Saxon termination 'holme' was added on the marriage of the Norman ancestor with a Saxon heiress, whose lands, from situation, were so-called." In the early records the name is written de Cheséholme, later de Chesehelme vel Chesholme, and eventually Chisholm as we now have it. The earliest document extant in which mention is made of the name, and relating to the family, is a bull of Pope Alexander IV., in which John de Chisholme is named in the year 1254. This

I. JOHN DE CHISHOLME

Married Emma de Vetereponte or Vipont, daughter of William de Vetereponte, Lord of Bolton, who grants him as a marriage portion a charter of the lands of Paxtoun, with the fishing of Brade-la-Tweed, in the county ,of Berwick, along with the pendicles in the village of Paxtoun and the fishings and pertinents thereunto belonging. In this charter the parties are described as John de Cheseholme and Emma de Vetereponte, his spouse. The Viponts or

Vetrepontes are now quite unknown even in the traditions of Tweedside, although, like the Vesis, the Moreviles, the Normanviles, and several other prominent families of that age, their forefathers ruled there as Princes. By his wife, Emma de Vetereponte, John had issue—

II. RICHARD DE CHESHOLME,

Described as " Del Counte de Rokesburgh," who married, with issue—

1. John, his heir and successor.
2. Alexander, forfeited at the same time as his brother, Sir John, along with Adam de Paxtoun.*

Richard was succeeded by his eldest son,

III. SIR JOHN DE CHESHOLME,

Designated as " Del Counte de Berwyke," whose name is attached to the Bond of Fealty to Edward I. in 1296, known as Ragman's Roll.   This Sir John, however, afterwards joined Robert Bruce and fought under his banner in 1314, at the battle of Bannockburn, where his kinsman Sir William de Vetereponte was slain.   In consequence of the part Sir John de Chesholme took on this glorious occasion his estates were forfeited by Edward II., who bestowed a considerable portion of them on Ranulphus de Holme, and on Sir Robert de Manners, ancestor of the Dukes of Rutland, who obtained from the English King two parts of the town of Paxtoun, and one-third of the Royalty of Bradewater on the Tweed.   In a mandate, dated at York, the 18th of April, 1317, and addressed to his "beloved James de Broughton, Chamberlain of Scotland," Sir John is described by Edward II. as " our Scottish enemy and rebel."†   Three years later, in 1320, some of his possessions were restored to Sir John by a charter from King Robert the Bruce, who is said to have granted him in addition several lands which had been forfeited by the

* *Rotuli Scot.* 10 *Edward* III.   † *Rot. Scot.* 2 *Edward II.*

Cummins in the county of Nairn. He married and had issue—

IV. ALEXANDER DE CHISHOLME,

Who is described as "Lord of Chisholme in Roxburgh and Paxtoun in Berwickshire." His name appears in a disputed case about fishings in the Tweed in 1335 as "Alexander de Chisholme of that Ilk."*
He married, with issue, a son and successor,

V. SIR ROBERT DE CHISHOLME,

Described as one of the "Magnates of Scotland." He fought and was taken prisoner at the battle of Neville's Cross, or Redhill, Durham, on the 17th October, 1346.† This Sir Robert de Chisholme married Anne, daughter and heiress of Sir Robert Lauder of Quarrelwood, Constable of Urquhart Castle, on Lochness. He is the first of the name of which any trace is found in the North of Scotland, and it will be shown that from him are descended all the Chisholms of the north. There were certain church lands, in the vicinity of Castle Urquhart, which, on the 6th of December, 1344, being the feast of St. Nicholas, were granted by John, Bishop of Moray, to Sir Robert Lauder. These lands were afterwards possessed by Robert de Chisholme. In 1345 there is a grant of them in his favour by John Randolph, Earl of Moray, probably on the occasion of Chisholme's marriage to Anne, Sir Robert Lauder's daughter and co-heiress. Sir Robert Chisholme's son subsequently, in 1386, resigned them in favour of Alexander, Bishop of Moray, who immediately disposed of them to Alexander, Earl of Buchan, the "Wolf of Badenoch." Both charters are given at length on page 33 of Mr. Fraser-Mackintosh's *Invernessiana*. By the first of these interesting documents, dated at Elgin in 1334, Bishop John has "given, granted, and in feu farm demitted, to the noble person Sir Robert de Lawadyr, Knight, for his

* *Rotuli Scotiae*, 342 and 402.   † *Foedera*, 20 *Edward* III.

manifold services done to our said Church, a half davoch
of our lands of Aberbreachy (Abriachan) lying between
the barony of Bonach (Bona) on the east on the one side,
and the barony of Urchard on the west on the other,
together with our lands of Achmunie, lying between the
lands of Drumbuie on the east on the one side, and the
land of Cartaly on the west on the other, within the barony
of Urchard foresaid, with the pertinents : To be held and
had by the said Sir Robert and his heirs of us and our
successors for ever, with their rights, marches and divisions,
freely, quietly, fully, peacefully, and honourably," etc., etc.,
for which Sir Robert and his heirs were taken bound to
pay to the Bishop and his successors, four merks sterling
per annum, in two equal instalments, at the accustomed
terms, in lieu of every other exaction, service and demand.
In the charter of 1386 granting the same lands to Alexander Buchan, Bishop of Moray, the lands are described
in identical terms, "which lands," Bishop Alexander says,
" with the pertinents, Sir Robert de Chishelme, Knight,
lord of that ilk, held of us in chief, and he, induced neither
by force nor fear, nor deceived by error, but by pure and
spontaneous free will, did give up and purely and simply
resign into our hands by staff and baton, the foresaid lands
with the pertinents, and all rights and claims which he,
the said Knight, or his heirs had or could in future have
in the said lands, with the pertinents." It will be observed
that the Sir Robert Chisholme who possessed these lands
in Abriachan and Glenurquhart, is in this last quoted
charter described as "lord of that ilk," or in other words,
the head of his house.

The same Sir Robert Chisholme refused to pay multures
for his lands of Quarrelwood to the prior of Pluscardine,
who appealed to the Bishop of Moray, and, in April,
1390, his lordship issued a monition to Sir Archibald
Douglas, in which it is set forth that " the mulctures of
the lands of Quarrywood, in the Sheriffdom of Elgin, at
that time (King Alexander's) unimproved, but now reduced
to cultivation, belongs and appertains to the mill of Elgin

from which it is scarcely a mile distant." The mills of
Elgin and Forres, and other mills depending on them,
had been gifted to the priory by "Alexander, King of
Scotland, of ·pious memory." The monition pleads undisturbed possession, with the full knowledge and tolerance
of Robert de Chisholme, Knight, during the preceding
reigns, and "further asserts and declares that the said
Robert had seized and bound a certain husbandman of
the lands of Kindrassie, to whom the prior had by contract let the said mulctures, and thrown him into a private
prison, by which he (Sir Robert) directly incurred the
sentence of excommunication." The civil judges are in
the same document threatened with similar punishment
if they interfere in the dispute or question the pretensions
of the ecclesiastical courts to determine the rights of the
parties in the quarrel. On the 16th of the same month,
Sir Thomas, the prior, records a solemn protest against
Sir Robert de Chisholme's proceedings. The two, however,
seem to have continued on the most friendly terms, for
on the 1st of May following they both witness a charter
by John of Dunbar, Earl of Moray, in favour of the town
of Elgin, by which the Earl granted to that burgh in all
time coming the ale of assize which belonged to him as
constable of the Castle of Elgin.

By his marriage with Anne, daughter and heiress of
Sir Robert Lauder of Quarrelwood, Sir Robert de Chisholme had issue—

1. Sir Robert, his heir and successor.

2. William de Chisholme, a churchman, and Treasurer
of Moray, whose name is mentioned in 1371 in an "Appeal
to the Pope on the part of the Abbot of Aberbrothoc
against the process before the Bishop regarding the tithes
of the Church of Inverness," and in which he is described
as "the venerable and discreet man Master William de
Chesholme, Treasurer of Moray."* He is mentioned as
attesting a sentence of reconciliation in a document dated
2nd November, 1389, in which Thomas de Chesholme

* *Invernessiana*, p. 73

along with Robert, Earl of Sutherland, and Alexander de
Moravia of Culbin, become security for the good behaviour
of the Wolf of Badenoch towards his wife, Lady Euphemia,
Countess of Ross,* the suit being "restituenda marito suo."
Between "the years 1360 and 1398 there appear in record
John of the Ard, Subchanter of Moray, William of Chesholm, Treasurer, and Thomas of Chesholm, a person of
some consequence at the time, all by birth apparently
connected with the families of the Ard."† Under the
designation of "William de Chesholm Clericus," he obtained a safe conduct ("salvus conductus") to pass into
England in 1364 with two horses and three companions, and in the following year a similar liberty is
granted to him with permission to remain one year along
with four companions for the purpose of study.‡ In 1371
his name appears in an appeal respecting the tithes of
the Church of Inverness, and in 1375, described as "cir-
cumspectus vir," a considerate person, he is appointed to
officiate as procurator to the Bishop "de bladis terrarum
de Cathboll," or to recover the corn lands of Cadboll from
pledge or wadset. On the 18th of July, 1378, he sub-
scribes a charter by Bishop Alexander to John Forbes of
the lands of Kinrossie. On the 2nd of September, 1393,
he is one of the witnesses to the execution of a solemn
deed and restoration of all the rights and immunities of
the Domus Dei, or God's House, a foundation for the
necessitous, by Alexander of Dunbar, brother german to the
Earl of Moray. In 1399 his signature is found attached
to a deed respecting the tithes due from the burgh of
Elgin. He must have lived to a very ripe old age.

Sir Robert was succeeded by his eldest son by his wife
Anne, daughter of Sir Robert Lauder of Quarrelwood—

VI. SIR ROBERT DE CHISHOLME.

In 1358, the Justices of the King, of whom Robert de
Chisholme, described as Lord of Chisholme in Roxburgh-

shire and Constable of the Castle of Urquhart on Loch
Ness, was one, remits a fine to Alexander de Chisholme.*
This Alexander appears to have been Sir Robert's second
son who afterwards succeeded to the Chiefship and estates
on the death of his elder brother John without male issue,
and who by his marriage with Margaret de la Ard acquired
the Erchless portion of the Bisset property and other
extensive estates in the North.

Sir Robert is said to have been appointed to the offices of
Constable of Urquhart Castle and Sheriff of Inverness-shire
in 1359 by David II., by whom he was knighted in 1357.
On the 8th of April, 1359, "Lord Robert de Chesholme,
Sheriff of the county of Inverness, gave in his accounts,
with all his expenses and receipts from Martinmas, 1357."†
He granted six acres of land to the Holy Rood of the
Church of Inverness, for the benefit of the poor of
the parish, by deed, dated the 14th September, 1362, being
the feast of the Holy Rood. In this deed he describes
himself as "Robert de Chesholme, Knight, and Lord of
the same." The lands are still partly in possession of the
Kirk Session of the parish, and are known as Diriebught,
or *Tir nam bochd*—the lands of the poor. The deed is
in the Inverness charter chest, and is in excellent preservation, with Sir Robert's seal attached fresh and entire.
It is printed at length by Mr. Fraser-Mackintosh,‡ beginning thus :—"To all who shall see or hear of this
charter, Sir Robert de Chesholme, Lord of the same,
wishes eternal salvation in the Lord ; since it is known
to all that all flesh returns into dust, and that there is
nothing after death except He who is the true safety
and who redeemed the human race on the cross." Then
follows a description of the lands, which he grants "for
the salvation of his own soul, and the souls of his ancestors
and successors, for making an increase of divine worship
forever to the altar of the Holy Rood of Inverness." The
charter is witnessed, among others, by Thomas de Fenton

---

* *Chamberlain's Accounts*, Vol. I., p. 381.   † *Chamberlain's Rolls*, 1359.
‡ *Invernessiana*, pp. 62-63.

"Alderman" of the burgh, and "Weland Shishlach," the exact phonetic equivalent of our Gaelic "Siosalach" of to-day, who is described as a burgess of Inverness.   In a deed dated 1364, Sir Robert speaks of his grandfather, after whom he has himself apparently been named, as Sir Robert Lauder of Quarrelwood.   This conclusively estab-lishes his father's marriage to Quarrelwood's daughter; and the fact that he succeeded to all his maternal grand-father's property in the counties of Inverness, Nairn, and Moray, clearly proves that his mother was Sir Robert Lauder's only child and sole heiress.

This Sir Robert Chisholme designates himself in a docu-ment, describing the proceedings of a court held at Balloch Hill, near Inverness, in connection with these lands, and dated the 25th of January, 1376, as "Robert de Ches-helme, Lord of that Ilk, Justiciary of the said Regality of Moray."*   His name appears four years later, in a Protest by the Bishop and clergy of Moray in opposition to claims made at that time by the Wolf of Badenoch to the superiority of the Bishop's church lands in Badenoch. The document is dated 11th October, 1380.   The Bishop makes protest that, "we lately, in the month of August last past, in the Church of St. Mary of Inverness, before our Lord the King and the illustrious men the Lords, the Earls of Carrick and Fife, sons of our Lord the King, and Lord and Earl of Moray, the reverend father in Christ, Lord John, by the Grace of God Bishop of Dun-keld, Chancellor of Scotland, John Lyon, Chamberlain of Scotland, Thomas de Erskine, Robert de Cheshelm, Knights, and many others, disclaimed you Lord Alex-ander and your consort, and acknowledged our Lord and King, (then follows the description of the lands in question) and we deny that we hold these lands of you."†

King Robert II. during his visit to Inverness in 1382 granted to his son, Alexander, Earl of Buchan, the Wolf of Badenoch, a charter of a half davoch of the lands of

* *Invernessiana*, p. 63.
† The document is printed in *extenso* pp. 80-82 of *Invernessiana.*

Invermoriston with the fishing and park, a fourth part of Blairy, three fourth parts of Incheberrys, with a fourth part of Lochletter, and one-fourth of Dalshangy, with the pertinents, within the Sheriffdom of Inverness, which lands, with the fishing and pertinents foresaid, belonged to Robert de Chisholme, Knight; and which the said Robert gave up and resigned to the King. In a deed dated at Elgin on the 23rd of February, 1386, he is again described as "Sir Robert de Chishelme, Knight, Lord of that Ilk." In the same year he voluntarily resigned the lands of Abriachan and others in Inverness-shire into the hands of the Bishop of Moray, which lands were afterwards granted to Alexander, Lord of Badenoch, in feu ferm.* In August of the same year "Robert de Cheshelme, dominus ejusdem," is a witness on an inquisition regarding the lands of Aldrochty, and on that occasion he appends his seal to the deed. On the 30th of August, 1393, he appended his seal to a mort ancestry award, finding that John Sibbald is the rightful heir to the lands of Aldrochty and others.

Sir Robert de Chisholme married Margaret, daughter of Haliburton of that Ilk, County of Berwick, with issue—

1. John de Chisholme, his heir.

2. Alexander de Chisholme, who, on the death of his brother John without male issue, succeeded to the Chiefship and Highland estates.

3. Robert, who is said to have succeeded to the original lands of the family in Roxburghshire and to have become progenitor of that branch of the house of Chisholme.

4. Janet, who, in 1364, married Hugh Rose, IV. of Kilravock. The marriage contract is dated 2nd of January in that year, and is witnessed and sealed by the Bishops of Ross and Moray, and by William, Earl of Ross and Lord of Skye.

To this Hugh Rose, IV. of Kilravock, who married Janet Chisholme, the author of the history of that family makes the following reference—" I finde him mentioned in a contract matrimoniall betwixt him and Joneta de

* _Register of the Great Seal_, p. 176, No. 39.

Chesholme, daughter of Sir Robert Chesholme, Constable
of the Castle of Urquhart. He was also Chesholme of
that Ilk, and in right of his mother, daughter of Sir
Robert Lauder, succeeded to Quarrelwood, Kinsterie,
Brightmannie, etc. This contract, because it is Kilravock's originall right of his lands in Strathnairn, and
through the character, contractions, and bad ink, is scarce
legible already, therefore I have here transcryved it." He
then quotes it at length in the original Latin.* We give
the following translation of the portion which, along with
the preceding quotation from the manuscript history of
the family of Kilravock, proves that the Sir Robert de
Chisholme who owned so much land in the Highlands,
and was Constable of Urquhart Castle, was also Sir
Robert Chisholme of that Ilk, and head of all the Chisholms, north and south :—

The present indenture bears witness that, on Thursday, the 2nd
of January, in the year of grace 1364, there was an agreement made
at the Church of Auldearn, between the noblemen, Sir Robert Chisholme, keeper of the Castle of Urquhart, on the one part, and Hugh
Rose, Lord of Kilravock on the other part, as follows—that is to
say, in the first, the said Hugh Rose shall marry Janet, daughter
of the said Robert, for which marriage the said Sir Robert shall
give to the said Hugh, and the heirs begotten between Hugh himself and the foresaid Janet, ten merks of land of   , with
all its pertinents within Strathnairn, and in case that the said lands
do not amount to ten merks, the said Sir Robert shall give to the
said Hugh as much of the land nearest to it as shall amount to the
said ten merks, and all this shall be done to the sight and satisfaction of worthy men. It is also fully agreed upon between the
said parties that from the day of the celebration of the said marriage,
the said Sir Robert shall keep and entertain his said daughter for
three years in meat and drink, but the said Hugh shall find and
keep her in all the needful garments and ornaments. It is also
agreed that if the said Hugh and Janet shall live beyond a complete year after their marriage, the said Hugh shall brook the said
land for his lifetime, but in case the said Hugh shall decease (which
God forbid) without heirs of his body begotten between him and
the said Janet, and in that case, the said lands shall return into
the hands of the said Sir Robert and his heirs, after the decease

* See pp. 36-38 *Family of Rose of Kilravock.*

of the said Hugh, and to the part of this indenture remaining with the said Hugh the seal of the said Sir Robert is attached along with the seals of the reverend Lords, by the grace of God Bishops of Moray and Ross, and of the high and noble man William Earl of Ross and Lord of Skye ; and to the part of this indenture remaining in the possession of the said Sir Robert the seal of the said Hugh Rose is attached, along with the seals of the same reverend Lords, the Bishops of Moray and Ross, and also of the said William Earl of Ross and Lord of Skye. Given and done on the day and year and in the place foresaid.

In this indenture a peculiar custom of the time is found recorded. Sir Robert Chisholme, the lady's father, agrees to keep and entertain his daughter from the date of her marriage "for three years in meat and drink," while her husband is only to " find and keep her in all needful garments and ornaments" during the same period.

Sir Robert de Chisholme was succeeded by his eldest son,

VII. JOHN DE CHISHOLME,

Designated " de la Ard," or of the Aird. He is repeatedly on record during his father's lifetime. We find him described in the reign of Charles II., by Sir George Mackenzie of Rosehaugh, Lord Advocate of Scotland, in his notice of the family of Chisholme, as "John Chisholme of that Ilk in the shyre of Roxburgh." In 1389 he receives a grant of the lands of Lower Kinmylies, near Inverness, from Alexander of the Isles, Lord of Lochaber. These lands were at once claimed by William Bishop of Moray, who, on the 20th of November in the same year, issued a warning against their occupation by "John de Chisholme de la Airde," and charging him. to quit claim, and to restore the Church's patrimony.* He is again mentioned in that year as "John of Cheshelm of the Arde."† On the 24th of April, 1420, he granted a charter, to his relative, John Rose, VII. of Kilravock, of the lands at Cantrabundy and Little Cantray.

He married Catherine Bisset, daughter of Bisset of

---

* *Invernessiana*, pp. 93-94.   † *Register of Moray*, p. 211.

that Ilk, in right of whom he succeeded, on the death
of her father, to a portion of the Bisset lands in the
Aird. By this lady he had issue—an only child, Morella,
who married Alexander Sutherland, Baron of Duffus,
grandson of Nicolas Sutherland, second son of Kenneth
Earl of Sutherland, who was killed at the battle of
Halidonhill in 1333. In right of Morella Chisholme, Alexander Sutherland obtained the following lands of Chisholme
—Quarrelwood, Clunie, and Clova, in Moray; Paxtoun in
Tweedale, Kinsterrie in Nairnshire, and other extensive
possessions. She is on record in 1424. From this
marriage the house of Duffus is said to carry the addition to their armorial coat armour, azure a boar's head
erazed, or. Dovach, a daughter of this union, married
Dunbar of Westfield, who, in her right, succeeded to
the lands of Clova and Clunie in Moray, which his wife
had inherited through her mother, Morella Chisholme.

If further proof be required that Sir Robert de Chisholme of Quarrelwood, and Constable of Urquhart Castle,
who came from the south and settled in the Highlands
early in the fourteenth century, was at the same time
progenitor of the Chisholms of Strathglass and the head
of the Chisholmes of the South, it will be found in the
documents after given. The lands which he then undoubtedly possessed on the Borders, as well as several
of his estates in the counties of Inverness, Moray, and
Nairn, are shown by these summonses and pleadings,
quoted below, to have been carried on her marriage by
Morella Chisholme, only child and heir of line of his
successor, John de Chisholme "de la Ard," or of the
Aird, to her husband, Alexander Sutherland, Baron of
Duffus, whose family inherited them after his death. In
the first summons, William Sutherland, Alexander's successor, is described as "of Duffus and Quarrelwood, heir
and successor to the umquhile Sir Robert Chisholme of
Quarrelwood," and the lands of the two Cantrays and
others conveyed by Sir Robert Chisholme to Hugh Rose
of Kilravock, as the dower of Sir Robert's daughter,

Janet, on her marriage to Kilravock in 1364 are referred
to in the same connection.	In the second summons,
Christian Sutherland, wife of the late William Urquhart
of Berriedale, in Caithness, is also described as "heir
and successor to the umquhile Sir Robert Chisholme of
Quarrelwood." The pleadings, which are endorsed the
20th of April, 1512, are still more conclusive. In them
most of the Chisholme lands, north and south, are mentioned. Christian of Sutherland, lady of Berriedale, is
shown to be the grand-daughter of Alexander Sutherland, laird of Duffus, who "married Muriel (Morella) of
Chisholme, daughter and heir to umquhile John of Chisholme of all and whole his lands" of Chisholme and Paxton,
in the South; Quarrelwood and Greshop, in Moray;
Kinsterrie in Nairn, and Brightmony, "the Clune, Clava,
and the half of Ouchterurquholl and the overlordship of
the two Cantrays and the other half of Ouchterurquholl,"
in the county of Inverness.	"Christian Sutherland, lady
of Berriedale, is heir of line to follow and pursue the
lands of Chisholme in Teviotdale, together with the lands
of Paxton and other lands of which she is the very heir
to," while "William Sutherland, now laird of Duffus, may
never have entry to the said lands of Chisholme (in Teviotdale) nor to any pertinents thereof but to so much as his
said grandame, Muriel of Chisholme, gave to him in her
widowhood by resignation." This is conclusive.

The first summons, which is as follows, bears the
messenger's execution upon William Sutherland "at his
dwelland place of Duffus," on the 15th day of July,
1511:—

"James . . . . charge William Sutherland of Duffus and
Quarrelwood, heir and successor to the umquhile, Sir Robert
Chisholme of Quarrelwood, Knight, to compear before us and our
Council at Edinburgh, or where it shall happen us to be for the
time, the 8th day of August next, to come, if it be lawful, and
failing thereof, the next lawful day thereafter following, in the hour
of cause, with continuation of days, to answer at the instance of
our lovite Hugh Rose of Kilravock, heir and successor to the
umquhile Hugh Rose of Kilvarock, his grandsire, to hear him be

decerned by the decreet of our Lords of Council, to warrant,
acquit, and defend to the said Hugh, as heir and successor to the
said umquhile Hugh, his grandsire, the lands of the two Cantrays,
and the half of the lands of Uchterorquhoil with the pertinents,
lying within our sheriffdom of Nairn, after the form and tenor
of the charter and infeftment made by the same umquhile Sir
Robert Chisholme's predecessor, to the said umquhile, Hugh's
grandsire, and his heirs, with clause of warrandice inserted in the
same, like as the said charter and infeftment more fully purports,
and also to make the said lands free of all recognition made of
the same in our hands, to be enjoyed by the said Hugh as heir
aforesaid, after the tenor of the said infeftment in time to come,
etc.   Given under our Signet at Elgin, the 10th day of June,
and of our reign the 23rd year."

The second summons is served upon Christian Sutherland, lady of Berriedale " at her duelland place of Ald-
weke," on the same day.

"James . . . . greeting. Our will is and we charge you,
that you peremptorily summon, warn and charge Christian Sutherland, the spouse of the umquhile William Oliphant of Berriedale,
heir and successor to the umquhile Sir Robert Chisholme of Quarrelwood, knight, etc.   Given under our Signet at Elgin, the 10th
day of June, and of our reign the 23rd year."

The pleading has no title, but is endorsed "anno, etc.,
VcXII years, the 20th day of April," and commences with
the pious invocation :—

"Jesus, Maria."

" Item, where it is alleged that Christian of Sutherland lady of Berriedale, that she has no entry, nor her forbears, lairds of Duffus, in the
Chisholme's lands of Chisholme and Quarrelwood, nor to no other
lands that might pertain to them ; the contrary of that is well
known, for her grandsire Alexander of Sutherland, laird of Duffus,
married Muriel (Morella) of Chisholme, daughter and heir to umquhile John of Chisholme, of all and whole his lands of Chisholme,
Paxton, Quarrelwood in Moray, the Greschip, Brechtmont, Kinsterry,
the Clune, Clava, and the half of Ouchterurquholl and the overlordship of the two Cantrays, and the other half of Ouchterurquholl ;
to the taking the forsaid Alexander gave of the forsaid Muriel's lands,
pertaining to her in heritage, to Sir Alexander Dunbar of the Westfield knight in marriage with his daughter and the said Muriel's lands
of Clune, Clava, and the half of Ouchterurquholl, with their pertinents.   And also the said Alexander Sutherland wadset the lands

of Greschip, and took upon them twelve score marks and gave that
in marriage to another daughter of his called Dovach Sutherland
with umquhile Alexander Ross, son and heir to the laird of Balnagown in Ross. And also the said Alexander Sutherland gave in
wadset to John Nicolson, burgess of Forres, the lands of Brouny-
scruk and the Milnfield, pertaining to the said Muriel in heritage.
And also the said Christian Sutherland, lady of Berriedale, is heir
of line to follow and pursue the lands of Chisholme in Teviotdale,
together with the lands of Paxton and other lands of the which
she is very heir to ; and William of Sutherland, now laird of Duffus,
may never have entry to the said lands of Chisholme nor to any
pertinents thereof but to so much as his said grandame, Muriel of
Chisholme, gave to him in her widowhood by resignation. And by
this reason the foresaid Christian of Sutherland as heir foresaid,
ought to free, relieve, and keep the baron of Kilravock scaithless
and to relieve him at the King's hands, and all others, of his lands
of the two Cantrays and the half of Ouchterurquholl, with their
pertinents, after the form of the charters and evidences made by
her forbears to him and his forbears thereupon."*

On the death of John de Chisholme de la Aird, in
1436, without male issue, he was succeeded in the remaining lands belonging to the family in the Highlands
and as head of the house by his next brother,

VIII. ALEXANDER DE CHISHOLME,

Who married Margaret, described as "Margaret de la
Ard and Lady of Erchless," daughter and heiress of
Weyland of the Aird, by his wife, Matilda, eldest daughter
and co-heiress of Malise *Dei indulgentia* Earl of Stratherne and *jure usoris* Earl of Orkney and Caithness, by
his wife, Isabella, eldest daughter and co-heiress of John,
Earl of Orkney and Caithness, by his wife, a daughter
of Patrick Graham of Lovat and the Aird. Margaret of
the Aird is mentioned in an indenture dated at Kinrossy,
in the Barony of Cullace, Perthshire, in 1403, and in
the same document her son, Thomas of Chisholme, is
also named. She had a brother Alexander, designated
"de la Ard," who was alive in 1375, and was made

* *General Register of Deeds*, Vol. 408. Contract recorded on the 3rd
November, 1628.

Captain of Orkney by the King of Norway. This Alexander, of the Aird, had in right of his mother, Matilda, eldest daughter of Malise, Earl of Stratherne, Caithness, and Orkney, succeeded as Earl of Caithness, but he subsequently resigned the title and the lands belonging to the earldom to King Robert II.

The male line of the Earl of Orkney failed in the person of Magnus the Fifth, and a new race, sprung from a female branch, succeeded to that dignity, who were not only natives of Scotland, but internally connected with that Kingdom. For several centuries in those days this Earldom had made a conspicuous figure in the annals of the North, not only on account of its territory, but for the spirit of its rulers and people, and its respectable and splendid connections. Besides Orkney, which was always considered as the centre of operation, and the seat of government, where the court and little parliament were kept, the laws enacted and justice administered, it contained not only Zetland, but the counties of Ross, Sutherland, and Caithness, and had rendered tributary the Hebudæ, which were for sometime subject to its dominion. Moreover, the ancient Counts that so long held it, were all of them men of high rank, and some of them of the most splendid talents. They were connected by ties of blood with all the monarchs that then ruled the North, and in the retinue they kept at home, as well as in the force they carried abroad, they had much more the appearance of sovereigns than of subjects.

The learned author of the *History of Orkney* says that Magnus the Fifth, the last of the Norwegian Earls, left an only daughter who "was marrried to Malise, Earl of Stratherne, in Scotland, who probably enjoyed the Earldom in right of his wife without question, as no formal investiture seems either to have been sought or obtained. A claim, however, was made for this purpose, by one Malise, in all probabilty a son of that marriage, and a caveat entered to secure the revenues in the country till he had time to take the steps that were necessary for obtaining what he considered his right. This Malise, who was also Earl of Stratherne, had been twice married, first to a daughter of the Earl of Menteith, by whom he had a daughter of the name of Matilda, afterwards married to Weyland de Ard. By his second wife, who was a daughter of the Earl of Ross, he had four daughters, the eldest of whom was married to William St. Clare, Baron of Roslin," whose son, Henry, afterwards succeeded to the Earldom. "Weyland de Ard had, by his wife, Matilda, a son named Alexander, who inherited the Earldom of Caithness and a certain proportion of Orkney, in right of his mother ; but he alienated the former to Robert the First, King of Scotland, and after he had resigned his share, and been governor of the latter only for a short time, he died without children, A.D., 1369."* Other writers place his death as late as 1376.

The following references will help to clear up many difficult and obscure points regarding the connection of the Frasers and Chisholms of the Aird and Strathglass with the county and Earldom of Caithness :—In 1296 Edward I. ordered John of Warren, Earl of Surrey, his warden of the Kingdom of Scotland, to cause to be delivered to Andrew Fresel, who was about to go into England beyond the Trent, a hundred marks of the dowry of his wife in Caithness for the maintenance of himself, his wife, and family. The Andrew Fresel here mentioned was Sir Andrew Fraser, son of Sir Gilbert Fraser, Sheriff of Stirling, and the first of the name who settled in the North.† The King further ordered that all the lands and tenements which were of his wife's dowry in Caithness should be restored to Sir Andrew for the same purpose.

In 1330 we find recorded "the complaint of Symon Fraser and of Margaret his wife, and one of the heirs of the Earl of Caithness, concerning the earldom of

---

* *The History of Orkney*, by the Rev. George Barry, D.D.
† *Anderson's Family of Fraser*, pp. 33-35.

Caithness, dated at Kinross, on the 4th of December in that year. This Simon was the son of Sir Andrew. He fell at the battle of Halidon Hill in 1333, about the same time that Malise, Earl of Stratherne, became Earl of Caithness. This Earl Malise married Johanna, daughter of Sir John, Earl of Menteith, who was dead in 1329. The offspring of this marriage, was a daughter, Matilda. In 1334 Malise styles himself "Earl of the earldoms of Stratherne, Caithness, and Orkney." In 1345 he forfeited the earldom of Stratherne. King David thereupon granted it to Maurice Murray, but Malise still " retained the earldom of Caithness, which was inherited by his daughter Matilda, and afterwards by Alexander of Ard, her son by Weland of Ard."

In Bishop Tulloch's manuscript we are informed "that Alexander of Ard, by the law and custom of the Kingdom of Scotland, succeeded in right of his mother as heir to Earl Malise of Stratherne, in the principal manor or mansion of the Earldom of Cathanes, and held it with the right and title of earl, and enjoyed also by the same right a perticate or quantity of the lands of Orkney, and acted as bailie and captain of the people on the part of the King of Norway."

In 1375 Alexander of the Aird sold or resigned to King Robert II. the earldom of Caithness, and the principal manor, with the title of earl and the other rights belonging to him by the law and custom of Scotland, in right of his mother as the eldest daughter of Earl Malise. These included lands in Banff, Sutherland, and Orkney. In the same year King Robert granted to his own son, David Stewart, who, in 1371, had been created Earl Palatine of Stratherne, the castle of Brathwell (Brawl), its lands, and all the other lands as well in Caithness as in any other part of Scotland inherited by Alexander de la Aird, in right of his mother, Matilda de Stratherne, and a few years before resigned by him.*   And thus the short connection of the family of the

* *Origines Parochiales Scotiae*, Vol. II. pp. 806-808.

Aird and of their Fraser and Chisholm descendants with Caithness seems to have for ever terminated. But it lasted long enough to become the basis of the theory that the Chisholms came originally from that county to Strathglass, and of the mass of fable to which it has given rise among the genealogists and chroniclers of the family. Alexander of the Aird appears not only to have resigned the earldom of Caithness, but his lands in Banff, Sutherland, and Orkney, and about the same time to have resigned his possessions in the Aird to his sister Margaret, and her husband, Alexander Chisholme ; for some twenty years earlier William of Fenton, Lord of Beaufort, Hugh Fraser, Lord of Lovat, and Alexander of Chisholme are found on record as the three portioners of the Aird.

Referring to these events Edmund Chisholm Batten says :—"Alexander del Ard had been induced in 1376 to resign to the King the davoch of Garthyes in Sutherland, part of the earldom of Strathern, which he inherited as the son of Matilda de Strathern. Afterwards he was appointed custodier of the earldom of Orkney by the King of Denmark in a deed given by Torfæus, and died without issue. Margaret del Ard, probably his sister, was anxious to recover these lands,† and consequently she entered into the contract, to be hereafter described, with Angus of the Isles on his marriage with her daughter, styled " Margaret the young " of the Aird.

But who was this Margaret de la Ard, or of the Aird, and what family did she belong to ? This is a question which cannot with absolute certainty be answered. In all the private pedigrees of the Chisholms in which any reference is made to her, she is said to be a Fenton. This has not been proved. The female representatives of the Fentons continued to possess their third of the ancient inheritance of the Bisset lands in the Aird long after this period, and so did the female representatives of the Grahams, who carried their third to the Frasers of Lovat in 1367. John Bisset had died in or about 1259, leaving

† *The Priory of Beauly*, pp. 94-95.

three daughters and co-heiresses—each of whom inherited
and carried to their respective husbands a third of the
Bisset lands in the Aird.

Marie, or Muriel, the eldest, married Sir David de
Graham, by whom she had a son, Patrick Graham, who
died without male issue. His mother, who, as her second
husband, married Fraser of Lovat, carried her portion of
the Bisset lands to the Lord of Lovat, whose representatives possess them at the present day. Cecilia, the
second, married William de Fenton; and the youngest,
Elizabeth, married, first—Rose of Kilravock, and secondly,
Andrew de Bosco, Lord of Redcastle.*

Andrew de Bosco died before 1291, leaving a son and
heir, John de Bosco, who, along with John Bisset, is
mentioned in Grace's *Annals of Ireland* as coming in
Edward Bruce's time with the Scots to Ulster. At Inverness, in the year 1327, Elizabeth, the daughter of this
Sir John de Bosco, and wife of Alexander de Strevelyn,
released in favour of the Roses any claim she had to the
lands of Kilravock. In 1332-33, Nelo de Carrick and
Johanna his wife, and in 1349, Joneta, a widow, the
daughter and one of the heirs of the late Sir John de
Bosco, both execute a similar release in favour of Rose
of Kilravock; and "we shall see hereafter," says Mr.
Chisholm Batten, "the third of the barony of the Aird,
which must have belonged to Elizabeth de Bosco, belonging to the family del Ard."†

Harold the son of Donald of the Aird—"Haroldo filio
Dofnaldi del Ard"—is one of the witnesses to a charter
by Cecilia Bisset, widow of William de Fenton, of her
third of the lands of Altyre, near Beauly, to God and
the Blessed Mary, and John the Baptist, and the brethren
of Valliscaulians serving God in the Priory of Beauly,
for the salvation of her own soul and the souls of her
ancestors and successors. The charter is not dated, but
it is supposed to have been granted about 1315. Another
charter by Patrick de Graham of his third of the lands of

* *Kilravock Papers*, pp. 27-28.   † *Priory of Beauly*, p. 67.

Altyre to the House of Beauly, dated about 1325, is witnessed, along with several others, by Lord William de Fenton, and John de Fenton, his son, " Johanne filio Christini de le Ard "—John, son of Christin or Christian of the Aird, and the same Harold, son of Donald of the Aird, who witnessed the charter of the same lands by Cecilia Bisset ten years before. William de Fenton, Lord of Beaufort, successor to the William de Fenton who married Cecilia Bisset, grants a charter dated at Beaufort on St. Valentine's Day, 1328, to the Priory of Beauly, of two merks out of the Mill of Beaufort. Among the witnesses are " Domino del Ard Milite ; Alexandro Pylche Vicomite de Innernyss ; Haroldo filio Dofnaldi " de la Ard, and several others.

Regarding these names Mr Edmund Chisholm Batten writes :—" The name of Christian del Ard, whose son John witnessed Patrick Graham's charter, and whose name was borne by Donald, whose son Harald witnesses the charter and also Cecilia Byset's, introduces us to a puzzle in the history of the north of Scotland. The name ' del Ard ' first occurs in the ' Ragman Roll.' In 1296, William Fitzstephen de Ard, of the county of Inverness, swears fealty to King Edward I. The same year Christian del Ard, then a simple esquire, is taken fighting against that King at the disastrous battle of Dunbar, and sent with others, knights and esquires, a prisoner to Corfe Castle, in Dorsetshire, on the 5th June, where he was allowed threepence a day by the Sheriff of Somerset and Dorset for his maintenance. The spectacle of the blue waters of the English Channel in the summer time must have chafed the spirit of the fighting Scottish esquire ; and on Hugh, son of Earl William of Ross, coming into England in 1297, Christian, not improbably got free with Earl William, and served Edward I. At all events, on Edward I.'s march to Scotland, Christian del Ard and his companion, Hugh de Ross, ask of the King a grant of the lands which they hope the King would take from his rebellious subjects ; and it is strange, as we find

3

Christian del Ard and Alexander Pylche together as
witnesses to this charter of William de Fenton, that
Christian should, in 1306, have fixed upon, not only the
lands of Laurence and Strathbogie, but also those of
'Alexander of Pylche, burgess of Inverness,' as his
chosen possessions.   Whether at this time Christian had
any lands in Inverness, near that belonging to Alexander
Pylche, does not appear ; but in 1361 a perch of land is
given to a chapel in a charter in the 'Register of
Moray,'* as lying between the land, which John, the son
of Hugh, held of Christian de Ard on the south on the
one side, and the land of William Pylche to the north
on the other.   In 1322,† the Abbot of Arbroath granted
to Sir Christian de Ard, Knight, the lands of Bught,
within the parish of Inverness, at a rent of four merks of
silver, and under the obligation to build houses sufficient
to enable the Abbot to find in them a hall, chamber, and
kitchen for his use when he visited Inverness.   A counter-
part of the charter is said to be left with the monks, with
the seal of the said Sir Christian, which he then used,
and with the new seal of his arms.   But he afterwards
appears under another name.   In Robertson's 'Index,'
among charters of 16 Rob. 1. (1322), the charter of
Deskford is to Christian de Ard, Knight ; but the actual
charter, which is printed in the 'Collections relating to
the shire of Banff,' is granted in 1325 to Sir Christian
de Forbes, Knight.   In 1329 the 'Register of Arbroath'
mentions him as Christian del Ard, Knight.   It does not
appear what became of his son, John, who was a witness
to Patrick de Graham's deed.   John de Forbes is the
first of the name mentioned in contemporary documents ;
this is in 1307.   There is no authority for the earlier
Forbes of the peerage books.   Fergus de Fothes is not
an ancestor ; Fothes and Forbes are two different places.
The story of Alexander de Bois defending Urquhart Castle
against Edward I., and being killed, and his son being
saved, and becoming the first Forbes suggests the family

* *Register of Moray,* p. 305.   † *Register de Aberbrothock,* Vol. I., p. 805.

originating from the de Bois or de Bosco family, and this identity of Christian del Ard and Christian de Forbes, when connected with the fact that Margaret del Ard afterwards possessed the third of the Byset property, which had belonged to Elizabeth Byset, the wife of Andrew de Bosco, may lead to the discovery of the real origin of the family of Forbes."*

It is thus almost certain that the family of De Bois or De Bosco, of Eddyrdor or Redcastle, on acquiring by marriage a third of the Bisset lands, immediately opposite the Aird, came to be known and described as "De la Ard," or of the Aird, and that Margaret de la Aird, who carried these lands to Alexander Chisholme on her marriage to that chief, was a De Bois or De Bosco. There is also the important fact brought out by Mr. Chisholm Batten—that the "Christian de Ard" of 1322 is the "Sir Christian de Forbes, Knight" of 1325; and the suggestion that the Alexander de Bois, who defended Urquhart Castle against Edward I., may have been the first Forbes deserves consideration as a factor in this inquiry; for, according to the traditions of the district, the lands afterwards acquired by the Chisholmes in the Aird and in Strathglass were originally possessed by the Forbeses.

In this way an obscure problem in genealogy hitherto inexplicable may possibly be solved. And further light is thrown on the point by the following facts—Between the years 1362 and 1372, William, Earl of Ross, exchanged with his brother Hugh of Ross, lord of Phylorth, and his heirs his lands of Argyle, which then included Kintail, Strathglass, and several parishes in Wester Ross, with the Castle of Eileandonain, in exchange for Hugh's lands in Buchan. Hugh died without issue and his brother, Earl William, re-acquired these lands. On his death, Philorth and Strathglass were carried by his daughter Johanna to her husband, Fraser, afterwards known as Lord of Philorth, progenitor of the family of Saltoun. In 1423 William Forbes of Kinaldie married Agnes,

* *Priory of Beauly*, pp. 84-86.

daughter of Fraser of Philorth, to whom she carried as dowry the barony of Pitsligo, and the Forbes possessions in Strathglass, which afterwards, in 1455, are found included in the barony of Pitsligo. In 1524, Isobell Wemyss, Lady of Pitsligo, released her terce of these lands to her son, John Forbes of Pitsligo, who has a charter dated the 20th of December, 1536, of Easter and Wester Aigais, with the island of the same name, which formed part of his Strathglass lands, and which he at once deponed to Hugh Fraser, fifth Lord Lovat.

Alexander Chisholme is on record again in 1368. In that year, on the feast of the Blessed Trinity, in the chamber of Alexander, Bishop of Moray, at Spynie, in the presence of the whole multitude of canons and chaplains and others invited thither to dinner, Alexander Chisholme of the Ard, comportioner with William de Fenton, with joined hands and uncovered head, did homage to the Bishop for the lands of the Ess and Kyntallirgy (Kiltarlity).

By Margaret of the Aird and Lady of Erchless, Alexander de Chisholme had issue—

1. Thomas, his heir and successor.

2. Margaret, who in 1401 married Angus, son of Godfrey of Uist and Garmoran, second son of John, First Lord of the Isles, the " Good John of Isla," by his first wife, Amie, heiress of the Macruaries of Garmoran. Godfrey's descendants are said to be extinct. His eldest brother, John, died before his father, leaving one son, also named Angus, who died without issue. Godfrey's next immediately younger brother was Ranald or Reginald, progenitor of the Macdonalds of Glengarry.* On the occasion of Margaret the Younger's marriage, a curious agreement was entered into between her mother, Margaret of the Aird, whose husband, Alexanner de Chisholme, was then dead, and young Margaret's husband, Angus. It is recorded that in 1401, by an indenture dated at Dunballoch between Margaret, Lady of the Aird, Lady

* Mackenzie's *History of the Macdonalds and Lords of the Isles*, p. 59.

of Erchless, and of that Ilk, and Angus, the son of
Godfrey of the Isles, it was agreed that Angus should
marry Margaret the Young, the daughter of the Lady
Margaret of the Aird, with whom he should have from
her mother fifteen merklands, namely, the davach of
Croicheal and the half-davach of Comar Kinbaddy, within
the bounds of Strathglass, to be held by Angus and his
heirs by Margaret his wife ; that should Margaret die
without heirs, the half of those lands and the half of the
goods then jointly possessed by Angus and his wife
should revert to Lady Margaret and her heirs,* the
other half to remain with Angus for his life ; that after
his death the whole should freely revert to the Lady
Margaret and her sons for recovery of the davach of
Brebach Carinnes, and Invernaver in Strathnaver, the
two Gartys in the earldom of Sutherland, and Larnys
in the earldom of Caithness ; and that in so far as the
Lady Margaret and her sons might recover the said
lands through the advice, assistance, and power of Angus,
he and his heirs by her daughter Margaret, should have
the fourth part of the recovered lands, and the other
three-fourths should remain with the Lady Margaret and
her sons ; the entry of Angus to be at the feast of
Penticost following, so that the fermes of that term
should remain with the Lady Margaret, and that the
lands should thenceforth be at the will of Angus.†
From this two important facts are made clear. First,
that the lands in Strathglass which Margaret de la Ard
brought to her husband, Alexander de Chisholme, continued under her own personal control after his death,
and second, that she still laid claim to some portions
of the lands in Sutherland and Caithness which had

---

* These lands of Croicheal are subsequently found in possession of
Haliburton, who married Catherine, the grand-daughter and heiress of
Margaret de la Ard, and Erchless, showing that Angus must have died
without issue.

† *Lib. Insulae Missarum*, pp. ⅃ and ·51 ; and the Pitsligo Charters,
quoted in *Origines Parochiales Scotiæ* pp. 515-516 Vol. II.

belonged to her late brother, Alexander, as Earl of Caithness.

Alexander de Chisholme was succeeded in the remain·ing portion of the lands inherited from his father and brother, which were still extensive, and as head of the house by his son,

IX. THOMAS DE CHISHOLME

Who is on record, during his father's lifetime, in 1389, 1390, and in 1391-92, 1394, and 1398.   His name has been already mentioned as one of the securities in an agreement, dated 2nd November, 1389, between the Wolf of Badenoch and his wife Euphamia, Countess of Ross; the other sureties being Robert, Earl of Sutherland, and Alexander de Moravia of Culbin.   He was Constable of Urquhart Castle in 1391-92, succeeding his father, who had at that date, from extreme old age, become too frail to perform the duties of that responsible office.

On the 10th of May, 1394, an agreement was entered into between Thomas Dunbar, Earl of Moray, and Alexander of the Isles, Lord of Lochaber, by which it was settled that Alexander of the Isles should have the custody of all the lands of the regality of Moray and the ecclesiastical lands, except those belonging to Hugh Fraser, Thomas de Chisholme, and Lord William de Fodrynham, regarding which there was an agreement among themselves.*   These three gentlemen were apparently at that time the portioners of the lands of the Aird, Thomas of Chisholme, holding his share in right of his mother, Margaret de la Ard, although his father was then, and for at least four years later, alive.

In 1403 there is an indenture, dated the 25th of April, at Kinrossie, in the barony of Cullace, Perthshire, between William de Fenton of Baky on the one hand and Margaret de la Aird Lady of Erchless, and Thomas Chisholme, her son and heir, on the other, dividing between them the lands

---

* _Register of Moray_, p. 354.

of which they were heirs portioners, and which, according
to this document, lay in the sheriffdoms of Forfar, Perth,
Lanark, Aberdeen, and Inverness. These extensive possessions are thus described in the deed—the barony of
Rethy, in Forfarshire ; the lands of Culase and Buthergask,
in Perthshire ; the lands of Quodqueen, in Lanarkshire ;
the barony of Gask, in Forfarshire ; the town of Kinrossie
and miln thereof, and the lands of Strathy and Prony,
in the earldom of Stratherne ; the barony of Dumblate,
the two Tollis and Culquhork, in the earldom of Mar ;
the two Arkethys and Craigtoun, in the barony of Crouden
and shire of Aberdeen ; and the lands of the Aird in Inverness-shire. By the same document it was agreed
between them that the lands of the Aird should stand
divided as of old. This agreement was confirmed by
Robert, Duke of Albany, Regent of Scotland, on the
13th of July, 1413, and it was again confirmed by James
IV. in 1513.*

Thomas married Margaret, daughter of Lachlan Mackintosh, VIII. of Mackintosh, by his wife Agnes, daughter
of Hugh Fraser of Lovat, who died in 1397 (and sister
of Hugh Fraser, the first lord), by his wife Elizabeth,
daughter of Sir David Wemyss of that Ilk.† By Margaret Mackintosh of Mackintosh Thomas had issue—

1. Alexander, his heir and successor.

2. Wiland, who, during his father's life, was designated
"of Comar," and, on the death of his brother Alexander
without male issue, succeeded to the chiefship and estates.

He was succeeded by his eldest son,

X. ALEXANDER DE CHISHOLME, ·

Described as "Lord of Kinrossy" in a deed dated at
Elgin on the 9th of August, 1422, in which Thomas of
Dunbar, Earl of Moray, as superior of the lands, grants
to Hugh, Lord of Lovat, the barony of Abertarff in

---

* *Register of the Great Seal, and Robertson's Index.*
† *Anderson's History of the Family of Fraser,* p. 52.

blench ferm, and the ward and relief of the late William of Fenton, Lord of the Baky, and of Alexander of Chisholme, Lord of Kinrosay, pertaining to the said Earl " within the Ard and Strathglass."* From this it will be seen that Alexander Chisholme, like his predecessors, was lord or proprietor of Kinrossy, in Perthshire, and of Strathglass and the Aird at the same time, and as late as 1422. In 1432 Alexander grants a charter to Catherine, his only child and co-heiress, of the barony of Pitcur, in the parish of Kettins, county of Forfar, on the occasion of her marriage to her cousin, Walter Haliburton, second son of Walter, first Lord Dirlton, to whom she carried the lands of Pitcur, which are possessed to this day by their descendents, and one-third of the Aird.

It is interesting to find that thirty years afterwards, as late as 1462, John Haliburton, described as "of Kinrossie"—the designation of Alexander de Chisholme in the deed of 1442—is pursued by the Abbot of Arbroath for alienating the lands of Bught, in the parish of Inverness, which had been formerly granted in 1322 to Sir Christian de la Ard, otherwise Sir Christian de Forbes, Knight, on the express condition that he must never alienate them.† The Haliburtons constantly turn up in documents connected with the Aird after the date of this marriage.

Alexander having died without male issue in 1432, he was succeeded by his brother,

XI. WILAND DE CHISHOLME,

Described "of Comar," whose name appears on record in 1443. About this period "the House of Redcastle is seized by Hector Mackenzie, and the country of Ardmeanach spulzied by William Forbes in Strathglass, Chisholme of Comar, and their accomplices; against whom he obtains a sentence upon 12th May, 1490.

---

* *Spalding Club Miscellany*, p. 256.
† *Lib. de Aberbrothock*, Vol. II., pp. 138-140.

And I find that George Earl of Huntly, Lieutenant of the North, gave commission to Mackintosh, Grant, Kilravock, and others, to the number of three thousand, to go against Kenneth Mackenzie and his kin for spulzieing Ardmeanach, and killing Harold Chisholm in Strathglass, and that they did harry, spulzie, and slay the Clan Kenzie by his command, as the King's rebels and oppressors of the lieges."* There is record of a decree or award respecting the lands of Croy and Kildrummy, in Morayshire, dated the 10th of April, 1492, in which the names of an Alexander and a William Chisholm appear among the arbiters in a dispute between Andrew, Bishop. of Ross, and Hugh Rose, baron of Kilravock, who at that time held the office of keeper of Redcastle.†

Wiland married a lady whose name we have been unable to ascertain, with issue—

1. Wiland, his heir and successor.

2. A daughter, who, about 1470, married Farquhar-of Invercauld.

3. A daughter, who married Ewen Maclean of Ardgour, with issue—three sons.

He was succeeded by his only son, .

XII. WILAND DE CHISHOLM,

The first of the name who was designated "The Chisholm." His descendants dropped the final E in the original name of the family, and from this point it may be as well that we should follow the same form, as it was adopted by the Chisholms of the north generally since they lost connection with the original Border possessions of their southern progenitors. We find Wiland on record in 1499. At Inverness on the 26th October in that year, James IV. issued letters, etc., in favour of Alexander Lord Gordon, and others, his Sheriffs in that part, to levy and distrain the goods of Donald Corbett, and many besides,

---

* *Kilravock Papers,* p 52.   † *Register of Moray,* pp. 237-239, 241, 243, 244.

who spulzied the lands of Ardmeanach and Redcastle, while Kilravock was captain or keeper of it, in consequence of former letters directed by the Lords of the Privy Council to David Ross of Balnagown not having been implemented. Among those mentioned in the letters addressed to Balnagown, and ordered to be distrained, were William Forbes *in* Strathglass, and "Welland Chisholm *of* Comar," and that "to the avail of certain cows, horses, sheep, goats, capons, hens, geese, victual, swine, sums of money, and other goods taken by them from the said Hugh, out of the lands of Ardmeanach and the Redcastle, the time that he was Captain thereof, and to have made him be paid of the same."* These gentlemen at once proceeded to execute their commission—to "burn, harry, and slay,"— and for their safety took the following warrant from the Earl of Huntly, His Majesty's Lieutenant in the north. The document proceeds—

Since it is meet and meritable to bear loyal and steadfast witnessing in the things that are true, that they keep innocents from skaith, I, George, Earl of Huntly, lieutenant to our Sovereign Lord, the King, whom God assoil, and sheriff of Inverness for the time, charged and "gerit" pass by the command of our Sovereign Lord's letters, Duncan Mackintosh, Captain of Clanchattan ; John the Grant of Freuchy ; Hugh the Rose of Kilravock [and several others], with their accomplices, men and friends, to the number of three thousand, upon Kenneth Mackenzie and his kin and friends, dwelling in Ross, for they were the King's rebels, at his horn in that time, and put to his horn by Sir Alexander Dunbar, our Sheriff-Depute for the time of Inverness, for the slaughter of Harrald Chisholm, dwelling in Strathglass, and for divers other herschips, slaughters, and spulzies, made by the said Kenneth Mackenzie, and his kin, accomplices of the Clan Kenneth, upon the King's poor lieges and tenants in the lordship of Ardmeanach, for the which we caused the forsaid persons to burn, harry, and slay, for their demerits ; declaring what skaith that was at that time to the said Clan Kenneth and their accomplices was by the King's command, and ours as Lieutenant, and after the form of our Sovereign Lord's letters directed to us and our deputies purporting at more length.

This warrant is dated at Newark-on-Spey, on the 15th of

* *Kilravock Papers,* pp. 168-170.

December, 1499, and is witnessed by Sir James Ogilvy of Deskford, Knight, Walter Ogilvy of the Boyne, William, Thane of Cawdor, and Patrick Barclay of Grantully.*

The "Harrald" mentioned in the preceding warrant as having been slain in the raid of Redcastle could not have been one of the chiefs of the family, as supposed by some writers. He is always referred to as dwelling *in* Strathglass—described exactly as William Forbes, another indweller, is described; while in the same document, Welland, or Wiland Chisholm, the head of his house, is described "of Comer," just as chiefs of clans and proprietors of lands are invariably described in such documents.

On the 26th of April, 1502, an undertaking is granted by Alexander, Earl of Huntly, to certain men who had suffered from the "Hership of Petty" at the hands of James Dunbar of Cumnock, Knight, David Dunbar his brother, and their accomplices, to follow and pursue these gentlemen "to the utter end of law and the rigour thereof," on certain specified conditions. The document is witnessed among others by "Weland Chisholm of Comar."†

In 1513 James IV. granted to Wiland Chisholm of Comar in heritage the lands of Knockfin, Comar Mor, the two Inverchannichs, and the two Breackachies, with the pertinents, all lying in Strathglass, and in the earldom of Ross, and which Wiland had resigned to the King as Earl of Ross, the title and lands of the earldom having been forfeited to the Crown in 1475, and the Lordship of the Isles in 1493. He has a precept under the Quarter Seal for infeftment of these lands, dated the 9th of April, 1513, and James IV. on the same occasion confirmed the indenture of 1403 between William Fenton of Baky, Thomas of Chisholm, and his mother, Margaret de la Ard. In the same year Wiland Chisholm, accompanied by Sir Donald Gallda of Lochalsh, and Alastair Macdonald of Glengarry, proceeded to Urquhart, and

---

* *Kilravock Papers*, pp. 170-171. † *Invernessiana*, p. 181.

stormed the Castle, expelled the garrison, and laid waste
the adjoining country. On the 26th of February, 1515,
Grant of Freuchy obtained a decree for this raid against
Sir Donald Gallda of Lochalsh, Chisholm of Comar, Alexander John Ranaldson's son in Glengarry, Donald Mac
Angus More in Achadrom, and others, "for the wrongous
and violent spoliation and takand of the fortalice of
Urquhart, frae the said John the Grant, and for £2000
as the value thereof." There was thus an interval of
two years between the raid and the decree.

In 1512 the same King had granted in heritage to
James Haliburton of Gask certain lands in the barony
of Aird and sheriffdom of Inverness, and the lands of
the two Erchlesses in the earldom of Ross which he
had previously resigned. These lands were then erected
into the free barony of Erchless, together with the lands
of Wester Struy, Easter Struy, Culguyry (Cuilgearan)
Easter Croicheal, Wester Croicheal, Wester Comar Kinbaddy, and Dalhenny, with the fishings and outsets of
the same, lying in Strathglass, in the earldom of Ross,
and in the sheriffdom of Inverness, which formerly
belonged to James Haliburton in heritage, and which,
after alienation by him, had now been redeemed. He
had at this date re-granted to him all the King's right
and title to the lands and their fermes which His Majesty
had, in consequence of the forfeiture of the Earls of
Moray and Ross, of whom, as the superiors, these lands
were formerly held. In 1529 the above-named James
Haliburton resigned the lands conveyed to him in 1512,
whereupon James V. granted them in heritage to Hugh
Fraser of Lovat.

Wiland Chisholm was, before his death, succeeded in
the lands by his son,

XIII. JOHN CHISHOLM,

Who, on the 2nd of October, 1529, during his father's
life-time, appears as a witness to a charter of endowment

for two chaplains to officiate in the Cathedral of Moray, executed by Gavin Dunbar, Bishop of Aberdeen. He is described in this document as "*Master* John Chisholm, son and heir of Wiland Chisholm of Comar." There is a charter under the Great Seal by James V. in favour of "John Chisholm, eldest son of the said Wiland Chisholm," of the lands mentioned in the charter of 1513, and which had in the meantime been apprised to James IV. for certain debts owing to the Crown. This charter, which is dated the 13th of March, 1538, erected the lands named into a barony in favour of John and his heirs whatsoever. On the same date we find an order and warrant under the Privy Seal by James V. to his comptrollers and auditors to delete the lands mentioned in these documents from His Majesty's Exchequer rolls.

On the 27th of May, 1539, there is an instrument of sasine on a charter by James V. granting in heritage to John Chisholm, the son and apparent heir of Wiland Chisholm of Comar, under reservation of his father Wiland's life-rent, the lands of Knockfin, Comar Mor, the two Inverchannichs, and the two Breackachies, with the outsets and the forests of Affric, Cullove, and Bramulich, in Strathglass, in the earldom of Ross, which formerly belonged to his father, Wiland Chisholm, but were apprised in the hands of King James IV. for certain sums of money due to him by Wiland, and which James V. in this year united into the barony of Comar Mor.

In the same year James V. granted to Hugh, Lord Fraser of Lovat, and his male heirs of the name and arms of Fraser, with remainder to his heirs whomsoever, the lands and baronies of Lovat, Stratherrick, Abertarff, Erchless or Strathglass, the fishings in the river of Forne or Farrar, the lands of Comer-na-kill in the barony of the Aird, and other lands in the sheriffdom of Inverness, the lands of Comer-na-kill, and some others having been apprised in the hands of James IV. for certain sums of money due to him by the deceased Thomas Lord Lovat, and the rest resigned by Hugh. All these lands were then erected into the free barony of Lovat.*

In 1542 John Chisholm receives a remission of all his offences from James V. The more recent of these appear to be offences óf which a detailed account is given in the Acts of Parliament, and in which " Maister John Chesholme is accused as 'one of the simulat and feugit assigns,'" who intromitted with "the gudis and errands of Archibald Douglas of Kilspindie " three years before, in 1539.†

From the fact that John is described as *Maister* in 1542, it is evident that his father was still alive at that date. He was dead, however, before 1555, for in that year Queen Mary granted to John, Earl of Sutherland, the lands of Comar in Strathglass, and all the other lands belonging to " the deceased John Cheisholme of Comyr, in her hands at his decease."‡ He could not write his own name ; for at Elgin, on the 7th of December, 1544, he and John Mackenzie of Kintail sign a bond of manrent to the Earl of Huntly, " Johne Chislome of Cummyr, with my hand at the pen, led by the said Maister James, notar publick."§ Lord Lovat, who was also one of the signatories, was able to sign with his own hand, but Mackenzie of Kintail required the same assistance as John Chisholm of Strathglass.

John was succeeded by his son,

XIV. ALEXANDER CHISHOLM,

Who has a sasine of the family estates on the 31st of May, 1555, as the son and heir of John Chisholm. This sasine follows upon a precept furth of Chancery for infefting Alexander as heir in special, served and retoured to his father John Chisholm of Comar. On the 15th of October, 1563, John Campbell of Cawdor was served

---

* *Origines Parochiales Scotiae*, pp. 516-517.
† *Acts of Parliament*, II. 354.
‡ *Register of the Privy Seal*, Vol. XXVII. p. 103.
§ *Spalding Club Miscellany*, Vol. II. p. 187.

in the barony of Strathnairn, before James Earl of Moray, then Sheriff-Principal. Among those whose names appear on the jury we find Alexander Chisholm of Comar, along with Kenneth Mackenzie of Kintail, Alexander Ross of Balnagown, Robert Munro of Fowlis, Hugh Rose of Kilravock, Hugh Fraser of Guisachan, William Fraser of Struy, Alexander Urquhart, Sheriff of Cromarty, and several others.* In 1577 James VI. confirmed a grant in life-rent by Alexander to his wife Janet Mackenzie, eldest daughter of Kenneth Mackenzie, X. of Kintail, ancestor of the Earls of Seaforth and sister-german of Colin Mackenzie XI. of Kintail, of the lands and mill of Breackachies, in the earldom of Ross, to be held direct of the Crown. There is a sasine of the lands of Comar Mor and Wester Invercannich, with the mill and pertinents, forming part of the barony of Comar Mor, in favour of Thomas Chisholm, son and apparent heir of Alexander Chisholm and Janet Fraser his spouse, proceeding on a charter dated the 26th of March, 1578, of the said lands granted them by Alexander. The instrument of sasine is dated the 12th of April immediately following.

Alexander's wife was the widow of Æneas Macdonald VII. of Glengarry, her mother being Lady Elizabeth Stewart, daughter of John second Earl of Athol, by his wife Mary Campbell, daughter of Archibald second Earl of Argyll. Through this marriage of Alexander Chisholm to Janet Mackenzie of Kintail, Lady Elizabeth Stewart's daughter, the Chisholms of Strathglass, of whom James Chisholm Gooden Chisholm, of Tavistock Square, London, is present heir of line, are descended from Edward I., Edward III., and from Mary, sister of King Robert the Bruce.† Alexander is again mentioned in a

---

* *Invernessiana*, p. 299.

† Janet Mackenzie of Kintail was Glengarry's third wife. His only issue by her was a daughter, Elizabeth, who married John Roy Mackenzie, IV. of Gairloch with issue, among others, Alexander Mackenzie V. of Gairloch, from whom the author is seventh in descent both on the male and female side.

retour in 1584 along with his third son, as "Alexander Cheisholme of Cwmer, and Wiland Cheisholme his youngest son."

Alexander married, as already stated, Janet, daughter of Kenneth Mackenzie, tenth Baron of Kintail, with issue—

1. Thomas, his heir and successor.

2. John, who succeeded his brother Thomas in the chiefship and estates.

3. Wiland, who is described in 1584, in a retour as Alexander Chisholm of Comar's "youngest son." We, however, cannot find any further trace of him.

Alexander, who died before 1590, was succeeded by his eldest son,

XV. THOMAS CHISHOLM,

Who has a sasine dated the 12th of April, 1578, during his father's life-time, on the occasion of his marriage to Janet Fraser, widow of John Glassich Mackenzie, II. of Gairloch, only daughter and heiress of James Fraser of Phoineas, brother of Hugh fifth Lord Lovat. On the 7th of June, 1539, the lady's father has a charter in his favour of the King's lands of Drumdervale (? Drumderfit) in the lordship of Ardmanoch or Redcastle, in Ross, and on the 25th of October, 1542, another of the lands of Kinkell, Culbokie, and Pitlundie, in the Black Isle. He was one of the principal men of the name of Fraser who fell at the battle of Blar-nan-leine in 1544, at the head of Loch Lochy.

In one of the Gairloch manuscripts it is said that by Janet Fraser her first husband, John Glassich Mackenzie, "got the lands of Kinkell, Kilbokie, Badinearb, Pitlundie, Davochcairn, Davochpollo, and Foynish, with others in the Low Country, for which the family [of Gairloch] has been in the use to quarter the arms of Fraser with their own."

Janet had three sons to John Glassich Mackenzie, each

of whom became in succession lairds of Gairloch. Her husband having been violently put to death at the instance of John Mackenzie, IX. of Kintail, she, according to an old family manuscript, fled with her eldest surviving son, John Roy Mackenzie, "to Lovat and her Fraser relatives." The same authority says that "she was afterwards married to Chisholm of Comar and heird his family; here she kept him in as concealed a manner as possible, and, as is reported, every night under a brewing kettle; those who, through the barbarity of the times, destroyed the father and the uncles, being in search of the son, and in possession of his all excepting his mother's dower. He was afterwards concealed by the lairds of Moidart and of Farr, till he became a handsome man, and could put on his weapon, when he had to wait on Colin Càm Mackenzie, laird of Kintail, a most worthy gentleman who established him in all his lands, excepting those parts of the family estate for which Hector and his successors had an undoubted right by writs."*

In 1574 John Roy Mackenzie acquired from Lord Lovat half the lands of Ardnagrask, partly for the rights he had inherited in Phoineas from his mother. In the disposition of these lands, Lord Lovat designates Mackenzie as "the son, by her first husband, of his kinswoman, Agnes Fraser." It appears from a charter of alienation by Hugh Fraser of Guisachan, dated the 29th of May, 1582, that John Roy Mackenzie had acquired Davochcairn and Davochpollo from this Hugh Fraser, in 1574, the same year in which he acquired Ardnagrask, and that in 1582 he obtained from him the lands of Kinkell-Clarsach and Pitlundie, in terms of a contract of sale dated the 26th of January, 1581.†

From this it would seem that part at least of the lands which Agnes Fraser on the occasion of her first marriage

---

* Quoted in Mackenzie's *History of the Clan Mackenzie*, pp. 315-316.

† Mackenzie's *History of the Mackenzies*, pp. 316-317. Her name must have been Janet Agnes, for she is as often called by the one as by the other.

carried to her husband, John Glassich Mackenzie of Gairloch, remained with herself, or returned to her Fraser
relatives, and that she did not carry them with her to
her second husband, Thomas Chisholm, Hugh Fraser of
Guisachan, who conveyed them to Mackenzie, being her
father's brother. It would, however, appear from the
sasine of 1578, that she carried some portion of her possessions to her second husband, Thomas Chisholm of
Comar, during his father's life-time.

This Thomas "Cheisholm of Cummer" is included in
"The Roll of the names of the landlordis and baillies of
landis in the Hielandis and Iles, quhair brokin men hes
duelt and presentlie duellis," appended to the Act of
Parliament passed in the year 1587, "for the quieting
and keeping in obedience of the disordourit subjects
inhabitants of the Bordouris, Hielandis, and Ilis," commonly called The General Band, or Bond.*

Thomas died very soon after his father (who was alive
in 1584), and before 1590, without surviving male issue,
and probably without making up titles, when he was
succeeded by his next brother,

XVI. JOHN CHISHOLM,

Who was the "son of Alexander and brother to Thomas,"
and was served heir to his father, Alexander Chisholm,
by a special service before the Sheriff of Inverness, on
the 19th of December, 1590, in the lands of Knockfin,
Comar Mor, the two Inverchannichs with the mill thereof,
the two Breackachies, the woods and forests of Affric,
Cullove, and Bramulach, extending to three davochs,
united into the barony of Comar Mor, in Strathglass,
in the earldom of Ross, excepting the lands of Wester
Inverchannich with the mill and the lands of Comar
Mor, of the old extent of £4.†

He has another special service of the same lands on

* Collectanea de Rebus Albanicis, pp. 33-34.
† Origines Parochiales Scotiae, p. 517.

the same date, as heir to his brother Thomas, and sasine
follows upon all his father's and brother's possessions with
an instrument of sasine following upon a precept from
Chancery, dated the 19th of July, 1591, for infefting him
therein as heir to his father Alexander Chisholm. The
sasine is dated the 19th of August in the same year. He
has a similar instrument following upon a like precept,
and on the same dates, infefting him in the said lands
as heir served and retoured to the said Thomas Chisholm
his brother-german.

He has an instrument of sasine of the lands of the
two Erchlesses and Comar-na-kill, with the pertinents,
following upon a precept of sasine contained in a tack of
nineteen years of the said lands, granted by Simon Lord
Fraser of Lovat, dated the 25th and 26th of February,
1594. On the 13th of May, 1606, there is a charter of
the lands of Erchless from the same Simon Lord Lovat,
in favour of John Chisholm of Comar and Janet Bayne,
his spouse. There is a charter of confirmation of this
deed under the Great Seal to John and his spouse,
dated the 28th of January, 1612 ; followed by a charter
of alienation by Simon Lord Lovat to John Chisholm
and his wife, Janet Bayne, of the lands of Comar Kirkton,
dated the 18th of May, 1614, along with a contract of
wadset between his lordship and the said John and Janet,
on the same date. From this it would appear that John's
first wife was the widow or daughter of one of the
Baynes of Tulloch.

In 1628 John Chisholm of Comar enters into a contract
with Colin first Earl of Seaforth, Simon Lord Fraser of
Lovat, Hector Munro of Clynes, John Grant of Glenmoriston, John Bayne of Tulloch, and others of their
respective names, for the preservation of deer and roe,
and the punishment of trespassers on their several estates.
In this contract "John Chisholme of Comer, and Alexander Chisholme, his eldest lawfull son and apperand air
for thameselffs," takes upon them the full burden " for
thair brether," men-tenants, and servants. The docu-

ment, modernised in spelling, is in the following terms :—

At   the year of God 1628 : It is appointed, contracted, and finally ended betwixt the noble and honourable parties
following, that is to say, a noble and potent Lord Colin Earl of
Seaforth, Lord of Kintail and Lewis, and with him his honourable
friends following, viz., John Mackenzie of Coigeach, George Mackenzie of Kildin, Mr. Colin Mackenzie of Kinnock, Mr. Alexander
Mackenzie of Kilcoy, Alexander Mackenzie, fiar of Gairloch, Alexander Mackenzie of Coul, and John Mackenzie of Fairburn for
themselves; and the said noble Lord taking upon him the full
burden for the remanent of his kin and friends and for his Lordship's men-tenants and servants, and his forenamed kinsmen taking
upon them the full burden each one respectively for their own men-
tenants and servants on the first part ; and a noble and potent
Lord Simon Fraser of Lovat, Hew master of Lovat, his eldest lawful son and apparent heir, and with them their honourable friends
after named, viz., Thomas Fraser of Strichen, Thomas Fraser of
Struy, Hucheoun Fraser of Kilbokie, and Hucheoun Fraser of Belladrum for themselves ; and the said noble lord and his said son
taking on them the full burden for the remanent of their kin and
friends and for their men-tenants and servants, and their forenamed
kinsmen taking upon them the full burden each one respectively for
their own men-tenants and servants on the second part ; and Hector
Monro of Clynes, Robert Monro of Assynt for themselves, and
taking on them the full burden for Hector Monro of Pitfure and
George Monro of Ardcharnich and the remanent of the tenants of
of the lands of Inverlael on the third part ; and John Chisholm
of Comar and Alexander Chisholm his eldest lawful son and
apparent heir for themselves, and taking upon them the full burden
for their brother, men tenants and servants, on the fourth part ;
and John Grant of Glenmoriston and Patrick Grant his eldest son
and appparent heir for themselves, and taking the full burden upon
them for their men-tenants and servants on the fifth part ; and
John Bayne of Tulloch, Ronald Bayne and Kenneth Bayne his
brother, for themselves, and taking on them the full burden for the
remanent, their brother, men-tenants and servants on the sixth
part ; In manner and effect as after follows.   That is to say, for
as much there is divers and sundry acts of Parliament made by
our sovereign lord's progenitors of worthy memory anent the stealing
of deer, doe, and roe, which is appointed to be punished as theft,
and anent shooting at them, which is appointed to be punished
with death and escheat of their goods movable ; which acts are,
and have been, daily contravened these many years bygone by
reason of the impunity of the offenders, whereby the wonted store

of deer, doe and roe, in special within the bounds pertaining to the aforesaid parties contracting, is greatly decreased ; For better preservation thereof in time coming the said six parties, each one of them for themselves, and taking on them the burdens respectively foresaid, by these presents bind and oblige them and their heirs each one to another respectively, that they nor none of them, their men-tenants nor servants shall, under whatsoever colour or pretext, steal or convey away by night or by day any deer, doe or roe, feeding within the bounds of any of their forests thereof to any other forest ; neither shall they hunt nor slay the said deer, doe or roe, by dogs, gun, or bow outwith the forest pertaining properly to themselves, nor tansport nor carry guns in hills or forest for that effect in no time hereafter, from the date hereof, without the special license of the owner of the forest, first had and obtained thereto in writing, under the pains following, viz., of one hundred marks money each person of the aforesaid parties contracting, and of forty pounds each one of their brother, men-tenants and servants that shall happen to contravene, as a liquidating fine presently modified by the said whole parties to be paid by each contravener to the person or persons within whose bounds and forest the contravention shall be committed *toties quoties*, the same shall happen and that within the space of fifteen days after the proving of each contravention in presence of the bailies to be nominated and appointed by the party contravening and the party contravened upon, in an open court to be held within the bounds of the party offended, where they shall appoint ; and if the said brother, men-tenants or servants of the contravening parties or either of the parties themselves refuse to compear before the said bailies, or that the bailie of the party contravening such like refuses to compear to hold court and hear probation led : In that case it shall be committed to receive witnesses and pronounce decree as well as if the other bailie were present, which decree being pronounced the said parties, each one for their own parts respectively, oblige them to satisfy and fulfil to the others without any exception and to cause their brother, men-tenants and servants, to satisfy their fines *toties quoties*, or else to present them each one to the other or to our sovereign lord's justice at the party offended's will and option to underlye the law for that effect : Consenting for the more security that these presents be inserted and registered in the books of Council and Session, and that a decree of the Lords thereof be hereto interponed, and that letters and executions of horning and others needful, the one without prejudice of the other hereupon be directed, and the horning in case thereof to pass upon a simple charge of ten days only : And for that effect constitutes Masters Alexander Cumming, Mathew Forsyth, John Sandilands, and David Heriot their procurators *promittentes de rato:* In witness thereof written by Alexander Ross, servitor to William Lauder, commissary clerk of Ross, the said parties have subscribed these presents with their hands, day, year, and place aforesaid, before these witnesses, Hugh Rose of Kilravock, James Fraser of Phopacy, Gavin Dunbar, Hew Macgill, and Alexander Dunbar, reader at Croy. *Sic subscribitur* Seaforth, Lovat, H. M. Lovat, Thomas Fraser of Struy, John Grant of Glenmoriston, Patrick Grant, apparent of Glenmoriston, "John Chisholme of Comer," Hugh Ross, witness, Gavin Dunbar, witness, Hew Macgill, witness, Alexander Dunbar, witness, James Fraser, witness, Alexander Dunbar, witness to Glenmoriston and his son's subscription, William Finlayson, witness to Thomas Fraser of Struy's subscription, Mr. Wm. Mackenzie, witness to the Chisholm's subscription, W. Fraser of Drumcharden.*

It is interesting to find that The Chisholm signs this document by his own hand as "John Chisholme of Comer," retaining the final E in the family name as late as 1628.

John, who does not appear to have had any issue by his first wife, married, secondly, the eldest daughter, by his second wife, of Alexander Mackenzie (natural son of Colin Càm Mackenzie, XI. of Kintail, by Mary, eldest daughter of Roderick Mackenzie, II. of Davochmaluag), progenitor of the families of Coul and Applecross. By this lady he had issue—

1. Alexander, his heir and successor.

2. Thomas of Kinneries, "Tanastair" of Chisholm, commonly called "Tomas Mor Mac-an t-Siosalaich," of whose family and descendants in their order.

3. Agnes, who married William Rose of Clava (who died on the 13th of August, 1664, aged eighty), second son of William Rose, XI. of Kilravock, with issue—one son, Hugh, his father's heir.

4. A daughter, who married Alexander Rose of Cantray, her brother-in-law (who died in his 36th year in 1622), third son of William Rose, XI. of Kilravock, with issue—four daughters, the eldest of whom married Grant of Corriemony, and the second, Macpherson of Nuide, in Badenoch.†

* *Transactions of the Iona Club*, pp. 193-195.
† *Kilravock Papers*, pp. 81-82.

5. A daughter who, about 1625, married Maclean of Dochgarroch.

John Chisholm was succeeded by his eldest son,

XVII. ALEXANDER CHISHOLM,

Who, during the life of his father, has a contract of disposition granted to him by Simon Lord Lovat, of the lands of Easter and Wester Erchless and Comar Kirkton, dated the 28th of March, 1621. On the same date he has from the same party, a feu charter of these lands in implement of this contract. A sasine follows on the 31st of the same month, which is registered in the Particular Register of Inverness and Cromarty, on the 22nd of April following. On the 25th of July, 1622, he receives a charter of confirmation under the Great Seal, of the foregoing lands, with infeftment following immediately thereon. He has an instrument of sasine in his favour of the whole lands and barony of Comar Mor, following upon a precept of Chancery, dated the 17th of July, 1630, for infefting him as heir, served and retoured, to his father, John Chisholm of Comar. The sasine is dated 4th of August following, and is registered in the Particular Register of sasines for the shires of Inverness and Cromarty on the 12th of the same month. There is a contract of feu in favour of Alexander by Hugh Lord Lovat, of the lands of Buntait and Mauld, dated the 31st of May and 1st of June, 1637, followed by a charter of implement on the same dates, and a sasine, dated the 19th of June, and duly registered on the 7th of July, in the same year. The whole is confirmed by a charter under the Great Seal in favour of Alexander, on the 16th of January, 1638, followed by infeftment in the usual form.

Alexander in 1639 married his cousin, a daughter of Alexander Mackenzie, V. of Gairloch, with issue—

1. Angus, his heir and successor.

2. Alexander, who, on the death of his brother Angus without issue, succeeded to the family estates.

3. Colin, from whom the Chisholms of Knockfin, and of whom in their order.

4. A daughter, who married Fraser of Belladrum.

Alexander was succeeded by his eldest son,

XVIII. ANGUS CHISHOLM,

Usually designated "An Siosal Càm," or the One-eyed Chisholm. He is on record in 1647. In 1658 he has a Colonel's commission for the command of horse or foot within the sheriffdom of Inverness, and by the Act for putting the country in a state of defence, his name appears in the list of persons whose station entitle them to the command of national troops,* which really means in ordinary phraseology, that he was empowered to arm and command his own clan.

He married Margaret, daughter of Murdoch Mackenzie, II. of Redcastle, without issue, and was succeeded in the family estates by his next brother,

XIX. ALEXANDER CHISHOLM,

Generally known as "An Siosal Og," or the Young Chisholm. On the 26th of November, 1657, we find a disposition by William Fraser of Culbokie (who on the 22nd of February, 1636, acquired the lands in question from Hugh Lord Lovat), by Hugh Fraser his son, and by Christina Chisholm, his wife, all with one consent, in favour of Alexander Chisholm, of the lands of Wester Comar, alias Comar Croy. This disposition was implemented by two charters of the same date, followed by an instrument of sasine, dated the 31st of May and registered, as in the last case, on the 8th of June, 1658. He has a precept of *Clare Constat* of these lands from Lovat's trustees already mentioned, dated the 23rd of March, 1678, upon which a sasine follows on the 8th,

* *Acts of Parliament*, Vol. VI. p. 303.

which is duly registered on the 15th of November in the same year.

Alexander is served as heir general on the 19th of June, 1677, and has a sasine following thereon on the 11th of April, 1678, duly registered in the Particular Register for Inverness-shire on the 19th of the same month. On the 23rd of March in the same year he has a precept of *Clare Constat* by Kenneth Mor Mackenzie, third Earl of Seaforth, Sir George Mackenzie of Tarbat, and Hugh Fraser of Belladrum, Lord Lovat's trustees, as heir of his father, Alexander, of the town lands of Comar Croy or Wester Comar. Sasine follows on this precept on the 8th of November in the same year, and it is registered in the Particular Register of Sasines for the county on the 15th of that month. On the same· date he has a similar precept from the same parties of the lands of Easter and Wester Erchless and of Comar Kirkton, with a sasine following thereon, duly registered on the 18th of November, 1678. He was Sheriff-Depute of the county of Inverness from 1689 to 1695.

In 1689 General Livingston found it necessary to send troops to disperse bodies of Highlanders, who, after the battle of Killiecrankie, which was fought in that year, continued in arms for the House of Stuart. A detachment of the Strathnaver and Grant regiments, from Brahan Castle, and the garrison of Castle Leod, accompanied by a party of horse under Lieutenant-Colonel Lumsden, were ordered to march against one of these bodies of Highlanders who had collected in Strathglass, and taken possession of Erchless Castle, the seat of the Chisholms, in which they resolved to defend themselves. It was, however, carried by storm, and a great quantity of provisions found within it was secured. Major Mackay, with four companies of the Grants, was left to defend the Castle and as a check on the disaffected, but the following summer he and his garrison were attacked by some five hundred Highlanders, by whom they would have been compelled to surrender had not Livingston promptly marched from Inverness and relieved them by a successful attack on the besieging Highlanders.

Alexander married the eldest daughter of Roderick Mackenzie, I. of Applecross, with issue—

1. John, his heir and successor.

2. Theodore, of whose family in their order.

3. Jean, who married Sir Kenneth Mackenzie, I. of Coul, created a baronet on the 16th of October, 1673, by Charles II., with issue—(1) Alexander, his heir and successor; (2) Simon, first of the Mackenzies of Torridon and Lentran; (3) John, first of Delvine; (4) Roderick, who married a daughter of Alexander Mackenzie, VIII. of Davochmaluag; (5) a daughter, who married Colin Mackenzie, IV. of Redcastle, with issue; (6) Agnes, who married Sir John Munro of Fowlis, with issue; (7) Jane, who married Alexander Baillie, IX. of Dunain; (8) Christian, who married John Dunbar, younger of Bennetsfield; (9) Lilias, who married John Munro of Inverawe, with issue; (10) Mary, who married Kenneth Mackenzie, VI. of Davochmaluag, with issue; and (11) a daughter, who married Gordon of Cluny.*

He was succeeded by his eldest son,

XX. JOHN CHISHOLM,

Known among his own countrymen as "An Siosalach Ruadh," or the Red Chisholm. He married Jane, third daughter of Sir Roderick Mackenzie of Findon, fourth son of Alexander Mackenzie, I. of Kilcoy, third son of Colin Càm, XI. of Kintail, by his wife Barbara, daughter of John, XII. of Grant, and brother of Kenneth, first Lord Mackenzie and twelfth Baron of Kintail. This lady brought John a considerable fortune in money, her eldest sister Lilias, as heiress, carrying her father's landed estate of Findon to her husband, Sir Kenneth Mackenzie, IV. of Scatwell, on the death of her only brother, when, on the 12th of

* Mackenzie's *History of the Mackenzies*, p. 448.

October, 1693, she was served heir of tailzie to her father in these lands, and carried them to Sir Kenneth, to whom she had been married in 1688. The other and youngest sister, Isabel, carried her portion, the estate of Allan, now Allangrange, to Simon Mackenzie, first of that family.*

By his wife, Sir Roderick Mackenzie's daughter, John had issue—

1. Roderick, his heir and successor.

2. Alexander of Muckerach, whose male representatives on the death of Duncan Macdonell Chisholm, on the 18th of September, 1858, without male issue, succeeded to the family estates as heir of entail, and of whom in their order.

3. Janet, who married one of the Macdonells of Leek.

4. Lilias, who married Fraser of Struy.

John was succeeded by his eldest son,

XXI. RODERICK CHISHOLM,

Sometimes called "Ruairi Mac Ian," but generally known among the people of Strathglass as "Ruairi 'n Aigh." He was born in 1697, and was a minor when he succeeded. At the age of eighteen, he led two hundred of his clan, accompanied by his cousin, John Chisholm of Knockfin, under the Earl of Mar in 1715, to Sheriff Muir, though both had signed, with many other chiefs and gentlemen, an address expressive of much loyalty to George I. and his family before he left for England to take possession of the throne of Great Britain, in the previous year. This document was, it is said, never seen by the King, but had been withheld by persons about the Court who were inimical to the Highland chiefs—a slight which they eagerly resented, believing that they had been unceremoniously insulted by His Majesty, who took no notice of their declared loyalty, but on the contrary, dismissed their leader, the Earl of Mar, from his office of Secretary of State after the King's arrival in

* Mackenzie's *History of the Mackenzies*, pp. 279-280, and 425.

England. This letter was signed by Sir John, Chief of the Macleans; Alastair Dubh Macdonell of Glengarry; Donald Cameron of Lochiel; Coll Macdonald of Keppoch, and his son, Alexander; Sir Donald Macdonald of Sleat; Lachlan Mackintosh of Mackintosh; Alexander Mackenzie of Fraserdale; John Macleod of Contullich; John Grant of Glenmoriston; Duncan Macpherson of Cluny; Roderick Chisholm of Comar, and John Chisholm of Knockfin, and was in the following terms:—

My Lord,—So soon as we heard of the afflicting news of the death of her late Majesty, Queen Anne, it did exceedingly comfort us, that after so good and great a queen, who had the hearts and consulted the true happiness of all her people, we were to be governed by his sacred Majesty, King George, a prince so brightly adorned with all the royal virtues, that Britain, under his royal administration, shall still be flourishing at home, and able to hold the balance in the affairs of Europe. Allow us, my lord, to please ourselves with this agreeable persuasion, that his Majesty's royal and kindly influence shall reach to us, who are the most remote, as well as to others of his subjects in this island. We are not ignorant that there are some people forward to misrepresent us, from particular private views of their own, and who, to reach their own ends against us on all occasions, endeavour to make us in the Highlands of Scotland, pass for disaffected persons.

Your lordship has an estate and interest in the Highlands, and is so well known to bear good-will to your neighbours, that in order to prevent any ill impressions, which malicious and ill-designing people may at this juncture labour to give of us, we must beg leave to address your lordship, and entreat you to assure the Government, in our names, and in that of the rest of the clans, who, by distance of place, could not be present at the signing of this letter, of our loyalty to his sacred Majesty King George. And we do hereby declare to your lordship, that as we were always ready to follow your directions in serving Queen Anne, so we will now be equally forward to concur with your lordship in faithfully serving King George, and we entreat your lordship would advise us how we may best offer our duty to his Majesty upon his coming over to Britain; and on all occasions we will beg to receive your counsel and direction how we may be most useful to his Royal Government. We are, with all truth and respect, etc.

Roderick Chisholm does not seem to have made up any title to the estates, and the result of his share in the

Rising of 1715 was that a great portion of his possessions was forfeited to the Crown. And his lands would
have been all lost were it not that the three Knockfins,
Affric, Quillove, and others were at the time, and as far
back as 1678, under wadset to Chisholm of Knockfin.
The following is a copy of the grant—

Contract of proper wadset betwixt Alexander Chisholm of Comar
and Colin Chisholm, whereby the former wadsets and impignorates
to the latter and his heirs and his assigns whatsomever the half
davoch, town and lands of Knockfin, commonly called Easter,
Middle, and Wester Knockfin, with certain other grazings, redeemable for 12,000 merks Scots, dated 19th August 1678.

The lands of Erchless, Comar, Breakachy, Glencannich,
Invercannich, and all the others belonging to The Chisholm, were specially mentioned in the forfeiture to the
Crown. These were afterwards sold by public auction
by the Commissioners of Forfeited Estates, and a disposition of them was made on the 21st of July, 1724,
to James Baillie, of the Dochfour family, at the time
practising as a Writer to the Signet in Edinburgh, who
bought them on behoof of the family.   He afterwards
disponed them to George Mackenzie of Allangrange, a
confidential friend of the House of Chisholm.   The deed
in favour of Baillie is registered in the records of Chancery,
on the 7th of August, 1724, and entered in the Auditor's
office in the Exchequer on the 12th of the same month.
There is an instrument of resignation of all these lands
and estates by James Baillie in favour of George Mackenzie of Allangrange, proceeding on the procuratory of
resignation contained in the original deed, on a disposition and assignation of the same by the former to the
latter, on the 2nd of September, 1724.   This instrument
is dated the 26th of July, 1725, and a charter of resignation under the Great Seal in favour of George Mackenzie
follows on the same day.   Sir George Mackenzie next dis-
'poses of the estates to Alexander Chisholm of Muckerach,
immediate younger brother of the forfeited Roderick ; and
on the 21st of July, 1727, we find an instrument of sasine

in favour of Muckerach, which was registered in the
Particular Register of Sasines at Fortrose, on the 27th
of September following.   The whole of these lands and
estates are ultimately granted, as was intended by all
the parties from the beginning, to Alexander Chisholm,
Younger of Comar.   There is a disposition dated the 9th
of November, 1742, and registered in the Books of Session
on the 25th of July, 1774, by Alexander Chisholm of
Muckerach, entailing the estates in favour of Alexander
Chisholm, eldest son of Roderick Chisholm, and the heirs
male of his body, whom failing, the other heirs mentioned
in the deed.   A procuratory of resignation by the one in
favour of the other follows on the 13th of May, 1743,
and an instrument of resignation in favour of the said
Alexander Chisholm, Younger of Comar, on the 22nd of
June following.   Then follows a charge of resignation
under the Great Seal in his favour of the same date,
and sealed on the 19th of July.   Sasine succeeds on the
29th of August, and is registered in the General Register
of Sasines on the 16th of September, all in 1743.

During the same period, similar transactions were carried
out regarding the lands of the Breackachies and Glencannich.   Chisholm of Muckerach secured possession of
these also, and, on the 20th of July, 1727, he disposes
of the Breackachies, with their teinds and pertinents, to
Robert Schevez of Muirtown.   A sasine follows next day,
and it is duly registered on the 6th of September in the
same year.   Robert Schevez disposes of these lands on
the 2nd of November, 1747, to John Baillie, Writer to
the Signet, who next conveys them to Alexander Chisholm, Younger of Comar, on the 10th of May, 1749.

On the 7th of December, 1763, Alexander Chisholm of
Muckerach and Alexander Chisholm, Younger of Comar,
disposes of the lands of Breackachies and Glencannich
to Captain James Chisholm, old Roderick's second son,
in life-rent, and his brother the said Alexander Chisholm,
Younger of Comar and his heirs in fee.   An instrument
of sasine in favour of the two brothers is registered in

the Particular Register of Sasines on the 4th of April, 1764. There is a second disposition by the same parties and on the same date as in the former case, in favour of William Chisholm, Alexander and Captain James' next brother, then practising as a surgeon in Inverness (of which he became Provost), of the lands of Buntait in life-rent, and to Alexander, his brother, in fee. A charter of resignation, under the Great Seal, by Muckerach in favour of William and Alexander follows, dated the 2nd, and sealed on the 5th of March, 1764. A sasine thereon succeeds on the 28th of the same month and is registered in the same Register as the other on the 4th of April following.

In 1725 Roderick took the necessary steps towards procuring a pardon for the part he had taken in the Rising under Mar in 1715. With this object he wrote a letter, of which the following is a copy, to Marshall Wade, then employed in disarming and receiving the submission of the clans, and opening up roads through the Highland glens for the more easy passage of the Royal troops. Roderick wrote :—

Sir,—The success your undertakings have always had has been more owing to your courteous and affable behaviour than the terror of your arms. I presume to throw myself under your protection, fully confident that so much goodness cannot decline representing my unhappy case to the best of Kings. I mean rebellion, which I now detest, and, Sir, I hope that my repentance will be judged the more solid that I am now in a mature age, whereas I had not attained to the years of manhood when, unnaturally, I allowed myself to be led to bear arms against His Majesty King George. I have disposed my clan to disarm, and for myself and them I promise faithfully henceforward to behave ourselves as becomes dutiful subjects to His Majesty King George, begging in the most profound manner his most gracious pardon for my life (my estate having been sold), which I assure myself of from instances of His Majesty's clemency to those of equal guilt with myself. Pardon, Sir, this trouble which your great and universal good character draws upon you, and alter not from yourself in neglecting the distress of one who is proud of being, Sir, your most obliged and most obedient servant,

(Signed)   RODERICK CHISHOLM.

Strathglass, 30th August, 1725.

In response to this appeal Roderick and others received a pardon under the Privy Seal, dated the 4th of January, 1727, and engrossed in a highly ornamental style, in the following terms :—

Pardonamus remittimus, relaxamus, pranfato, Robert Stuart de Appin, Alexander Macdonald de Glenco, John Grant, Domino, Anglice Laird, de Glenmorriston, Joanno Mackinnon, Anglice Laird de Mackinnon, Roderick Chisholm de Strathglass, etc.

The way being thus cleared, George Mackenzie of Allangrange, on the 27th of July, 1727, as already stated, disposed of the lands to Alexander Chisholm of Muckerach, Roderick's brother, who obtained infeftment on the 6th of September following, handing over the open charter in his own favour of 2nd September, 1724. The wadsets of the Knockfins were redeemed by Muckerach, and John Chisholm of Knockfin granted him a discharge and renunciation of these lands, dated the 1st and recorded the 6th of August, 1728.

On the 3rd of May, in the last-named year, Chisholm of Muckerach, by consent of Roderick, now pardoned, granted Chisholm of Knockfin a wadset of the lands of Buntait in Glenurquhart, by a document entitled "Contract of wadset twixt Chisholm (Muckerach) and John Chisholm of Knockfin, of the Davoch, town and lands of Buntait, mill and pertinents—Wadset to Knockfin for 12,000 merks."

On the 26th of May, 1721, a Bailie Court was held at Erchless for the whole lands of Roderick Chisholm, late of Strathglass, by William Ross, of Easter Fearn, Bailie appointed by the Commissioners on forfeited estates when

The said William Ross, of Easter Fearn, aforesaid, insists and craves that John Chisholm, of Knockfin, make payment to him of the rents of the lands of Wester, Easter, and Middle Knockfin, the shealings and grazings of Cullovie, and shealings and grazings of Arnamulach (Affric.) John Chisholm, present, acknowledges possession of the lands, and contends that he cannot be obliged to make payment of the rents of any part thereof, in regard he possesses the same by virtue of a contract of wadset passed betwixt the deceased Alexander Chisholm of Comer, grandfather of the person attainted, and Colin Chisholm of Knockfin, his (own) father whereby the said lands and impignorate and wadset to him for the sum of 12,000 merks Scots money, and redemption of the lands, he has good right to uplift the rents for his own use, for proving whereof he produces his father's sasine [dated 24th July, 1679] in the said lands, under the hand of Alexander Fraser, notary public, and registered at Chanonry, the 15th August, 1679.

Roderick took up arms again in 1745, notwithstanding the professions of loyalty poured forth in his letter to Marshall Wade in 1725, and his fulsome praises in the same document of "the best of kings." Though two of his sons, Captains James and John, held commissions in the Duke of Cumberland's army, his youngest son, Roderick Og, led the clan to the fatal field of Culloden, where the brave youth received a mortal wound at the commencement of the battle. It is not surprising, keeping in view Roderick's conduct in connection with the Rising of 1715, and the lenient manner in which he was dealt with by the Government for his treasonable conduct on that occasion, that he should be among the chiefs excluded from the Act of Pardon passed in 1747 in favour of so many of the other leaders engaged against the Government in 1745-46, under Prince Charles. Through the interest of Lord President Forbes of Culloden, however, he again soon after got off very easily by the mere payment of a fine.

The following, recorded by Mr. Colin Chisholm in his *Traditions of Strathglass*, is characteristic of Old Roderick and his friend, the Laird of Gairloch, and illustrates the familiar relations which in those days existed between chiefs of clans and their retainers. The author of these interesting local reminiscences informs us that Old Rory was in treaty with the laird of Gairloch for the purchase of Glasletter, at that time belonging to him, in Glencannich. The then Laird of Gairloch was Sir Alexander Mackenzie, ninth baron and second baronet, locally known as "An Tighearna Breac." About 1720 he purchased some lands in the low country of Ross, and continued for a few years

afterwards to add to his estates. This rendered it necessary for him to dispose of the most distant portion of the
barony of Gairloch, situated in Strathglass. The Chisholm made up his mind, if possible, to buy it. With
this view the two met, and proceeded to the place.
Passing through the west end of Glencannich on their
way, they called on "Fearachar na Cosaig," a very eccen-
tric character, who convoyed them for about two miles
up the glen. When about to part with Farquhar, Sir
Alexander asked him:—"Ciod i do bharail ormsa Fhear-
achar? tha mi dol a chreic na Glasleitreach!" "Ma ta,"
arsa Fearachair, "Alastair, cha 'n eil ach barail a bhruic
de ladhran, barail bhog. Ach ciod a tha thu faighinn air
a son? am bheil thu faighinn uiread Beinn-Fhionnla
air a son?" "Cha 'n eil idir," arsa Tighearna Ghearrloch, "cha 'n eil mi faighinn uiread na cloiche sin air
a son," 's e bualadh a bhrog air sconn cloiche bha'n laimh
ris. "Tha thu faoin Alastair," arsa Fearachair, "Ged
thoisicheadh tu an diugh aig bun Beinn-Fhionnla, agus
a bhi gabhail di fad laithean do bheatha, cha chaith thu
i, ach faodaidh tu uiread na cloiche sin, a chaitheamh an
uin ghoirid agus bithidh a Ghlasleitir a dhith ort." "Tha
thu ceart, ro cheart, Fhearachair," arsa Tighearna Ghearrloch, "agus bithidh 'bhuil." Thug an Siosalach suil air
Fearachair mar gun abradh e, "Rinn thu 'n tubaist."
Thuig Fearachair mar bha, agus thuirt e, "Ach co ris
a ghaolaich, Alastair, tha thu dol a reic na Glasleitreach?"
"Ri do charaide fhein, an Siosalach," arsa Tighearna
Ghearrloch. "Puthu! mas ann mar sin a tha," arsa
Fearachair, "'s beag eadar ribh i; 's cloinn chairdean
sibh fein. Turas math dhuibh a dhaoine uaisle," arsa
Fearachair, 's e cur cul a chinn ri na tighearnan. *Anglice*
—"What do you think of me now," said the Laird of
Gairloch addressing Farquhar, "I am going to sell the
Glasletter?" "My opinion of you is the same as the
badger's opinion of his hoofs, a soft one; but how much
are you getting for it, are you getting as much as Ben-
Finlay (of gold) for it" (one of the highest mountains in

the district)? "Oh! no, Farquhar, not even the size of this stone," striking his foot against a boulder that lay near them. "Well, then, I beg to tell you that you are very foolish, for if you were to begin this day at the foot of Ben-Finlay and continue at it for the rest of your life, you could not spend it, but you could soon spend the size of this stone in gold, and then it and the Glasletter would be gone from you for ever." "You are right, quite right, Farquhar," replied the Laird of Gairloch. The Chisholm looked askance at his vassal, as much as to say, "you have spoiled my bargain." Farquhar, discovering that he had committed a mistake, then said, "But, my dear Alexander, who are you going to sell the Glasletter to?" "To your friend, The Chisholm," replied Mackenzie. "Oh, then," answered Farquhar, "if that is the case, it's a very small matter between the two of you, children of relations as you are. A good journey to you, gentlemen;" and Farquhar turned on his heels and left them. The result was that Gairloch did not offer the Glasletter to The Chisholm again for some five or six years after this interview, when Roderick succeeded in buying it.

Soon after the purchase Roderick entered into an agreement with a contractor to drain Loch Mulardich, a fresh water lake in Glencannich which measures from east to west about five miles, and in some parts about one mile in breadth. It was thought that by draining the loch some valuable grazings could be reclaimed and added to the already fine pastures about its upper end. The great depth of the lake at the intercepting rock was an encouragement to proceed with the operations. The contractor began with great vigour by blasting the intervening mass, and removed piece after piece, until there was only a thin breast of the obstructing rock left to keep back the water. Part of the smithy wall which the workmen erected for sharpening their tools still remains. Everything was going on so successfully that the draining of the loch was considered almost an accomplished fact,

when the contractor accidentally lost his life. Subsequently
Roderick was on a visit to his father-in-law, Macdonell
of Glengarry, when he accompanied a shooting party
on an expedition to Cuileachaidh, where a man resided
named Alastair Mor, who considered himself no mean
poet. Approaching The Chisholm he addressed him
with reference to these operations, in the following
lines :—

> Mo ghaol an Siosalach Glaiseach,
> Chunnaic mi an Cuileachaidh an de thu,
> Cha 'n eil agad ach aon nighean,
> Gheibh thu Tighearna dha 'n te sin ;
> Thug thu 'n cuid fhein do na Tailich
> 'S mor gu'm b fhearr leo agad fhein e,
> Leig thu ruith do Loch Mhulardaich,
> 'S rinn thu fasach dha 'n spreidh dhi.

John Tulloch, the contractor, a native of Redcastle, was
a man of great energy and reputation in his business.
While the operations at Loch Mulardich were in progress
he joined a salmon-spearing party at the Falls of Kilmorack, and accidentally over-balanced himself while aiming
at a salmon, when he fell into the caldron below, and
with his life ended the scheme for draining this loch.

After the Rising, in 1746, a body of troops was sent
into the Strathglass district under command of Captain
Campbell, a notorious blood-thirsty Government officer,
immortalised by the Aireach Muileach, a Mull Gaelic
poet, in the following scathing lines :—

> Caimbeulach dubh Earraghaidheal
> Mac a mhurtair, odha mhearlaich,
> Air an t-sraichd a fhuair e arach
> 'S bhiodh e 'm pairt ri mearlaich a chruidh.

When Beaufort Castle and all the buildings on the •
Lovat estates had been reduced to ashes by Government forces, a strong party under Campbell was sent
out from camps formed at Convent Bank, Dounie, and
Raonfearna, at Struy, to burn and destroy everything

they could lay their hands on. So completely did Campbell and his party do their work, that they drove before
them to Browlin every cow and other animal worth eating,
and burned every house and hut in the glen. But before
setting fire to them the dwellings were ransacked, and
any articles of value found in them were carried away by
the soldiers. After selecting such of the smaller valuables
as were to be forwarded to the camp at Raonfearna, a
white horse was loaded with a portion of the spoil and
sent in charge of two of the soldiers across Bacaidh—
one of the hills between Glencannich and Glenstrathfarrar,
and the ridge of which is the boundary in that part between the lands of Chisholm and Lord Lovat. This road
was probably chosen by the soldiers from prudential
reasons, and to avoid the burning embers of the smoul-
dering villages through Glenstrathfarrar. But whatever the
motives, the expected security for the unfortunate men
turned out worse than useless. They were met on the
Chisholm's side of the hill by two Glenstrathfarrar men close
to a place called Ruidh-Bhacaidh. These men disputed
the right of the redcoats to the booty which they were
carrying away on the white horse. Mortal combat ensued,
and one of the soldiers very soon fell to rise no more.
The other took to his heels with the speed of a hare
before the hounds, leaving his pursuers far behind. He
soon landed at Lub-mhor, a shieling between Lietrie and
Carrie. Here there remained only a few women and
children herding cattle. On the approach of the half-
naked and half-maddened fugitive, shouting and praying
for mercy and protection, the women and children at the
shieling betook themselves to the hills, and the soldier,
if possible, increased his speed, following the course
of the river, shouting and roaring until he reached the
camp at Raonfearna, twelve miles distant.

The soldier having soon out-distanced his pursuers, the
natives returned and resumed their ugly work. The white
horse was taken to a bog, the valuables stript off his back,
a pit dug, and a dirk thrust in each side of his heart,

when he was thrown into the pit. A second pit was prepared for the dead soldier, to which he was dragged and thrown in. The story was related by an eye-witness, a girl named Cameron, who happend at the time to be herding her father's goats on the slope of Tudar, an adjacent hill. From the first sight she had of the soldiers she crouched down in a hollow to hide herself, where she remained quietly until she saw the corpse of a fellow-creature pulled by the ankles and thrown into the yawning bog. Unable to control her feelings any longer, she gave way to a wild coronach, and in a frenzy left her hiding-place and ran away. Observing her, and alarmed at their unexpected discovery, the gravediggers gave chase, seizing and questioning her as to the cause of her grief. She assured them that she had fallen asleep while herding her father's goats, and that she could not now find them, a dereliction of duty for which she was sure to incur her mother's displeasure. Upon this excuse, and in the hurry to finish their unholy work, the men allowed her to return to Carrie, where her father was a farmer.

The result of this tragedy upon the soldiers was perfectly natural. It caused great commotion in the four camps in the district, as well as at Inverness. Every officer and man was seized with a determination to retaliate, and eagerly wished for any opportunity to avenge the death of their comrade. The news was promptly conveyed to Major Lockhart, who was at the time commanding-officer at Inverness. He at once ordered the companies in which two of Roderick's sons, James and John, held commissions, to proceed next morning to their father's estate at the head of a body of troops to burn his castle and plunder his property. The selection was considered cruel, even in military circles. The young officers sought and procured an interview with Lockhart, and urged upon him to institute such an enquiry as they were sure would bring the murderers to condign punishment, but without avail. He instantly ordered them out of his presence. Nothing but fire and sword would

satisfy him. But as he was retiring to bed the same
night, a bullet from a window opposite his lodgings
in Bridge Street, Inverness, found a billet in his body.
The house from which the bullet came was occupied by
Chisholm's two sons and other officers of the Royal Army.

About the same time two murders were committed by
a soldier at the farm of Tombuie and at another place in
Glencannich. The account preserved of them among the
people and handed down to the present generation at
once illustrates the brutality of Cumberland's soldiers and
the superstitions which then prevailed among the natives
of Strathglass. The tenant of the farm and members of
his family were shearing corn on the dell of Tombuie,
when, much to their horror, they observed a party of
soldiers approaching their house. They immediately made
for the hills. But the frantic screaming of a woman, who
had gone to the field to assist her husband and the other
members of her family, reminded them that her baby
was left fast asleep at home. There was no way of
reaching the house or extricating the infant before the
redcoats could reach it. The people, greatly terrified,
made all haste to the rocks at the east side of Glaic-
na-Caillich. While concealed here, they noticed one of
the soldiers entering the house within which the child
was peacefully asleep. It afterwards transpired that in
drawing his sword from the scabbard to murder the
occupant of the cradle, the rays of the sun, flashing on
the polished steel, reflected a blaze of light upon its face.
The little creature clapped its tiny hands and laughed at
the pretty light which thus played upon its eyes. At the
sight of the baby's smiles the would-be assassin stood
awed, and hesitating between the orders he had received
and the dictates of conscience and humanity, he put the
sword back into its scabbard, and was walking out of
the house when he was met by a companion, who asked
him if he had found any one inside. Answering in the
negative, his suspicious comrade dashed into the house
and emerged from it with brutal triumph carrying the

mangled body of the innocent child transfixed on the
point of his sword. Not satisfied with this horrid act,
the monster turned to his companion and threatened to
report him for sparing the life of the infant. His more
humane comrade, however, incensed at the fiendish spectacle before him, instantly unsheathed his sword, planted
the point of it against the breast of the cowardly murderer,
and vowed that in another moment he would force the
blade to the hilt through his merciless heart if he did
not at once withdraw his threat, and promise on his oath
never to repeat it. Thus the ruffian was compelled at
the point of the cold steel to beg for his own dastard
existence.

Here is another Strathglass tradition. When the Cloth-
ing Act was in force and the feileadh-beag and breacan
-uallach were proscribed by law, a company of soldiers
were loitering on their way through Glencannich. They
spied a young man dressed in tartan kilt and hose,
engaged loading a sledge cart with black stem brackens
which were to be used for thatch. Two girls were assisting him in collecting them, and on their unchallenged
statement it has been carried down to the present day,
that, as they began to make the load, standing on Tom-na-
cloich-moire, in Badan-a-gharaidh, half-way between Lietrie
and Shalvanach, their young man companion turned suddenly round towards them and exclaimed—" Oh, God!
look at the dead man in the cart, look at his kilt, hose,
and garters." But the girls could see nothing except
the brackens he had himself just placed there.

The youth was chaffed and heartily laughed at for his
credulity. Soon finishing his load, he led his horses down
the hill, until he came to the side of a lake at Fasadh-
coinntich, at the end of which is a small promontory
jutting out into the water. When turning this point he
observed for the first time that his movements were being
watched, and he was almost immediately surrounded by
a cordon of soldiers, disposed in line to prevent any
attempt on his part to escape. Determined not to be

caught alive or disgrace his dress by surrender, he jumped into the water and swam across the lake, but while climbing a small rock on the opposite shore he was fired at by the soldiers, when he fell back into the water, and perished in presence of his pursuers. His companions, observing his fate, ran off and informed the people of Lietrie of what had happened. His neighbours, proceeding to the spot, found his lifeless body at the edge of the water where he fell. They then turned the brackens out of the cart, placed his body in it, just as it was taken from the water, dressed in kilt and hose, and the unfortunate youth was thus carried to his own residence.

The same belief in the supernatural is further illustrated by the following interesting legends. On the return to their homes of those who survived Culloden, the people of Strathglass were not at all surprised to learn that Ian Beag, The Chisholm's piper, should have performed feats quite beyond the powers of any other of his craft. He had, in addition to his natural abilities, other great advantages. Exceptional and extraordinary powers had always been attributed to the Black Chanter, the famous "Feadan Dubh." The tradition regarding it was that long ago a chief of Chisholm stayed for a time in Rome, and on his return brought home, among other valuables, the celebrated Black Chanter, which combined in itself all manner of musical charms. But though manufactured of the hardest and blackest ebony, it was not impervious to the gnawing effects of time. Consequently it had been strapped with bands and hoops of silver by successive chiefs. This gave it the familiar name of "Maighdean a Chuarain," or the Maiden of the Sandal. It is said that along with its musical charms it had other qualities the reverse of charming. When a member of the chief's family was about to die, the Black Chanter would be quite silent, or if not entirely mute the best piper that ever handled a set of pipes could not get a correct note out of it. So say the legends. A native poet, Donald Chisholm, determined to perpetuate his admiration of the Feadan Dubh, says in one of his sweet effusions—

> Fraoch Eadailteach binn,
> 'S e gu h-airgiodach grinn,
> Cha robh an Alba
> Na fhuair cis deth an ceol.

James Logan, author of *The Scottish Gael*, in an unpublished manuscript note left by him, makes the following reference to this famous instrument. "There is," he says, "a curious relic preserved from time immemorial at Erchless Castle. It is a feadan or bagpipe chanter, to the possession of which a superstitious importance is attached by the clan. Whenever the laird died, this sympathetic instrument is said to have announced the event, at whatever distance it might then be, and it is related that the piper, when one night playing it at a wedding in a part of the country far distant from Strathglass, heard his chanter suddenly crack, on which, starting up, he exclaimed: 'It is time for me to be gone, for The Chisholm is no more!' It was found that he died at that very moment. This instrument, cracking so often, is now considerably shattered, and has been very carefully bound together, whence it has got the name of 'Maighdean a Chuarain,' from a fancied resemblance to the lacing of the cuaran, or Highland buskin, now disused. The Chisholms," he continues, "were accounted excellent musicians, and the chiefs had often both fiddler and piper in their establishment, and two of these, being contemporaries, were remarkable for having each had five wives."

Comar, in the heart of the district, was usually the residence of the chiefs of Chisholm when the heir-apparent was unmarried. When the heir was married his father always established him in Comar, while, until the Castle was built, he himself resided at the old House of Erchless. The practice was continued long afterwards Thus a Highland Court on a moderate scale was established in the very centre of the people. From these centres of genuine hospitality a virtuous and exemplary mode of life used to flow. If tradition speaks aright the ties of friendship and mutual confidence never stood on a firmer basis anywhere between landlord and tenant than they generally did in the country of the Chisholms. The alacrity with which, when asked, the tenants furnished their chief with the requisite number of men to procure commissions for such of his sons as made choice of the profession of arms was simply wonderful, and nothing could illustrate the feeling of good-will which existed between them better than their action on such occasions. Roderick was one of the most popular of the Chisholm chiefs. Domhnull Gobha, a popular local poet said of him—

> Chaill sinn Ruairi an aigh,
> Fear a dh'fhuasgladh gach cas,
> An diugh cha'n aithne
> Dhomh 'aicheadh beo.

He married first, Elizabeth, daughter of the famous Alastair Dubh Macdonell, XI. of Glengarry, by his second wife, Lady Mary, daughter of Kenneth Mor, third Earl of Seaforth, with issue—

1. Alexander, his heir and successor.

2. James, who had a commission in the army, dated the 25th of October, 1744. He afterwards served in the Gordon Fencibles, was for several years Governor of Fort-Augustus, and, after he retired from the service, lived for many years at Wester Moniack. He subsequently died, unmarried, at Inverness, in February, 1789.

3. John, who held a commission in the same regiment as his brother James. They were both lieutenants in the King's army in 1746, when they fought under the Duke of Cumberland at the battle of Culloden, on which occasion their youngest brother was killed fighting for Prince Charles.

4. William, who was bred to the medical profession, which he practised with much success. He was Provost of Inverness from 1773 to 1776, and again from 1779 to

1782, and he died there in 1807. He married, first,
Janet, daughter of John Mackintosh, IX. of Kyllachy, by
whom he had issue—a son William who also followed
and became eminent in the medical profession. He practised for many years in Clifton, near Bristol. William
had a daughter who married Thomas Waddington, son
of the Rev. Joshua Waddington, Vicar of Haworth
and Walkeringham, Nottinghamshire, by his wife, Ann,
daughter of the Rev. Thomas Ferrand, Vicar of Bingley,
in whose right Thomas, who was at the same time the
owner of cotton spinning mills at St. Ledger, near
Rouen, in France, succeeded to the estate of Towes in
Lincolnshire. By his marriage with Miss Chisholm,
Thomas Waddington (who died in 1868) had issue,
among others, Henry William Waddington, at one time
Prime Minister of France. He was appointed French
Ambassador to the British Court in July, 1883, and holds
that position now. By his first wife Provost Chisholm
hada daughter Mary, who married, as his first wife, John
Mackintosh of Aberarder, who also became Provost of
Inverness. Provost Chisholm married, secondly, Catherine,
daughter of Baillie of Dochfour, with issue—a son, Alexander, who emigrated to Demerara and died there, without
male issue, on the 16th of July, 1799. By this marriage
the Provost had also four daughters, Emilia, who married
William Mackintosh of Balnespick ; Jamesina, who married
an officer named Macpherson, who afterwards rose to the
rank of Lieutenant-Colonel in the army ; Sarah, who
married Colin Munro of Granada. " She accompanied
her husband, Mr. Munro of Granada, several times to
the West Indies, was a lady of great beauty, and so
attractive in manner as to be the toast and admiration
of all who had the happiness of her acquaintance."* Isabella, who eloped with and married Captain Henry Morrit
of Rokeby, with issue—two daughters, the Mina and
Brenda of Sir Walter Scott in the "Pirate."

* *Letters of Two Centuries*, by Charles Fraser-Mackintosh, M.P., p. 291.
A. & W. Mackenzie, Inverness.

In a letter from Mrs. Macbean, wife of Robert Macbean of Nairnside, to her husband, dated Inverness, May
5th, 1798, Miss Chisholm's elopement is fully described.
Another interesting incident which occurred on the same
day—Glengarry's duel with Lieutenant Macleod, Flora
Macdonald's grandson—is referred to in the same letter.
Mrs. Macbean, herself a Mackintosh of Dalmigavie,
writes :—

Such wonderful events have happened here within these ten days
past ; the like have not been heard of in this corner of the world
this many a year—an elopement and a duel in one day. I am sure
your curiosity is raised, but you must have a little patience until
I relate the circumstances as they happened. Well, to begin, there
was a grand ball, given by the officers and some of the county
gentlemen—among the rest Glengarry. He paid Miss Forbes, Culloden, a deal of attention. Lieutenant Macleod, of the 42nd, asked
her to dance and she did. Glengarry wished her not, and spoke
rough to Macleod. After the ball was over they quarrelled. Macleod challenged Macdonald ; they fought, and Macleod has got a
severe wound, but not mortal ; the other has escaped without a
scratch ; some people would not be sorry if he got a slight wound.
Well, now for the elopement. Can you guess who ? But to keep
you no longer in suspense, the night after the ball Captain Morrit
and Miss Bell Chisholm set off at twelve o'clock at night in a carriage
and four, accompanied by another officer. She was not missed until
eight o'clock in the morning, and you may be sure her parents were
in great distress. Provost John, Mr. Munro, and Mr. Fraser, Kirkhill, set off after them—they went the coast road. It is said the
young people asked Mr. Stalker in Fort-George to marry them,
but he would not. They were in Elgin that morning at eight
o'clock, and would be in Aberdeen that night. Where they intend
for I do not know, but the other gentlemen have continued the
chase. It was never suspected that she was fond of him, nor was
he ever within their house or Mr. Munro's. He did all he could
to be introduced, but when any offer Mrs. Chisholm always de-
clined it. Her sister (Emily) knew it ; all the officers knew it ;
perhaps you will meet them. Their intention is to marry her
whenever they meet her, and I hope that Captain Morrit never
intended anything but what was honourable.*

5. Roderick Og, who held the rank of Colonel in the

* *Letters of Two Centuries*, by Charles Fraser-Mackintosh, M.P., pp.
335-336. A. & W. Mackenzie, Inverness.

army of Prince Charles, and was killed at the battle of
Culloden, during his father's lifetime, at the head of his
clan.   He received his fatal wound at the commencement of the battle, and was being carried a short distance
to the rear by Domhnull MacUilleam, when they were
both struck by a cannon ball which killed Roderick out-
right and seriously wounded Donald. It is said that his
brothers, James and John, made a diligent search for
Roderick's body, after the action in which they were
engaged on the King's side against him, and that they
found and buried one whom they believed to be him.
He left no legitimate issue.

Roderick " Mac Ian" married, secondly, his cousin,
Isabel, daughter of Sir Kenneth Mackenzie, baronet, IV.
of Scatwell, and widow of Kenneth Bayne of Tulloch
(marriage contract, 1728), with issue—a daughter, Lilias,
who married Colonel Alexander Fraser of Culduthel,
with issue—James Fraser of Culduthel, Roderick of the
H.E.I.C.S., and Simon, killed in a duel; also three
daughters, Grizell, the eldest of the family; Isabell, who
married the Rev. Dr. Fraser, of Kirkhill; and Jean, who
married the Rev. Roderick Morison, of Kintail.   Grizell
married the Rev. Alexander Grant, minister of Daviot
and Cawdor, who died in 1828, aged 84 years, 65 of
which were in the ministry.   He is mentioned in
Dr. Johnson's *Tour to the Hebrides* by Boswell.   By
Grizell Fraser of Culduthel, the Rev. Alexander Grant
had issue, among others—James Grant, minister of Nairn,
who married Christian, daughter of John Mackintosh,
Midcoul, with issue—four sons and one daughter.   Three
of the sons died unmarried.   The daughter is married
to the Rev. Dr. Mackenzie, Ferrintosh, without issue;
and the only surviving son is the distinguished Colonel
James Augustus Grant, C.B., of Nile celebrity.   Colonel
Grant was born on 11th of April, 1827, and married
Margaret Laurie, with issue—two sons, James Augustus,
and Alister, and three daughters, Mary, Christian, and
Margaret.   The Rev. Alexander Grant had a son, George,

who married Robina, daughter of the Rev. Dr. Rose, of
the High Church, Inverness, without issue; also Ann,
who married Captain William Fraser of the 92nd Gordon
Highlanders, and afterwards of the 6th Royal Veteran
Batallion, stationed at Fort-George, with issue—(1) Alexander, who died unmarried; (2) George, a merchant in
Liverpool, who also died unmarried; (3) Robert Fraser,
Brackla, who married Mary, daughter of Robert Gordon
of Croughley, Banffshire, with issue—(*a*) a son, William
Alexander, who died unmarried; (*b*) Mary Helen, who
married Frederick Jerdein, a merchant in China, without
issue; (*c*) Anne Georgina; (*d*) Robina Gordon, who
married Lieutenant-Colonel Colin George Lorn Campbell, Senior Ordinance Officer of the North British head-
quarters, Edinburgh. Colonel Campbell died on the 15th
of August, 1890, leaving issue—a son, Charles William,
and a daughter, Isla Gavine; (*e*) Emily Forbes. (4)
Anne, who married Alexander Mackintosh, merchant,
Calcutta, now resident in London, with issue—three sons
and a daughter; (5) Grace, who died unmarried. The
Rev. Alexander Grant's second daughter, Grace, married
John Mackintosh of Firhall, with issue.

Roderick died on the 19th of August, 1767, aged
seventy years * (his wife having died in 1755), when he
was succeeded by his eldest son,

XXII. ALEXANDER CHISHOLM,

Who is on record in 1742, 1744, and 1746. He succeeded to the remaining portions of the estate on the
death of his father in 1767. It has been already .told
how the estates were purchased from the Commissioners
of Forfeited Estates by James Baillie, W.S., on the 21st
of July, 1724, and how George Mackenzie of Allangrange subsequently, on the 21st of July, 1727, conveyed
them to Alexander Chisholm of Muckerach, who, in the

* *Scots Magazine.*

same year was duly infeft in the lands as Crown vassal. By deed dated 9th of November, 1742, and registered in the books of Session on the 25th of July, 1774, Alexander Chisholm of Muckerach disponed the estates to Alexander Chisholm, then designated "Younger of Comar," during his father's lifetime. Two years earlier, on the 10th of January, 1740, Alexander, with the consent of his father, Roderick, and of his uncle, Alexander Chisholm of Muckerach, the trustee in possession of the estate, entered into a contract of marriage with Elizabeth, or Lilias, only daughter of Roderick Mackenzie, IV. of Applecross, by his second wife, Margaret, daughter of Sir Kenneth Mackenzie, first baronet and IV. of Scatwell, and widow of Æneas Macleod, II. of Cadboll. On the 11th of March, 1777, ten years after he succeeded, Alexander made a strict entail of all the old family inheritance, as well as of the lands which he had personally acquired in the county of Ross, in favour of himself and, after his death, in favour of Captain Duncan Chisholm, his eldest son, whom failing, in favour of the other heirs substitutes mentioned in the deed, which is recorded in the Register of Talzies on the 2nd of July in the same year, and in the Books of Council and Session on the 22nd of August, 1787. The deed, on which so much has turned since, is in the following terms :—

I, Alexander Chisholm of Chisholm, Esq., for the well and standing of my family, and for the preservation of my lands and estate after-mentioned with my own posterity and other relations after-mentioned, do by these presents, always with and under the express burdens, conditions, provisions, declarations, limitations, restrictions, clauses, irritant and faculties after-mentioned and no otherwise, Give, grant, and dispone to, and in favour of myself, and after my decease to Captain Duncan Chisholm, my eldest lawful son, and the heirs male of his body, whom failing to Alexander Chisholm, my second son, and to the heirs male of his body, whom failing, to Roderick Chisholm, my third son, and to the heirs male of his body, whom failing, to William Chisholm, my fourth son, and the heirs male of his body, whom failing, to James Chisholm, my fifth son, and the heirs male of his body, whom failing, to any other sons yet to be procreated of my body, and the heirs male of their bodies, whom failing, to Major James Chisholm of Carrie, my brother, and the heirs male of his body, whom failing, to Dr. William Chisholm, Bontait, also my brother, and to the heirs male of his body, whom failing, to Archibald Chisholm, eldest son of the deceast Alexander Chisholm of Muckerach, and the heirs male of his body, whom failing, to Lieutenant John Chisholm, second son of the said Alexander Chisholm of Muckerach and the heirs male of his body, whom all failing, to my nearest and lawful heirs whatsomever, the eldest heir female and the descendants of her body, excluding all other heirs portioners, and succeeding always without division through the whole course of female succession in all time coming, heritably and irredeemably, all and whole, the lands and estate which formerly pertained to Roderick Chisholm, late of Comar, viz., the lands and mains of Erikless, with the manour, place, yeards, and pertinents thereof; the lands of Breachachy, the lands of Inverchannich, the lands of Comar, the lands of Glencannich, the lands of Comar Kirktown, the lands of Wester Comar, the lands of Bontait, the lands of Mauld, with houses, biggings, yeards, orchards, lofts, crofts, outsets, insets, mosses, muirs, grazings, commonties, woods, parks, meadows, and whole parts, pendicles, and pertinents thereof belonging, all lying within the parish of Kilmorack and Kiltarlity, and Sheriffdom of Inverness, with any right of reversion of the lands of Knockfin, and Forest of Apharrick, and Breamulloch, which by law was competent to the said Roderick Chisholm at the time of his attainder, and all right and title which the said Roderick Chisholm had, or might pretend to the teinds, parsonage, and vicarage of the lands above disponed, with the pertinents and sicklike, all and whole, these parts and portions of the lands and barony of Gerloch after specified, viz., the forest, pasturage, and grasings of Glassletter and Corrienacullen, with houses, biggings, parts, pendicles, outsetts, shealings, and pertinents of the same, lying in the parish of Croe, in Kintail, and Sheriffdom of Ross, and sicklike all and whole the town and Davoch lands of Rhindown, with the towns and lands which are parts and pertinents thereof called Tobermorosk, Altnabreck, Scalling, Teandsdalloch, and Clashintorran, with the multures, sucken, thirlage, and knaveships thereof, and whole houses, biggings, yards, orchards, mosses, muirs, meadows, shealings, commonties, woods, and whole other parts, pendicles, privileges, and universal pertinents belonging to the said lands, lying within the united parish of Urray and Kilchrist, and Sheriffdom of Ross, together with all right title, or interest which I have or may have, claim or pretend to the lands and others before disponed, or to any part or portion thereof, or to the teinds, parsonage, and vicarage of the same in time coming,

6

with this provision always, as it is hereby expressly provided and
declared, that the said Duncan Chisholm, my eldest son, and his
heirs substitutes and successors above mentioned, shall by their
acceptance hereof be holden obliged to content, satisfy, and pay all
the just and lawful debts that shall be resting and owing by me
to whatsoever person or persons the time of my decease, and particularly the life-rent and annuity and other provisions granted by
me to Mrs Margaret Mackenzie, my present wife, and the provisions to my younger children, and with this provision also that
my said eldest son and his heirs substitutes and successors above
mentioned, shall possess and enjoy the lands and others before
disponed by virtue of these presents and the charters and infeftments to follow hereon, and by no other title whatsoever, and
likewise with this provision, that the said Duncan Chisholm, my
eldest son, and his heirs substitutes and successors above-men-
tioned, as well male as female, and the descendants of their bodies
who shall happen to succeed to the lands and others before disponed, and the husbands of such of the said heirs female (if any
be) shall be holden and obliged to assume, and constantly retain,
use, and bear the surname, arms, and designation of Chisholm of
Chisholm as their own proper arms, surname, and designation
in all time thereafter, and farther, it is hereby expressly provided
and declared that it shall not be leisome or lawful to my said
eldest son, or to any of the heirs substitutes or successors above
mentioned, to alter, innovate, or change the order of succession
above specified, or to do any other act or deed directly or
indirectly whereby the same may be anyways altered, innovated,
or changed, also that it shall not be leisome or lawful to my
eldest son, or to any of the other heirs substitutes and successors
above mentioned, to sell, dispone, wadsett, or impignorate the
lands and others above specified, or any part thereof, to contract
debts thereon, or to grant infeftments of annual rent furth of the
same, or any right or security redeemable or irredeemable of the
said lands and estate or any part thereof, nor to grant tacks or
leases of the same for a longer space than the granter's life and
nine years, nor even to grant tacks of any part of the said lands
and estate until the current tacks thereof for the time shall be
fully expired (the said tacks when granted for a longer space than
the granter's life being always without diminution of the rental),
nor to do any other act or deed, civil or criminal, or even treasonable, whereby the said lands and estate and pertinents thereof
may be adjudged, evicted, or confiscated in any sort, as also,
That it shall not be lawful to my said son or to any of the heirs
substitutes or successors above mentioned to suffer the duties of
nonentry and relief, or the feu blench or teinds duties, or other

public burdens or duties whatsoever, payable furth of the said lands and estate to run on unsatisfied so as the lands and others foresaid may be evicted or adjudged for any of the said casualties of superiority or public burdens, and, That the said Duncan Chisholm, my eldest son, and the other heirs substitutes and successors above mentioned, shall be obliged to obtain themselves timeously entered, infeft, and seased in the said lands and estate and not to suffer the same to lye in nonentry, and in any adjudication or other legal diligence shall happen to be led and deduced for any of said burdens, duties, or casualties or superiority above mentioned, or for any debts due and contracted by me or any of my predecessors, or for any other debts whatsoever, That then the said Duncan Chisholm, my eldest son, and the other heirs substitutes and successors above mentioned who shall possess the said lands and estate for the time, shall be bound and obliged to purge and redeem the said diligences three years before the expiry of the legal reversion thereof, in case any of the said heirs shall succeed so long before expiry of the said legals, and if the said heirs succeed not so soon, they shall be obliged to purge the same within six months after his or her succession, Declaring hereby that if the said Duncan Chisholm, my eldest son, and the other heirs substitutes and successors above mentioned, or any of them shall act or do in the contrary of the particulars above specified or any of them, or neglect to fulfil the provisions and conditions above written or any of them, Then, and in that case, all and every one of such debts, acts, and deeds, withal that shall happen to follow or may follow therein shall *ipso facto* be void and null and of no strength or effect, sicklike and in the same manner as if the said debts, acts, and deeds had not been contracted, acted, and committed, and declaring also that the person so contravening or failing to fulfil the conditions and provisions above mentioned, shall for him or herself alone, immediately upon the contravention or failing to fulfil and observe the said conditions and provisions or any of them, admit, lose, and forfeit all right or title he or she hath or can pretend to the said lands or estate, and the same shall in that case *ipso facto* fall, accressce, pertain, and belong to the next heir or substitute hereby appointed to succeed thereto although descending of the contravener's own body, sicklike and in the same manner as if the contravener were naturally dead, and it shall be leisome and lawful to the next heir or substitute to establish the right thereof in his or her person, and that either by declarator or serving heir to the person who died last vest and seased in the said lands and estate, preceding the contravener or by adjudication or any other manner of way consistent with the laws of Scotland for the time, without respect to any alteration, innovation, or charge foresaid to be made by the person contra-

vening, and without the burden of any act of ommission or
commission or any other act, debt, or deed whatsoever, which,
according to law, may be interpreted to impart a contravention of
the said clauses irritant or any of them, and the person so succeeding upon the contravention is to be subjected and liable to
the said irritancies to which my said eldest son and the whole heirs
substitutes and successors above specified are to be subject and
liable through the whole course of succession in all time coming,
excepting and reserving from the said clauses irritant full power
and liberty to the said Duncan Chisholm, my son, and to the heirs
substitutes and successors above mentioned to grant liferent provisions to their wives or husbands by way of locality on any part
of the said lands (excepting the mansion house of the family) not
exceeding £100 stg. of yearly rent, the said locality liferent provisions being allenarly in lieu of their terce and courtesy, from
which they are hereby excluded, as also excepting and reserving
power and liberty to my said eldest son and the heirs substitutes
and successors above mentioned to provide their younger children
beside the heir in provisions to the amount in all of £1500 stg.,
Declaring that after the foresaid faculty of granting provisions to
younger children shall be once exercised it shall not be in the
power of my said son or his said heirs substitutes or successors to
burden the said lands and estate further with new provisions till
the former provisions be satisfied and paid in whole or in part, and
in case of partial satisfaction, new provisions may be granted only
to such an extent as that the same, together with the former provisions in favours of younger children, shall not at any one time
exceed the said sum of £1500 stg. in whole, and which provisions
in favours of younger children are hereby expressly so qualified, and
shall be so qualified by the bonds or other securities to be granted
for the same that they shall never be increased to burden the said
lands and estate by growing annual rents, nor so as any diligence
may follow on the same against the said estate further than for
securing the principal sums and that the annual rents and expenses
may affect the persons or personal estates of the said heirs or substitutes or current rents of the said estate or their separate estates,
but in no ways really to affect the lands and estates hereby disposed, and my said son and the heirs substitutes and successors
above mentioned shall be bound and obliged to satisfy and pay the
annual rents of the said provisions and thereby effectually to dis-
burden the said lands and estate thereof and not to suffer any
diligence to pass against the same for payment of such annual
rents or penalties wherein if they fail the right of the person so
contravening or doing in the contrary shall *ipso facto* become
void and null for him or herself alone, and the right of succession

to the said lands and estate shall fall and devolve to the next heir
hereby appointed to succeed although descending of the contravener's body in manner above specified in all points. And further
in regard that by the irritancies before mentioned, it is provided that
the contravener shall only for him or herself alone amit lose and
forfeit their right to the said lands and estate, but that the descendants of his or her body are nowise by the contravention cut off from
the right of succession. Therefore it is hereby expressly provided
and declared that albeit the next heir of Tailzie existing may upon the
contravention obtained established in his or her person the right of
the said lands and estate by declarator, adjudicaton, service and retour,
or any other legal manner, yet notwithstanding thereof in case a nearer
heir of Tailzie shall happen to exist after obtaining the foresaid declarator or adjudication or service and retour upon the contravention
as by procreation of a child or children of the contravener's body,
In that case the person so succeeding upon the contravention shall
not only be holden and obliged immediately thereafter to denude
in favours of the said nearest heir and other heirs of Tailzie above
written, under the conditions and irritancies above mentioned, so
that the course of succession be no further diverted than to exclude
the contravener only, but also the right of the person so succeeding upon the contravention and their heirs of Tailzie aforesaid
shall *ipso facto* become extinct, void, and null so soon as the said
nearer heir shall exist, and the right of the said lands and estate
shall fall and devolve to the said nearer heir, who shall have access
to establish the right thereof in his or her person in the same way
and manner as was competent by the contravention, so that the
right of succession shall always and unalterably fall and belong to
the nearest heir of Tailzie, according to the course of succession
above specified, except the contravener, whose right shall be extinct
for him or herself alone, and nowise to prejudge the next heir in
order although descending of the contravener's own body, Reserving always to the person who shall succeed by virtue of the contravention, the rents, and profits of the said lands and estate until
the term of Whitsunday or Martinmas, inclusive, immediately
preceding the birth of the said nearer heir, with the burden of
the current annual rent of the debts, real or personal, and other
annual burdens, which do or may affect the said lands and estate,
and that for the years and terms to which the said remoter heir
is provided by these presents, with and under which express conditions, provisions, burdens, restrictions, limitations, clauses, irritant
and faculties above written, which are hereby appointed to be
contained in the Instruments of Resignation, Charters, Infeftments,
Retours, and other writs to follow hereupon, these presents are
granted by me and no otherwise, and I hereby bind and oblige me

and my heirs and successors to make due and lawful resignation of
the lands and others before disponed in the hands of my immediate lawful superiors thereof, in favours of and for new infeftments
of the same to be made and granted to myself, and after my
decease to the said Duncan Chisholm, my eldest son, and the
heirs male of his body, whom failing, to my other heirs substitutes and successors above mentioned, according to the order of
the substitution and destination of succession above specified, whom
failing to my nearest and lawful heirs and assignees whatsoever,
the eldest heir female and the descendants of her body, excluding
all other heirs portioners, and succeeding always without division
through the whole course of succession in all time coming, and
that with and under the express conditions, provisions, burdens,
restrictions, limitations, clauses, irritant and faculties, above written
allenarly, and no otherwise, and for that effect I hereby make,
constitute, and appoint   and
each of them conjunctly and severally my lawful undoubted and
irrevocable procurators for me and in my name to resign, surrender,
upgive, overgive, and deliver as I by these presents resign, surrender, upgive, overgive, and deliver all and whole the several lands
and others before disponed, all lying and described as aforesaid, and
here held as repeated *brevitatis causa*, together with all right, title,
or interest which I have or may have, claim, or pretend to the lands
and others above mentioned, or to any part or portion thereof in
time coming, in the hands of my immediate lawful superiors, or of
their commissioners in their names, or any others having power
for the time to receive resignations thereof and grant new infeftments thereupon, in favours of and for new infeftments of the same,
to be made, given, and granted to myself, and after my decease to
the said Duncan Chisholm, my eldest son, and the heirs male of
his body, whom failing to my other heirs snbstitutes and successors
above mentioned, according to the order of substitution and destination of succession above specified, which is here holden as repeated
and with and under the conditions, provisions, burdens, restrictions,
limitations, clauses, irritant and faculties above written, which are
all holden as here repeated and exprest allenarly, and no otherwise,
heritably and irredeemably in due and competent form as effeirs,
acts, instruments, and documents, one or more, as needful in the
premises, to ask, lift, and raise, and generally all and sundry other
things, requisite and necessary thereanent, to do use and exerce in
the same manner and as freely in all respects as I might do therein
myself if I were personally present, or which to the office of procurators in such cases by the law of Scotland is known to pertain,
all which I promise to hold firm and stable, and in like manner I
by these presents, always with and under the conditions, provisions,

burdens, restrictions, limitations, clauses, irritant and faculties, above written and no otherwise, assign, transfer, and dispone to and in favours of myself, and after my decease to the said Duncan Chisholm, my eldest son, and the heirs male of his body, whom failing, my other heirs substitutes and successors above mentioned according to the order of the substitution and destination of the succession above mentioned, the whole Charters, Infeftments, Procuratories of Resignation, and Precepts of Sasine, as well executed as not executed Instruments of Resignation and Sasine dispositions, apprisings, adjudications, tacks, assedations, decreets of plat, prorogation, valuation or vendition, assignations, translations, and other conveyances, and all other writs, rights, evidents, titles, and securities whatsoever made, granted, and conceived, or that may be any wise interpreted in favours of me, my predecessors, or authors of and concerning the lands and others above disponed or any part or portion thereof, or to the teinds parsonage or vicarage of the same, or the annuities of the said teinds, with the whole clauses of warrandice and other clauses tenor and contents thereof, together with all action, diligence, and execution competent, or that may be competent, upon the premises and with all that has followed or may follow thereon. And lastly I hereby reserve full power and liberty to myself at any time of my life, even in sickness and on deathbed, to revoke, recal, rescind, after innovate and change these presents in whole or in part and to declare the same void and null at my pleasure and to add such other provisions, conditions, and limitations upon my said eldest son and the heirs succeeding him in the said lands as I shall think proper. But declaring that if these presents shall not be revoked by me the same shall remain a valid evident to my said eldest son and to his heirs substitutes and successors above mentioned, although found in my custody or in the custody of any other person to whom I may have entrusted the same undelivered at my death with the not delivery whereof I hereby dispense for ever and I hereby recommend to all or any of the heirs substitutes, or successors above mentioned, or to the nearest agnate of any of them under age at the time at and upon my death to cause duly record this present Deed of Tailzie in terms of the Act of Parliament, 1685, made anent Registration of Tailzies and that without delay and also to cause expede Charters and Infeftments thereon with all convenient diligence that so this present deed may have its full force and effect, consenting to the Registration hereof in the Books of Council and Session or others competent therein to remain for preservation, and for that effect I hereby constitute my procurators, etc., in witness whereof, etc. Signed at Inverness, 12th March, 1777. Registered in the Register of Tailzies, 2nd July, 1777, and in the Books of Session, 22nd August, 1787.

This deed and the results which followed from it will be discussed later on.

By Elizabeth Mackenzie of Applecross, Alexander had issue—

1. Duncan, a Captain in the 71st Regiment, or Fraser Highlanders. He was born in 1747, and died before his father, in London, on the 23rd of October, 1782. Dr Gilbert Stewart, author of a *History of Mary Queen of Scots*, at the time contributed the following curiously-phrased notice of Captain Duncan to a London newspaper— "Upon the 23rd day of October, died at his apartments in Oxenden Street, Haymarket, Duncan Chisholm, Esquire, the younger of Strathglass, and late first Captain of the 71st Regiment of foot. He received his education at Edinburgh, and profited under the instruction of the great masters who adorn the University of that place. He followed the profession of arms, and served his country with gallantry in America. In figure he was tall and athletic ; in his spirit he was high and not to be insulted with impunity, but he was not of a humour that took delight in broils and quarrelling. Being the apparent heir to the chieftain of a numerous Highland clan, there was a portliness in his walk and carriage which is not common in this country. He exhibited the ideal of a Scots baron in ancient times. He was stout, fearless, hospitable, and bountiful. His indulgence in conviviality was beyond the polite bounds of fashionable manners. His gaiety was without capriciousness, and there was an honest and vehement sincerity in his laugh. His virtues were more solid than shining. He respected his country and mankind, liberty, and patriotism. His pride was without insolence ; his vivacity without sarcasm ; his resentment without revenge ; his firmness without obstinacy. There was in him much of the milk of human kindness. His heart was warm and his affections generous. In the 35th year of his age he was called from this world to a better, and he submitted to his fate with the most entire resignation. His relations, his friends, and acquaintances,

who loved him when living, will remember long, with a tender sorrow, his immature death and the amicableness of his virtues and his failings." He died unmarried.

2. Alexander, who, on the death of his brother Duncan, in 1782, became his father's heir.

3. Margaret, who married Hugh Fraser of Dunballoch and Newton, who fought in the Scots Guards at Fontenoy, which his uncle, Lieutenant-Colonel Hugh Fraser, then commanded, being killed at that famous battle at the great age, for an officer on active service, of seventy-eight years. Lieutenant-Colonel Hugh Fraser bought the estate of Kilmuir and West Kessock, in the Black Isle, county of Ross, and married Christian, daughter of William MacNaghten of that Ilk, with issue—Henrietta, who married Sir Charles Erskine of Alva, with issue—two daughters. By Margaret Chisholm Hugh of Dunballoch, the Colonel's nephew, had issue—Thomas Fraser of Newton, a Major in the First Royals, born on the 20th of March, 1758 ; he succeeded his father in 1787. He married Katharine, daughter of Alexander Mackintosh, of the family of Drakies, and Provost of Inverness, with issue (among twenty-two children)—(1) Hugh Fraser of the H.E.I.C.S., who was born on the 27th of April, 1797, succeeded his father in 1839 or 1840, and died, without issue, on the 7th of December, 1843. (2) Alexander Fraser, born on the 15th of June, 1807, and died on the 7th March, 1848. He succeeded his brother Hugh in Newton in 1843, and married Emilia Walker (who still survives), with issue—Katharine and Margaret, both unmarried. (3) Elizabeth, who died unmarried on the 10th of January, 1867 ; (4) Margaret, who married Major Ludovic Stewart of Pityvaich, Banffshire, with issue— several sons and daughters. She died in October, 1859. One of Mrs. Stewart's daughters, Katharine, married Alexander Ewing, Bishop of Argyle, with issue. Another, Elizabeth, married Henry Gordon Cumming, brother of Sir A. P. Cumming of Altyre, with issue ; and a third, Margaret Clifford, married the Rev. C. K. Robinson,

Master of St. Catherine's College, Cambridge, with issue.
(5) Katharine, who married Benjamin Goldsmid Elliot,
and died at Inverness on the 7th of February, 1890,
without issue.   (6) Isabella, who married James Wilson,
for many years agent for the Commercial Bank at Inverness, with issue—several sons and daughters.   (7) Emily,
who resides, unmarried, at Inverness.   (8) Wilhelmine,
who, on the 26th of November, 1844, married Thomas
Porter Bonell Biscoe of the H.E.I.C.S.   She died on
the 27th of April, 1878.   In 1850 he purchased the
estate of Newton from the trustees of Alexander Fraser.
He had issue—(a) Thomas Ramsay Biscoe, now of Newton, who married Cecilia Laura, daughter of Adolphus
Meetkerke of Julians, Herts, with issue—John Vincent
Meetkerke, born on the 20th July, 1880, and Cecilia
Benigna Meetkerke ; (b) William Fraser Biscoe, now of
Kingillie, who married Mary Alice, daughter of Francis
Crozier of Delawarr, Lymington, Hants, with issue, an
only son, Francis Ramsay Fraser, who was born in 1883 ;
(c) Katharine Emma, who married William Munro, of
Marchbank, Midlothian, without issue ; and (d) Frances
Anne Benigna, unmarried.   Hugh Fraser of Dunballoch
and Newton had, by Margaret Chisholm of Chisholm, a
second son, Alexander, whose descendants, since the death
of Alexander Fraser of Newton in 1848, without male
issue, represent the family in the male line.   This Alexander, who was born on the 30th of July, 1759, settled
at St. Christopher's, and married Miss Duff of Muirtown,
with issue—Evan Baillie Fraser of Balconie, a Captain in
the 88th Regiment of Foot, now residing at Redburn.
Hugh Fraser had also, among several others, a daughter
Margaret, who married David G. Sandeman of Springfield,
Perthshire, by whom she had a daughter, Margaret Chisholm, who married William Fraser, father of Lieutenant-Colonel William Fraser of Culbokie, now residing
at Nairn.

    4. Anne, who married Roderick Mackenzie, II. of Scots-
burn, with issue—Alexander Mackenzie, III. of Scotsburn,

who sold the estate in 1843; Duncan Chisholm Mackenzie, Commander, Royal Navy, who died unmarried;
and three daughters, Elizabeth, Anne, and Lilias, the last-
named of whom married James Walker of Dalry, with
issue. Roderick's wife died in 1816. Alexander of Scotsburn had a son, Charles Roderick Mackenzie, who, on the
28th of March, 1846, married Madeline, daughter of Sir
William Murray of Clermont.

Alexander married, secondly, Margaret, daughter of
George Mackenzie, II. of Allangrange, with issue—

5. Roderick, mentioned in his brother Alexander's entail
of the estates, in 1786, as his father's then second surviving son. He must, however, have predeceased his
brother Alexander, without issue male, as his immediate
younger brother, William, succeeded to the family inheritance and chiefship of the clan.

6. William, mentioned in the same deed, as his father's
third surviving son, and who, on the death of his brother
Alexander, in 1793, without male issue, succeeded to the
chiefship and estate.

7. James, mentioned in the deed of entail as his father's
fourth surviving son. He died abroad, unmarried.

8. Mary, who, on the 20th of December, 1789, married
Major William Robertson of Kindeace, Ross-shire, with
issue—Charles, his heir, and Alexander, an officer in the
24th Regiment, and 42nd Highlanders. Alexander was
born in 1794, and died, unmarried, in 1821. Major
Robertson having died on the 7th of April, 1844, was
succeeded by his eldest son Charles, who was born on
the 26th of July, 1790. He was a Major in the 78th
Highlanders, and was present at the capture of Java. He
married on the 12th of August, 1812, Helen, fourth
daughter and co-heiress of Patrick Cruickshank of Strath-
cathro, county of Forfar, with issue—William Cruickshank,
born 17th of May, 1817, and married on the 5th of September, 1860, Euphemia Garden, youngest daughter of
Major Donald Mackay, of the 70th Regiment, with issue—
two daughters; Patrick Gerard, born on the 3rd of Feb-

ruary, 1819, and died unmarried in Australia on the 17th
of April, 1854; Charles Henry, born on the 14th of
June, 1821, and died in the following year; Charles, now
of Kindeace; Mary Chisholm, who on the 15th of July,
1845, married Alexander Hamilton, Edinburgh, with issue;
and Margaret Amy, who on the 27th of July, 1852,
married James Falconer Gillanders of Highfield, with
issue.   Major Charles Robertson of Kindeace died on
the 17th of October, 1868, when he was succeeded by
his eldest surviving son, Charles Robertson, now of
Greenyards and Glencalvie,' who was born on the 20th
of April, 1831.   He married on the 10th of December,
1868, Helena Emma, youngest daughter of Sir John
Maryon Wilson, baronet of Charlton, Kent, with issue—
six sons and two daughters.

9. Lilias, who married General John Mackenzie of
Belville, second son of Sir Alexander Mackenzie, third
baronet and tenth baron of Gairloch, and brother of Sir
Hector Mackenzie, fourth baronet, with issue—Alastair,
who, after serving for a time in the army, settled and
was appointed a magistrate in the Bahamas, where he
married Wade Ellen, daughter of George Huyler, Consul-
General of the United States of America, and French
Consul at the same place, with issue—(1) the Rev. George
William Russel Mackenzie, an Episcopalian minister; and
(2) Lilias Mary Chisholm, unmarried.   Alastair subsequently left the Bahamas for Melbourne, Australia, where
he received the appointment of Treasurer to the Government of Victoria, and died there about the year 1854.

10. A daughter who, at an advanced age, died unmarried.

Alexander, who died in December, 1785, was succeeded
by his second and eldest surviving son,

XXIII. ALEXANDER CHISHOLM,

Generally known as "An Siosal Bán," or the fair-haired
Chisholm.   To make a title he epede a general service

on 7th June, 1786, before the Sheriff of Edinburgh, as nearest and lawful heir male and heir of entail and provision of his father, which carried the personal right to the deed of entail of 1777, and the procuratory of resignation therein contained. On these he expede a Crown Charter of Resignation and Tailzie under the Great Seal, dated the 7th of August and sealed on the 4th of September in the same year, on which he was duly infeft on the 23rd of that month, the sasine being registered at Inverness on the 29th.

This charter conveyed the estate of Chisholm to himself, "Alexander Chisholm, now of Chisholm, Esquire, formerly second, now eldest son of the deceased Alexander Chisholm, late of Chisholm, and the heirs male of his body, whom failing, to Roderick Chisholm, formerly third, now second son of the said late Chisholm, and the heirs male of his body, whom failing, to William Chisholm, formerly fourth, now third son of the said late Chisholm, and the heirs male of his body, whom failing, to James Chisholm, formerly fifth, now fourth son of the said late Chisholm, and the heirs male of his body," whom failing, to any other brothers of the entailer in their order and the heirs male of their bodies, whom failing, to the heirs male of the said Chisholm of Muckerach and his heirs male in their order, whom failing, *to the nearest lawful heirs whatsoever of the entailer, the eldest heir female and the descendants of her body, excluding heirs portioners throughout the whole course of succession,* following exactly his father's entail of 1777.

Alexander, in 1776, married Elizabeth, daughter of Dr George Wilson, Edinburgh, with surviving issue—an only child, Mary, born on the 25th of March, 1780, and of whom and her descendants after the male heirs of entail are exhausted. He died on the 7th of February, 1793, and was buried in the chancel of the Priory of Beauly, where, affixed to the wall is an unpretentious white marble monument, placed there by his daughter, with the following simple inscription :—

Sacred to the memory of Alexander Chisholm, Esq. of Chisholm, who died 7th February, 1793, aged 44 years, and was here
interred. And of Elizabeth Wilson, his relict, who died in London,
23rd January, 1826, aged 66 years. This tablet was placed as a
tribute of affection by their only child, Mary Chisholm, wife of
James Gooden, Esq., Anno Domini MDCCCXXVII.

The Chisholm had wisely made provision for his
widow in a form which subsequently proved a great
blessing to a very considerable number of his brother's
tenants in Strathglass. He left her a specified sum of
money per annum, or alternately the rents of certain
townships or joint farms on the estate as jointure. On
the death of her husband in 1793, Mrs. Chisholm, on
the advice of her daughter Mary, made choice of the
farms, with the result that when, eight years later, in
1801, nearly all the rest of the population of the Strath
were evicted by her late husband's half brother, she found
herself in a position to keep all the tenants of these farms
in possession of their holdings, where they remained in
comfortable circumstances until her death on the 23rd of
January, 1826, when the whole of the estate, unfortunately
for them, reverted to Alexander William, the twenty-fifth
chief, who, a few years afterwards, cleared Strathglass of
every remaining tenant of his name and clan within its
bounds, with the exception of two.

Of this chief James Logan, author of the *Scottish Gael*,
in a manuscript note in our possession, writes:—" Of
Alexander it must be recorded to his honour as a chief
and a generous landlord, that he did not suffer himself to
be infected with the mania for sheep farming, which has
proved so lamentable a scourge to a deserving and unob-
trusive race. He firmly resisted the importunities of his
friends, and, unaffected by the prospect of an increased
rental, he preferred allowing his lands to be occupied by
his attached clansmen, whose natural father and protector
he was, to a forcible expulsion of his faithful descendants,
to give room for sheep and their heartless attendants.
The southland shepherds could not tempt him with their

golden offers. The cheerless glens, and the reproaches of those who had once enlivened the scene by their rustic joys were not to be endured by a feeling heart, and the utmost reasoning of Coiremonaidh [Grant of Corriemony], of whom better might have well been expected, backed by others, failed in persuading him that the change was just. Time has shown whose views were most correct. Affluence has not always followed the introduction of sheep, but many who depopulated their lands to form sheep walks have themselves been forced to abandon a country which ought to have been ever their paternal homes. Fortune may again restore a Highland laird to his native hills—but his clansmen! He may exclaim 'Where,' and he will be answered by Mac Talla, with the sure and mournful response, 'Where!'"

This patriotic feature of Alexander's character is fully set forth in the traditional history and native poetry of the district. Not only his own people, but those who lived in the neighbouring straths and glens ever spoke of him as the most considerate and, in all respects, one of the best proprietors in the Highlands. A Glengarry bard, speaking of the esteem in which he was held by his own as well as by other people, said :—

> 'S beag ioghnadh iad bhi dileas dhuit,
> 'S do chis a dhioladh durachdach,
> 'S nach d' fhuair coin no ciobairean
> 'N ad thir a steach dha 'n ionnsachdainn,
> Bho'n chuir thu cul ri tairgseachan
> Bho Ghalla-bhodaich nan luirichean,
> Gun d' fhag sud cliu an Albainn ort,
> 'S tha farmaid aig gach duthaich riut.

The following interesting colloquy between himself and his relative, Bishop John Chisholm, who died at Lismore in 1814 deserves record. The Bishop first began his clerical career in his native district of Strathglass, and he was often invited to Erchless Castle. During one of these

visits Alexander asked him—" How do you get on, Mr.
John, with our mutual friends in the Strath ?" "Well,"
replied his reverence, " I have only one complaint against
them. I can scarcely make them believe or understand
that it is wrong for them to cut as much of your wood
as they require for their own use." "Oh, if that is your
only complaint against them, Mr. John," replied The
Chisholm, "I will undertake that, if you absolve them
from all their other sins, I shall give them absolution
for cutting what they require of my wood."

On the death of the Fair Chisholm, the well-known
Gaelic bard, Donald Chisholm, locally known as " Domhnull Gobha," composed an elegy to his memory, to his
father's, and to his grandfather's, all three of whom died
within a comparatively short period of each other. The
following verses refer specially to Alexander — " An Siosalach Bàn:"—

> Och nan ochan 's mi fein,
> Chaidh mo chadal an eis,
> An diugh cha leir dhomh,
> Ach eiginn sgleo.
>
> 'S tric mi 'n iomadain truagh
> Mu'n eug thug Alasdair bhuainn,
> Craobh nan abhall
> A b' uaisle meoir.
>
> Crann seudmhor nam buadh
> Dh'fhag fir Alba fo ghruaim
> 'N uair a dh'ionndraich
> Iad bhuath' thu, sheoid.
>
> 'S iomadh fear a bha 'm breis',
> Eadar tuath agus deas,
> Iad fo ghruaim,
> 'S ann an deise-bhroin.
>
> Cha b'e ardachadh mail
> Dh'fhag do bhancaichean lan,
> Ach torc-sona
> Bhi ghnath ad choir.

'S gur a fiosrach tha mi
Gu'n robh meas ort's gach tir,
Ann am Parlamaid Righ,
'S aig mòd.

'Nuair a shuidheadh tu'n cuirt
Bu leat eisdeachd 's tu b' fhiu—
Chuireadh d'fhocal
Gach cuis air seol.

Bha gach fasan a b' fhearr
Ann am pearsa mo ghraidh,
Ach co mhealas,
An dràsd a chòt'?

Bu leat faghaid nan gleann,
'S fuaim nan gaothar na 'n deann,
Fhir a leagadh
Na maing le sgòrr.

Leat a chinneadh an t-sealg,
Ann am frith nan damh dearg,
Eadar Finne-ghleann,
Is Cioch an fheoir.

Eadar Comunn-nan-allt,
Agus garbh-shlios nam beann,
Eadar Fairthir
'S an Caorunn gorm.

Allan Macdougall, better known among his own countrymen as "Ailean Dall," Glengarry's family bard, and a
contemporary of "The Fair Chisholm," commends his
refusal of the tempting offers made to him to evict the
native tenantry to make room for the Southern sheep
farmers in a Gaelic poem of eleven stanzas, from which
we quote the following four:—

Gu seasach, duineil, faoilteachail,
    Mu d' dhaoine tha thu curamach;
Air gheard mu 'n eirich baoghal dhoibh,
    'S cha leig thu aomadh cùil orra;
'S gur mairg a nochdadh aobhar dhuit,
    Nuair dh' eireadh laoich do dhucha leat
Chum seasamh ri uchd caonnaige,
    Le 'n claidheannaibh cha diùltadh iad.

Nuair thogteadh piob a's bratach leat
 A mach bho chaisteal Eirchealais,
Bu lionmhor oigeir spalpara,
 Fo ordugh grad chum seirbheis dhuit :
Gu dagach, gunnach, acfhuinneach,
 Gu ruinn-gheur, sgaiteach, eirbheartach,
Ag gearradh smuais a's aisinnean,
 La cruas nan ealt' gun mheirg orra.

Le 'n ceannard uasal Siosalach,
 Gu suairce, measail, giùlanta,
Cha mheall an t-òr le sitheadh thu,
 Gu bristeadh air do chumhnantan ;
Cha'n fhàillinnich do ghealluinnean,
 De t'fhearann thug thu cùnnradh dhoibh
Air làraichean a' seanairean.
 A's ceangal ac' air ùine dheth.

Cha 'n ioghnadh iad bhi dileas dhuit
 'S do chis a dhioladh durachdach ;
Cha 'n fhaicear coin no ciobairean
 A steach 'na d' thir 'g an iunnsachadh ;
'S bho 'n chuir thu cul ri tairgseachan
 Bho Ghall-bhodaich nan luirichean,
Gu 'n d' fhag sid cliù an Albainn ort
 'S tha farmad aig gach duthaich riut.

Alexander died on the 7th of February, 1793, without
male issue, and was succeeded, in terms of the entail
of 1777, and his own charter of resignation dated 7th
of August, 1786, by his eldest surviving brother,

XXIV. WILLIAM CHISHOLM,

Who has a retour of special service, as nearest and lawful
heir male of tailzie and provision of Alexander Chisholm
his brother, of the lands of Breackachy and others, dated
the 8th of August, 1793, on which infeftment follows on
the 30th of August, with a sasine on the 25th of September, registered at Inverness on the 26th of October
in the same year.   He has a charter of resignation in
his favour of the lands of Wester Comar, called "Comar
Cruaidh," Easter and Wester Erchless, Comar Kirkton,

Buntait, and Mauld, by the trustees of the deceased Lieutenant-General Simon Fraser of Lovat, the superior of these lands, dated the 24th of October, 1797, with an instrument of sasine thereon, on the 12th of April, 1798, registered in the Particular Register of Sasines on the 16th of the same month. He has another charter of resignation from the same trustees, dated the 26th and 27th of May, 1800, with sasine thereon on the 1st of August and registered at Inverness on the 5th of the same month.

He married, on the 12th of March, 1795, Elizabeth, eldest daughter of Duncan Macdonell, XIV. of Glengarry (who, as her second husband, married Sir Thomas Ramsay, Baronet of Balmain, an officer in the H.E.I.C.S. in the Presidency of Bengal), with issue—

1. Alexander William, his heir and successor.

2. Duncan Macdonell, who on the death of his brother Alexander, unmarried, succeeded to the chiefship and estates.

3. Jemima, who, on the 1st of August, 1843, married Edmund Chisholm Batten, M.A., F.R.S.E., of Thornfalcon, county of Somerset, author of a volume entitled *The Charters of the Priory of Beauly*, published by the Grampian Club in 1877. On the death of her brother, Duncan Macdonell Chisholm, in 1858, she and her husband acquired by purchase his unentailed lands of Aigais. They at the same time assumed the surname Chisholm before that of Batten by Royal license. She died in August, 1883, leaving issue—two sons and four daughters, (1) James Forbes Chisholm Batten, B.A. Oxon., Major A.P.D., late Captain 34th Foot He was born on the 13th January, 1847, and educated at Westminster, and at Exeter College, Oxford. He married on the 9th of August, 1883, Anne Douglas (widow of Captain William Bothwell Potter), eldest daughter of John de Havilland Uttermarck, Attorney-General of Guernsey, by his wife Helen Douglas, youngest daughter of John Guthrie of Guthrie, Forfarshire, and his wife, Helen,

daughter of William Douglas of Brigton, with issue—*(a)* James Uttermarck, born on the 29th of May, 1884; *(b)* Harry Copeland, born on the 25th of October, 1885, and died in 1886; *(c)* Edmund Rodolphe, born on the 10th of May, 1887; and *(d)* John de Havilland, born on the 14th of October, 1889. (2) Alexander William, Commander, Royal Navy. He was born in September, 1851, and is still unmarried; (3) Jemima Emily, who died in 1882, unmarried; (4) Edith Ursula; (5) Sarah Annette Eliza; (6) Amye Fanny; and (7) Rose Jane. Lady Ramsay died at Thornfalcon, Somersetshire, the residence of her daughter, at the advanced age of eighty-two years, on the 17th of October, 1859.

William died at Cullumpton, Devonshire, on the 22nd of March, 1817. His body was removed by sea to Inverness, and thence to the family burying place, "with all the pomp and circumstance which marked the last scene in a chief's earthly sojourn." A letter from the famous Colonel, afterwards Lieutenant-General James Macdonell, K.C.B., the hero of Hougomont, to Major Thomas Fraser of Newton, intimating the death of The Chisholm, and giving directions regarding the funeral of that chief in a manner worthy of his position, will be found interesting. It is as follows :—

Bristol, March 29th, 1817.

Dear Sir,—I was at Clifton on the 24th inst. preparing to receive my sister and her family, when I was called to Collumpton by the melancholy tidings of the Chisholm's death. I joined my sister during the night of that day, fearing the injury her health might sustain from continuing a witness to the sad scene, particularly as she is in the family way. I prevailed on her to continue her journey to this place on the morning of the 26th, taking upon myself to do all that could be done in this country for our deceased relation and friend. The body is enclosed first in a lead coffin, and then in one of wood, with a temporary covering of black cloth ; of course on the remains reaching Inverness it will be proper and necessary to replace that covering with new cloth, and the coffin properly finished with brass nails, plate, etc. Upon the leaden coffin there is the following inscription—"William Chisholm, Esq. of Chisholm, died at Collumpton, County of Devon,

March 22nd, 1817." A similar inscription, *without any addition or alteration whatever*, my sister wishes to be put on the brass plate on the outer coffin. On my sister's departure from Collumpton, I proceeded to Exeter and the sea port of that city, Topsham. At the latter place I succeeded in hiring a vessel to convey the remains to Inverness. On the 27th I saw the body removed from Collumpton, and put on board the ship "Liberty," at Topsham ; on the 28th she proceeded on her voyage. The coffin has been put into a large case for its greater security, and consigned to Mr Alexander Anderson, banker, Inverness, to whom, on the 27th, I enclosed one of the bills of lading, which mentions that the case contains a coffin. I had the body removed from Collumpton in a hearse and four, and followed it myself in a carriage to the quay, when it was embarked. Nothing should have prevented me accompanying the remains of my deceased brother-in-law to the burial ground of his ancestors but the absolute necessity I find myself under of returning to France so soon as I have in some degree seen my sister and her boys settled. As an arrangement had been made some time ago for the reception of the boys into the family of a highly respectable clergyman in this neighbourhood, my sister has determined on taking up her residence at Bristol, at least till after her confinement. As the nearest male relation of the family of Chisholm, from the warm interest you have ever taken in all that concerns it, as well as the particular regard she has always felt for you, Mrs Chisholm delegates to you the melancholy and sacred duty of seeing the remains of her late husband and your uncle consigned to the tomb of his forefathers, with all the respect which she feels for his memory, and which is due to the head of a family so ancient and respectable. On the arrival of the remains at Inverness, which will be intimated to you by Mr Anderson, it will be necessary that you give directions that they shall be properly lodged till you have issued the funeral letters and fixed the day of interment. When the obsequies are over, my sister requests to hear from you, addressed to her at the Post-Office, Bristol. I beg you will believe me, my dear sir, with sincere regard, your obedient servant,

(Signed)   JAS. MACDONELL.

Major Fraser of Newton, etc., etc.

It may be interesting to remark that the postage of this letter, as marked on the cover, cost 2s. 8d.

The following account of William's funeral is taken from Anderson's Essay—" His corpse was taken to Inverness by sea, and lay in state there for several days in one of the inns ; where wines and refreshments were laid out for all visitors; after which it was removed to the family burial place in Beauly priory, attended by almost the entire population of the town. The tenants of the deceased met the funeral procession at Beauly Bridge, resolved on removing their chief from the hearse and carrying him on their shoulders; but the coffin being a leaden one, they were glad to desist from their purpose. A granary adjacent to the priory was the scene of the banquet after the interment. The company were so numerous that it was apprehended the floor would have given way. Those of the 'gentle kindred' occupied the upper room, whilst the commons caroused in the lower storey. To use a rude but familiar phrase—the claret ran like ditch water—and the old women of the village brought pails to carry off the superfluous whisky, when those for whom it was intended could drink no more ; nay, further, the voice of scandal has hinted that everyone of them kept public houses for six months afterwards, from the relics of the feast. When the fiery beverage had inflamed their blood, the tenants, at being debarred from tasting the claret, made an irruption into the quarters of the more favoured class, but were easily repulsed. Night closed on the revellers ; several of whom (if my information be correct) were to wake no more, for a sharp fall of snow overpowered individuals of the senseless and straggling people."*

Although the body left Devonshire on the 28th of March it did not arrive in Inverness until the 10th of May. The expenses of the funeral, including £60 for the conveyance of the body by sea from Topsham, near Exeter, to Inverness, amounted to £747 7s. 1d. This sum the tutors of the heir at first refused to pay, and they took the opinion of counsel, who, in giving his decision, was to keep in view "that as the executry may be thrown into the hands of the creditors this claim

* *Essay on the State of Society and Knowledge in the Highlands*, by John Anderson, 1827. pp. 143-144.

would undoubtedly be objected to by them," and counsel
was to say "whether the tutors of the heir would be
justified in paying any part of a sum where the waste
had been so improvident." The opinion of counsel was
not encouraging. The widow, Mrs. Chisholm, never saw
the memorial, and from a letter written by Robert Scott,
her factor, dated the 22nd of June, 1818, it appears that
she did not at all approve of what had been done by
some of her son's tutors without consulting her, though
she was herself one of them. The account was ultimately
paid by the tutors.

On his death, in 1817, William was succeeded by his
eldest son,

XXV.   ALEXANDER WILLIAM CHISHOLM,

Born at Castlehill, Inverness, on the 15th of February,
1810, and consequently a minor only seven years old
when he succeeded to the chiefship and family estates.
He is specially served as nearest lawful heir-male of
tailzie and provision of his father to all the Chisholm
lands held of the Crown, on the 28th of July, 1817, and
duly retoured to Chancery; and there is a precept for
his infeftment, dated the 27th of August, with an instrument of sasine following thereon on the 15th of September,
and registered at Edinburgh on the 16th of October in the
same year. On the 24th of May, 1818, he has a precept
of *Clare Constat* in his favour by Duncan Fraser of Fingask, the superior of the lands of Wester Comar, Wester
and Easter Erchless, and Comar Kirkton, with an instrument of sasine thereon dated the 22nd of June and
registered in the Particular Register of Sasines, at Edinburgh, on the 24th of the same month. He has a similar
precept in his favour of the lands of Buntait and Mauld
by James Fraser of Belladrum, the superior, dated the
2nd of June, 1818, followed by an instrument of sasine,
dated the 22nd, and registered in the Particular Register
of Sasines, on the 24th of the same month.

His guardians, as also of his brother and sister, were his mother; Charles Grant, afterwards Lord Glenelg; John Peter Grant of Rothiemurchus, subsequently one of the judges of the Supreme Court at Calcutta; Sir Hugh Innes of Lochalsh, baronet; and William Mackenzie of Muirton, W.S., Edinburgh. The charge of seeing after the children's education was however mainly left to Mrs. Chisholm, who, soon after the death of their father, sent the two boys to a school under the care of the Rev. William Reid at Midsummer Norton, Somerset. In consequence of the weak state of Alexander's health, brought on by a severe attack of rheumatic fever, he was removed successively to Clifton, Weymouth, Malvern, and Bath. When his health improved, he and his brother were entrusted to the charge of the Rev. Mr. Fendall, Nazing, Essex, with whom they remained until the autumn of 1822, when, on the advice of Charles Grant, they were both sent to Eton. Mr. Ollivant, Fellow of Trinity College, Cambridge, and subsequently Bishop of Llandaff, accompanied them as private tutor. In the end of 1825 Mr. Ollivant resigned his charge, and on their return to Eton the following year the two boys were placed under the tuition of the Rev. Edward Coleridge. They left Eton in 1828, and were placed under the charge of the Rev. James S. M. Anderson, Chaplain in Ordinary to the Queen, until, in the following October, Alexander went to Trinity College, Cambridge, where he entered under the tuition of the Rev. George Peacock, afterwards Dean of Ely. He remained there for three years.

In 1824, at the age of fourteen, he authorised his guardians to pay all his father's debts, with interest at 5 per cent., and to remit all arrears to certain petitioning tenants. In a letter written to his mother, dated Eton, 12th October, 1824, he says in reference to this matter, "I should think that it would be the best way to grant the petitioners a remission of all the arrears of their rent, and to assist them, if possible, to resume the tenancy of Kerrow and Clachan."

In 1825 the brothers paid a visit to Strathglass, on which occasion they received a warm Highland welcome from the tenantry on the estate.   In 1829 Alexander entered Trinity College, Cambridge.   On his coming of age two years later, in 1831, he took possession of the family inheritance, and is said to have taken "an active part in plans for ameliorating" the condition of the people on the property, which amelioration took the form of evicting a large number of the ancient tenantry of his forbears in accordance with the mistaken views which then so extensively prevailed of improving the condition of the Highland people by clearing them out of their native glens to make room for sheep and deer.   Alexander's mode of "improvement" we shall describe in the words of an eye-witness.   For a few years after the death of the Dowager Mrs. Chisholm, in 1826, whose power over a portion of the estate will more fully appear later on, the people were allowed to remain in their holdings.   This, however, our authority adds, "was in order to adjust matters for future and more sweeping arrangements, as all the leases in Strathglass were about to expire.   To the best of my recollection it was in the year 1831 that all the men in Strathglass were requested to meet the young Chisholm on a certain day at the Inn of Cannich.   The call was readily complied with, the men were all there in good time, but The Chisholm was not.   After some hours of anxious waiting, sundry surmisings, and well-founded misgivings, a gig was seen at a distance driving towards the assembled tenants.   This was the signal for a momentary ray of hope.   But on the arrival of the vehicle it was discovered that it contained only the 'sense carrier' of the proprietor, viz., the factor, who told 'the men that The Chisholm was not coming to the meeting, and that, as factor, he had no instructions to enter into any arrangements with them.   I was present," says Colin Chisholm, who is still hale and hearty as we write, "and heard the curt message delivered, and I leave the reader to imagine the bitter grief and disappointment of men who attended that meeting with glowing hopes in the morning, but had to tell their families and dependents in the evening that there was no alternative before them but the emigrant ship, and to choose between the scorching prairies of Australia and the icy regions of North America. In a short time after this meeting, it transpired that the best farms and best grazing lands in Strathglass were let quite silently, without the knowledge of the men in possession, to shepherds from other countries, leaving half the number of the native population without house or home."*

When Thomas Lord Lovat heard of the cruel treatment dealt out to this fine body of Highlanders, he took pity upon them and entered upon negotiations with Mr George Grieve, then occupant of the sheep farm of Glenstrathfarrar, with the view of placing upon it the evicted Chisholm tenants. His lordship agreed to take over the whole stock at valuation, and offered farm and stock to the evicted tenantry from Strathglass. And the best proof that can be given of their ability to hold their own and pay their rents where they were, is that they were not a penny in arrears, and that, at the following Martinmas, they were able to pay Mr. Grieve in cash for the whole stock on the farm of Glenstrathfarrar.

But the unfortunate people were, like many others in the Highlands, soon after doomed to another clearance. "Some fourteen years afterwards," continues Colin Chisholm, "when the rage for deer forests began to assert its unhallowed territorial demands," Lord Lovat informed the evicted men of Strathglass that he required their new holdings for the purpose of enlarging his deer forest in the neighbourhood, and they were again removed to holdings provided for them by his lordship on other portions of his estate. "In short," says the writer, "the management of the Chisholm's estate left only two of the native farmers in Strathglass, the only surviving man of whom

* *The Clearance of the Glens*, by Colin Chisholm, in the *Celtic Magazine* for 1878, Vol. III., pp. 378-388.

[1878] is Alexander Chisholm, Raonbhraid. He is paying rent as a middle-class farmer to the present Chisholm
for nearly twenty years, and paid rent in the same farm
to the preceding two Chisholms from the time they got
possession until they died.   He was also farmer in
a townland or joint-farm in Balnahaun, on the 'Fair
Lady's' portion of Strathglass.   This far, he has satisfied
the demands of four proprietors and seven successive
factors on the same estate.   And, like myself, he is
obeying the spiritual decrees of the fifth Pope, protected
by the humane laws of the fourth Sovereign, and living
under the well-meaning but absent fourth chief."   All the
other Strathglass tenants found a home on the Lovat
estates, where their sons and grandsons are still among
the most respectable middle-class farmers in Inverness-
shire.   Mr Chisholm continues—"There were only two
native farmers left in Strathglass.   The only one who
left his native country of his own accord at that time
was my own father.   So that, when the present Chisholm came home from Canada to take possession of
the estate about nineteen years ago, there were only two
of his name and kindred in possession of an inch of
land in the whole of Strathglass.   At the first opening
he doubled the number by restoring two more from the
Lovat estate.   But I am sorry to say that restoration is
a plant of slow growth.   It is, however, only right to
state that the Chisholm generously re-established and
liberally supported one of the tenants in the farm from
which he was evicted nineteen years before.   This man's
father and grandfather lived and died as tenants on the
same farm, and his great-grandfather, Domhnull Mac-
Uilleam, was killed on Drumossie-moor.   This faithful
clansman was shot when carrying his mortally-wounded
commander, The Chisholm's youngest son, in his arms
from the field.   In Glencannich, even within my own
recollection, there were a number of people comfortably
located.   Of the descendants of Glencannich men there
lived in my own time, one Bishop and fifteen Priests;

three Colonels, one Major, three Captains, three Lieutenants, and seven Ensigns. Such was the class of men
reared and who had their early education either in this
glen or in Strathglass. And now there are eight
shepherds, seven gamekeepers, and one farmer in Glencannich!" Mr Chisholm adds that, when he wrote, in
1878, there was not one of the men in Strathglass or
any of the descendants of the men who were instru-
mental in driving the native farmers out of it.

In 1832, a number of Chisholms who had settled in
Canada, many of them in high and responsible positions,
transmitted an address to their chief through Dr. Stewart
Chisholm of the Royal Artillery, who had for many
years resided and rendered distinguished service in the
Dominion. This address was presented by Dr. Chisholm
to Alexander, on behalf of his Canadian countrymen,
at the St. James Hotel, Jermyn Street, London, in
presence of his mother and several members of the clan.
There is nothing in the document itself which would
justify its reproduction here, but the names attached to
it, many of them historical, and the positions occupied
even then by so many of the clan Chisholm in Canada,
make the completed document, with the signatures as we
now have it, particularly interesting. The version which
we give is from a lithographed copy, apparently published in or soon after 1845. This difference of dates
between the address itself and the published copy, by
the carelessness of those who prepared it for the press,
introduces a good deal of confusion. Some of the facts
and incidents recorded regarding the signatories are com-
puted from the date of the address, while others, it is
quite apparent, are calculated from the date upon which
it was lithographed, thirteen years later. Thus, it is now
impossible to say whether some of the gentlemen whose
names are adhibited to the address occupied the positions
ascribed to them in 1832 or in 1845, or whether the
number of years given as elapsed since they or their
predecessors emigrated are to be reckoned from the first

or last mentioned year. The document, with the names attached, is as follows :—

Glengarry, Upper Canada,
September, 1832.

Dear Chief,—It is with great pleasure that we embrace the present opportunity of transmitting to you through our respected clansman, Dr Stewart Chisholm of the Royal Artillery, who is now on his route to Scotland, our warmest expressions of regard and attachment to you, Chief of our clan.

It is true that a wide sea rolls between us, our native glens and heathclad hills, the land of our forefathers, but divided as we are we have still hearts to appreciate the value of the institutions of our country.

At a time like the present, when Britain seems to be insulted by a Democracy that would destroy all order, and when her ancient and perhaps noblest enemy * has made order a song, we, clansmen of yours inhabiting the wilds of Upper Canada, declare that whatever the rest of governors or governed may do, we at least shall still be proud to act upon the old principle. It may not be irrelevant perhaps to say that, while all other institutions are on the wane, our patriarchal ones remain firm.

> The king can mak' a belted knight,
> A marquis, duke an' a' that,
> A Highland chief's aboon his might,
> Gude faith he mauna fa' that.

The Highland chief of a thousand years is still the father of his family, and we are proud to acknowledge him. Dear chief, that you may long live to enjoy health and prosperity is the ardent and sincere wish of your clansmen.

SIGNED,

George Chisholm, of Burlington Bay, head of Lake Ontario, now in his eighty-seventh year. Sixty years ago he emigrated from Springton on the Leys, near Inverness, N.B. [He died in the year 1843, aged 98.]

John Chisholm, of East Flamboro, Gore District, J.P., Colonel Commanding 4th Regiment of Gore Militia, and Collector of Customs and Tolls.

William Chisholm, of Oakville, Member of Parliament for the county of Halton, Colonel Commanding 2nd Regiment Gore Militia.

George Chisholm, Lieutenant-Colonel 2nd Regiment Gore Militia. The three above are sons to Mr George Chisholm of Burlington Bay.

* In allusion to the abolition of the hereditary peerage in France.

A. M. Chisholm, W. D. Chisholm, John B. Chisholm, James B. Chisholm, sons of the above Colonel John Chisholm.

George R. Chisholm.

John A. Chisholm, Robert K. Chisholm, William Mackenzie Chisholm, sons of the above William Chisholm, Esq. of Oakville, M.P.

Alexander M. Chisholm.

Duncan Chisholm, George B. Chisholm, William K. Chisholm, sons of the above Lieutenant-Colonel G. Chisholm.

George Chisholm of Queenstown Heights, Niagara.

Angus Allan Chisholm, Archibald Charles Chisholm, James Halking Chisholm, sons to the late Mr. Alexander Chisholm, who emigrated 47 years ago from Middle Knockfin, Strathglass.

Charles Alexander Chisholm, James Allan Chisholm, sons to the above Mr. Angus Chisholm.

Alexander Chisholm, Lieutenant-Colonel 1st Regiment Hastings Militia, emigrated 47 years ago from Middle Knockfin, Strathglass, named after the chief Alexander, grandfather to the present chief.

Colin Chisholm, James Chisholm, John Chisholm, Stephen Gilbert Chisholm, Allan Taylor Chisholm, William Fraser Chisholm, sons to the above Lieutenant-Colonel Alexander Chisholm.

Archibald Chisholm, Captain 1st Regiment Hastings Militia, brother to the above Alexander, and emigrated at the same time.

John Chisholm, William Henry Chisholm, Murcheson Chisholm, sons to the above Colin Chisholm.

Donald Chisholm, from Achlian in Glenmoriston, and emigrated from thence about ten years ago. He is grandson to that celebrated and noble-minded Highlander, Hugh (Macphail) Chisholm, who spurned at the reward of £30,000 offered for betraying Prince Charles Edward Stuart, and who never gave his right hand to a man after having bid farewell to his Royal Master. Mr. Donald Chisholm is the son of Alexander, eldest son to the hero of Corrigho, and now lives near Lochiel, County of Glengarry, Upper Canada. The sword of his grandfather is in the possession of Dr. Stewart Chisholm, Royal Artillery, with affidavits attached to it from Isabella, his daughter and others. [The following foot-note is added—"London, 21st March, 1845. The above sword was this day placed in possession of The Chisholm, where it ought to be. Signed, Stewart Chisholm, Senior Surgeon, Royal Artillery." On the death of The Chisholm the sword was returned by his housekeeper to Dr. Chisholm. When Dr. Chisholm died, on 30th September, 1862, the sword came into the possession of his son, Captain Archibald Macra Chisholm (late of the Black Watch, Royal Highlanders), Hartfield House, Applecross, now (1890) residing at Glassburn, Strathglass.]

John Chisholm ; Alexander Chisholm ; Peter Chisholm, sons to the above Mr. Donald Chisholm.

William Chisholm, son of John Chisholm, from Strathglass, now in Lochiel, Glengarry, Upper Canada.

Valentine Chisholm, from Strathglass, now in Lochiel, Glengarry, Upper Canada.

John Chisholm, from Strathglass, now living at Roxburough, Eastern Division, Upper Canada.

John Chisholm; Alexander Chisholm, sons of the above Mr. John Chisholm.

Donald Chisholm; Charles Chisholm, grandsons to the celebrated Hugh Chisholm, by his daughter Katherine, and sons to John Chisholm from Strathglass, now in Glengarry, Upper Canada.

Duncan Chisholm, son of Donald (Macphail) Chisholm, brother to the hero of Corrigho, emigrated from Blairie, Glenmoriston, in the year 1769.

Hugh Chisholm; Donald Chisholm; Alexander Chisholm; William Chisholm, sons to the above Mr. Donald Chisholm, residing near Bishop Macdonell's, in Glengarry.

Archibald Chisholm, son of Hugh, son to said Donald (Macphail) Chisholm.

Alexander Chisholm, son to the above Archibald Chisholm, both living on the Black River, Glengarry.

Lewis Chisholm, Captain 1st Regiment Glengarry Militia, son to the above Donald (Macphail) Chisholm, residing on the Black River, Glengarry; emigrated with his father and brother from Blairie, Glenmoriston, in 1769.

Alexander Chisholm; Donald Chisholm; John Chisholm, sons of the above Captain Lewis Chisholm.

William Chisholm, son of John Chisholm, and grandson to Alexander, brother to the hero of Corrigho, living in Glenmore, Glengarry; emigrated years ago from Glenmoriston.

John Chisholm; Alexander Chisholm; Donald Chisholm, Peter Chisholm; Duncan Chisholm; William Chisholm; sons to the above William Chisholm.

John Chisholm from Strathglass, emigrated previous to the American Revolutionary War, and was the first settler on the Indian Reserve, north branch of the Black River, Glengarry.

David Chisholm, eldest son of the above John, being the first European christened in that part of the country.

John Chisholm; Hugh Chisholm; Donald Chisholm; Ronald Chisholm; Alexander Chisholm; James Chisholm; Roderick Chisholm; sons to the above John Chisholm, who emigrated from Strathglass previous to the Revolutionary War.

Alexander Chisholm; John Chisholm; Duncan Chisholm; sons to the above Mr. David Chisholm (the first christened).

William Chisholm, son of John Chisholm, and grandson to the above John Chisholm from Strathglass.

Archibald Chisholm; John Chisholm; two sons of Donald Chisholm, and grandsons to J. Chisholm, from Strathglass.

Kenneth Chisholm, from Strathglass years ago.

John Chisholm, St. Andrews, Knoydart, near Glengarry, Upper Canada.

Colin Chisholm, brother of the above.

Alexander Chisholm, emigrated with the Honourable and Right Rev. Bishop Macdonell from Strathglass, gardener to the Bishop at his palace, St. Raphaels.

Archibald Chisholm, emigrated from Craskie, Glenmoriston, in 1830.

Archibald Chisholm, from Strathglass in 1828, residing near Bishop Macdonell's, Glengarry, Upper Canada, brother to Dr. A. B. Chisholm, Portland Place, London.

Duncan Chisholm, from Invercannich in 1828.

Alexander Chisholm, student of Divinity, son to Colin Chisholm, Strathglass, carrier.

James Sutherland Chisholm, son to Roderick Chisholm (who died at Montreal during the cholera of 1832), and nephew to Captain Donald Chisholm, H.P., Royal Highlanders. He is heir of entail to the Chisholm estates, failing issue to the present chief, Duncan Macdonell Chisholm, Captain and Adjutant of the Coldstream Guards. His sister Jemima Chisholm, was married at Kingston, Upper Canada, on the 8th January, 1840, to Mr Milner, a Government contractor.

Alexander Chisholm, J.P., late a Lieutenant of the Royal African Corps, emigrated from Kerrow in 1817. He is now Member of Parliament for Glengarry, and Colonel-Commandant of the 2nd Battalion Glengarry Militia.

Duncan Chisholm, father to the above, emigrated in 1822; resides on his farm, which he has called Achagiad.

Duncan Chisholm, Colin Chisholm, Roderick Chisholm, Theodore Chisholm, sons to the above Achagiad, all living in his neighbourhood.

Christopher Chisholm, brother to Roderick and Duncan Chisholm, of Middle Crochel, lives on south side of Lake St. Frances, at a place called Kintail; has twelve sons.

Alexander, who was always in delicate health, is said to have been a young man of more than average ability. In 1835 he was returned to Parliament, in the Conservative interest, for the county of Inverness, after a keen contest with James Murray Grant of Glenmoriston, by a majority of twenty-eight. At the general election of 1837, caused by the death of King William IV., and the accession of Queen Victoria, Alexander again came forward as a candidate for the county. He on this occasion was opposed by Sir Charles Grant, whom he succeeded in defeating by a majority of fifty-four. His Parliamentary duties, however, proved too much for his delicate constitution, and finding himself obliged to be often absent from the House on account of the state of his health, he, in the following spring, determined to resign his seat, and this resolution he intimated to his supporters in an address dated, London, May the 18th, 1838. He almost immediately proceeded to the North, where he proposed

the Master of Grant as his Parliamentary successor—a
proposal which was given effect to without opposition.*
He remained at Erchless during the remainder of the
season, but on the 1st of August he had occasion to go
to Inverness on business, where he was seized, in the
Caledonian Hotel, with the sudden illness which shortly
afterwards terminated his life.   He died there unmarried
on Saturday, the 8th of September, 1838, at the early
age of 28 years.   From a post-mortem examination it
was found that he died of aneurism of the aorta.

His funeral and character are set forth in glowing
terms by a contemporary.   The oldest inhabitant of the
district does not, his eulogist says, remember any funeral
in the North which excited an interest so intense.   At
ten o'clock in the forenoon an immense assemblage, com-
prising individuals of opposite sides in political sentiment
met to show their respect for the memory of the departed chief.   The procession moved slowly from the
Caledonian Hotel, and proceeded by the old bridge and
along the western bank of the river Ness towards the
road leading to Erchless, the equipages and vehicles of
every description extending to more than a mile in
length.   A great many joined on the way, and few of
those who had conveyances returned until they saw the
grave closed over the remains of the young chief amid
his own mountains.   The magistrates of Inverness walked
in deep mourning before the hearse, attended by the
town's officers.   Glengarry, his cousin, followed the body
as chief mourner ; the sheriffs of the northern counties
came next, after whom followed a numerous body of the
gentry and clergy of the Highlands, and of the town's
people of every rank.   Every eminence from which a
view of the procession could be obtained was crowded

* On the preceding page, which was printed off before the error was discovered, it is stated, ninth line from bottom, that Alexander Chisholm was
opposed in his second contest for the Parliamentary representation of Inverness-shire by Sir Charles Grant.   This should have been his unsuccessful
opponent of the previous contest in 1835, James Murray Grant of Glenmoriston.

with spectators, and both banks of the river were lined
with an orderly and sympathetic throng, as the mortal
remains of the young chief were borne away from the
place where his early death had excited the liveliest
feelings of regret and sorrow.   As the cavalcade passed
along the road to Erchless, the country people crowded
to the wayside to express their sympathy.   A body of
the Strathglass tenantry, as well as of the rural population in the neighbourhood, joined the procession some
time before it arrived at Erchless Castle, which it reached
at four o'clock in the afternoon.   When the hearse entered
the policies, the coffin was taken out and slowly borne on
the shoulders of his clansmen and tenants to a wooded
hill in the immediate vicinity, where the body was interred after the burial service of the Church of England
had been read by the Rev. Mr. Fyvie, of Inverness.   A
broad pathway wound round the hill.   The body was
deposited in the centre of a level area on the summit
surrounded by ancient trees, the loveliest spot in that
picturesque vicinity.   The personal appearance of The
Chisholm was very prepossessing ; his manners engaging.
" In speaking or writing his style was chaste, elegant,
and copious ; his eloquence was peculiarly graceful ; and
his stores of literature and erudition were extensive and
varied, though his natural unobtrusiveness prevented him
from giving so many public specimens of his talents as
others of much inferior acquirements had done."   After
stating that his principles were those of the Revolution
of 1688, his eulogist proceeds—" Religion was not used
by him as a convenient tool for accomplishing secular
purposes, but formed the sacred principles to which all
his political sentiments were uniformly subjected.   To
the religious establishments of both Kingdoms he was
firmly attached, while anxious to see them disencum-
bered of every real abuse.   He had studied the Confession
and Laws of the Church of Scotland, and signified his
readiness to become one of its office-bearers.   Had his
valuable life been prolonged he would soon have taken

his place in its General Assembly as an elder, an office which he was well qualified to fill, from his independent bearing, and uniformly consistent character. He bore a near resemblance to our ancient Scottish barons, whose talents and zeal defended, while their lives adorned, and their prayers formed a mighty munition to the often persecuted Church of their beloved Scotland. The religion of Chisholm was deep and fervent, and such as produced the greatest strictness of domestic, social, and personal deportment. To the last moment of his life he cherished a profound feeling of his own unworthiness, a confident reliance on the power and grace of his Divine Redeemer, and an ardent devotedness to His service by whose death he lived, and in whose arms he closed his eyes on this evanescent scene. In Erchless Castle he assembled his numerous family circle every morning and evening for the social worship of God, and his youthful countenance on those occasions contrasted strikingly with the fervent and ripened aspect of his devotional feeling. In prayer his language was strikingly beautiful and expressive, and still flowed forth as the natural aspirations of his own mind. The stated intercourse which he kept up with God and his Word in the retirement of his own chamber gave him at once a readiness of expression and a richness of devotional feeling when he led the worship of his family. And even amidst the bustle and agitating discussions of the House of Commons, he formed one of a group of its members who statedly met during the session for social worship. When his grave was prepared in the sequestered and beautiful spot where his body now reposes, one who marked his habits said, 'that was the place to which, I believe, he often retired for the purpose of secret meditation and prayer.' Sweet is the remembrance of such a man, and long will his name be mentioned with reverence by the inhabitants of his own mountain land, where his religious, and patriotic, and benevolent demeanour will long surround his name with a brighter halo than the antiquity of his house, or the

proudest emblazonment of earthly heraldry, which often
only adds a deeper melancholy to the coldness of the
sepulchre."*

Alexander William Chisholm died unmarried, and was
succeeded in the chiefship and estates by his brother,

XXVI. DUNCAN MACDONELL CHISHOLM,

Who was born on the 5th of August, 1811, and had therefore at the date of his accession entered on his twenty-
eighth year.   When his brother died he was serving as
Adjutant with his regiment, the Coldstream Guards, in
Canada, whither he sailed from Portsmouth on the 18th
of April previously.   We have already seen how he had
been educated along with his brother Alexander, finishing
at Cambridge University.   He obtained his commission
in the Coldstream Guards through his maternal uncle,
General Sir James Macdonell, K.C.B., the hero of Hou-
goumont.   He was aide-de-camp to his uncle when the
General commanded the Northern District of Ireland.
His brother, Alexander, visited them at Armagh, in 1834.
On learning of his brother's death he sold out of the
Guards, immediately returned home and took the necessary steps to secure legal possession of the family estates.
On the 25th of March, 1839, he was specially served heir
to the lands of Breackachy and all the others held direct
from the Crown as the only brother german and nearest
lawful heir male of tailzie and provision of his late brother
Alexander, and was duly retoured to Chancery.   Infeftment followed on the 4th of April, with a precept of
slipterm from Chancery in his favour, dated the 26th
of June, and an instrument of sasine thereon, dated the
17th of September, recorded in the General Register of
sasines on the 16th of October, all in 1839.   On the
9th of September in the same year he is specially served
in the lands of Wester Comar, the two Erchlesses, and
Comar Kirkton, of which, as previously stated, Duncan

* *Inverness Herald* of 21st September, 1838.

Fraser of Fingask was the superior, and against whose heirs, successors, and representatives he has Special Letters, charging them to enter heir to him in these lands, dated the 10th and signeted on the 11th of September. Upon this follows a decree of Declarator of Tinsel of Superiority obtained on the 22nd of January, 1840, at his instance before the Lords of Council and Session against the heirs and representatives of Duncan Fraser of Fingask. He has a precept of infeftment in these lands, dated the 5th of February, and written to the seal on the 12th of March, with an instrument of sasine thereon, dated the 1st, and registered in the General Register of sasines on the 8th of April, 1840. He has a precept of *Clare Constat* in his favour by John Stewart, the superior of the lands of Buntait and Mauld, on the 2nd of April, with an instrument of sasine thereon, dated the 24th of the same month, and recorded in the Particular Register of sasines, at Inverness, on the 19th of June, 1839.

Duncan Macdonell Chisholm spent most of his time in London and for many years before his death fixed his residence there, only occasionally visiting his property in the Highlands, and attending the Inverness county meetings. He took a prominent position among his Highland countrymen in the Metropolis, having occasionally taken the chair at the annual meetings of the Scottish Corporation and similar institutions, and presided or took a leading part at the celebration of important military anniversaries. He is described as a fluent and accomplished speaker.

Mr. Colin Chisholm, writing in 1857, a year before Duncan died, observes that, "it is a question whether the present Chisholm could muster six tenants of his own name on the whole of Strathglass. Sheep and deer now graze on its lonely hills and glens. As for the people or Clan Siosal, they were almost to a man banished from the place occupied by their forefathers for centuries and had to seek an asylum in other lands." Matters are not much better as we write in 1890.

Duncan Macdonell Chisholm died, unmarried, in London, on the 14th September, 1858, aged forty-seven years, when the property reverted, in terms of the entail, to

XXVII. JAMES SUTHERLAND CHISHOLM,

Great grandson, in the direct male line, of Alexander Chisholm of Muckerach, immediate younger brother of Roderick, the twenty-first chief, and uncle of Alexander, The Chisholm who, in 1777, entailed the estates. He has a decree of special service as heir of entail and provision expede before the Sheriff of Chancery, on the 14th and recorded in the General Register of Sasines on the 23rd of December, 1859. His descent is as follows—ALEXANDER CHISHOLM of Muckerach, who married a daughter of Archibald Chisholm of Fasnakyle, of the Knockfin family, had a son ARCHIBALD, who married Catherine, third daughter of John Matheson, V. of Fernaig and Attadale, by his second wife, Margaret, daughter of Kenneth Mackenzie, I. of Pitlundie, son of Alexander Mackenzie, II. of Belmaduthy, by his wife, Catherine, daughter of Sir Kenneth Mackenzie, I. of Coul, Baronet.* Alexander Chisholm of Muckerach had also a second son, Captain John Chisholm, Fasnakyle, who married a daughter of Fraser of Fingask, with issue—one son, who died in the West Indies, unmarried, and two daughters, who married respectively, Fraser of Kinmylies, and Colonel James Chisholm of the 71st Regiment. By Catherine Matheson, Archibald Chisholm had issue—(1) Roderick ; (2) Captain Donald Chisholm of the 42nd Highlanders, and afterwards of the H.P. Royal Highlanders, Canada. Donald was twice married. His eldest son died in China in the house of Jardine, Matheson & Co., and his second son died at Blairs, Aberdeenshire, both without issue. (3) Alexander, who married Janet, daughter of one of the Grants of Glenmoriston, and afterwards settled in the county

* Mackenzie's *History of the Mathesons*, pp. 41-42.

of Antigonish, N.S. RODERICK CHISHOLM married Miss
Sutherland, North-West Territory, with issue — James
Sutherland Chisholm, and a daughter, Jemima, who, on
the 8th of January, 1840, married Mr. Milner, a Government contractor, in Kingston, Upper Canada.

Roderick Chisholm emigrated to Glengarry. Ontario,
early in the present century.   He died at Montreal in 1832.
When, in 1858, James Sutherland Chisholm succeeded to
the Strathglass estates, he was considerably advanced in
years, about fifty-two, and unmarried.   In 1861, however,
he returned to Canada, and on the 13th of November
in that year married a relative of his own, Annie Cecilia,
daughter of Angus Macdonell, residing in Upper Canada,
son of Captain James Macdonell, a distinguished and
loyal British officer, who settled in Montreal after the
American Revolutionary War.   Captain James was a son
of Allan Macdonell of Ardnaslishnish, third son of Æneas
Macdonell, III. of Scotos (brother of Alastair Dubh Macdonell, XI. of Glengarry), by Catherine, third daughter of
Sir Norman Macleod, I. of Bernera, and widow of Alexander Macleod, .VII. of Raasay.   The Chisholm, during
the whole of his rule in Strathglass, lived a quiet and
retired life ; was a good-hearted Highlander, and, as things
were understood in his day, a kindly and generous landlord.

When his son came of age, in 1883, they at once
took steps to disentail the estates, which, failing heirs
male—as they did two years later, on the death of Roderick
Donald Matheson Chisholm, the twenty-eighth chief, unmarried, in 1885—would have reverted to James Chisholm
Gooden Chisholm, London, in terms of the entail of 1777,
as heir of line and nearest heir female of Alexander
the entailer.   Here was a most selfish procedure on
the part of James Sutherland Chisholm and his son,
considering all the circumstances.   Had it not been for
this entail of 1777—for the Muckerach family was excluded
from the entail of 1742, which in all other respects was
identical with that of 1777—neither father nor son would

have succeeded to the estates, and yet as soon as they
found themselves in a legal position to do so, they took
advantage of the Act of 1848, and barred the entail, in
right of which alone they themselves inherited the property,
against the next heir mentioned in that deed. It was
perhaps a natural step to take, but that it was a just one,
no impartial judge, we believe, will for a moment maintain,
when all the circumstances of the case are considered.
The estates were finally disentailed by James Sutherland
Chisholm, with consent of his only son, in 1884.

By his wife, Cecilia Macdonell, he had issue—

1. Roderick Donald Matheson, his heir.
2. Mary Isabella, who died young.
3. Louisa Jane.
4. Annie Margaret.

James Sutherland Chisholm died at Erchless Castle, on
Thursday, the 28th of May, 1885, having just entered
on his eightieth year, and was interred on the Thursday
following, in the family burying-ground near the Castle.
He was succeeded in the chiefship and estates by his
only son,

XXVIII. RODERICK DONALD MATHESON
CHISHOLM,

Who was born on the 20th of September, 1862. He was
thus in his twenty-third year when he came into possession of the Chisholm estates. Being always in delicate
health, he never took any very active part in public life,
even in the Highlands. In 1884 he obtained a commission as Lieutenant in the 3rd Battalion Seaforth Highlanders. Dying of diabetes, unmarried, at his mother's
residence, March Hall, near Edinburgh, on Monday, the
4th of April, 1887, he was interred in the family burying
ground near Erchless Castle, Strathglass, when the estate,
with a rental of £10,000 a year, went by trust disposition to his mother, who is now in possession, but which,

in terms of the same deed of entail, in virtue of which alone the Muckerach family obtained possession of it, would have reverted, had not the entail been barred, to

JAMES CHISHOLM GOODEN CHISHOLM, of Tavistock Square, London, grandson of Alexander, the twenty-third chief, and great-grandson of Alexander, the twenty-second chief, as follows—ALEXANDER, the twenty-second chief married first, Elizabeth, daughter of Roderick Mackenzie, IV. of Applecross, with issue — (1) Captain Duncan, who died before his father ; (2) Alexander, who in 1785 succeeded his father in the chiefship and estates; (3) Margaret, who married Hugh Fraser of Dunballoch and Newton ; (4) Anne, who married Roderick Mackenzie, II. of Scotsburn. This Chisholm, married secondly Margaret, daughter of George Mackenzie, II. of Allangrange, with issue—(5) Roderick, who died before his brother Alexander, the twenty-third chief, without male issue ; (6) William, who, in 1793, succeeded his brother Alexander as twenty-fourth chief ; (7) James, who died unmarried ; and three daughters. The last *male* heir of all these sons died out in the person of Duncan Macdonell Chisholm, the twenty-sixth chief, on his death, unmarried, in 1858, when the representative of the Muckerach family, James Sutherland Chisholm, who died in 1885, succeeded. On the death of his only son and successor, Roderick Donald Matheson Chisholm, unmarried, in 1887, the last male heir of all those mentioned in the deed of entail of 1777 became extinct. In order to pick up the succession of the heir of line next mentioned in the deed of entail we must now revert to

ALEXANDER, the twenty-second chief, who first introduced the Chisholms of Muckerach into the entail of the estate in 1777. He died in December, 1785, when he was succeeded in the chiefship and the family estates by his eldest surviving son by the first marriage—

ALEXANDER, the twenty-third chief, who, as already stated, in 1776 married Elizabeth, daughter of Dr. George

Wilson, Edinburgh, with issue, an only daughter—

MARY CHISHOLM,

Born in March, 1780. Any account of the Chisholms of
Strathglass would be incomplete without a record of
what the native tenantry owed to this lady, afterwards Mrs. James Gooden, London, and to her mother,
the Dowager Mrs. Chisholm, widow of Alexander, the
twenty-third chief. While Mary was a young girl, having
scarcely entered upon her teens, influence was brought
to bear upon her father, by neighbouring proprietors
and friends, to follow the example of the Macdonalds of
Glengarry and other Highland landlords, who had cleared
out the native tenantry on their estates for the purpose
of consolidating their holdings and letting them to southern
sheep farmers.

On one occasion four of these southerners, one of whom
was the grasping Gillespie, of Glencuaich, called at
Comar House, where The Chisholm at that time resided.
They remained all night and were, of course, hospitably
entertained. During the evening they introduced the
subject of their mission, and used all their uncouth
eloquence to impress upon their host the great advantages which would accrue to him if he would only agree
to evict his native tenantry and let his guests have the
principal portions of his estates—the best parts of Strathglass—as sheep farms. They pointed to what had been done
so recently by Glengarry, and strongly urged upon The
Chisholm that he should deal with his tenantry and estate
as Mac' ic Alastair had dealt with his property and people a
few years before, so much, according to them, to his own
advantage. Father and child listened quietly but respect-
fully to the cold-blooded proposals of these strangers,
but Mary, at last losing patience, mildly protested against
the ruthless eviction of her father's clansmen and retainers
to make room for such a rough, selfish, unfeeling set as
she had been just listening to. The girl was rewarded by

being at once ordered to her room ; but instead of retiring there, she found her way to the kitchen, with tears
in her eyes, and explained to the servants, who gathered
around her, the cause of her grief. "Never," says Colin
Chisholm, "was *Crann-Tara* sent through any district
with more rapidity than this unwelcome news spread
through the length and breadth of Strathglass.   Early
next morning there were about a thousand men, including young and old, assembled on the ground at Comar
House.   They demanded an interview with The Chisholm.
He came out and discussed with them the impropriety
of alarming his guests.   But he was told in reply that
his guests were infinitely worse than the freebooters who
had on a former occasion come with sword in hand to rob
his forefathers of their patrimony—an allusion to a sanguinary battle which was fought on the plain of Aridh-dhuiean
many years before, between Clann-'ic-an-Lonathaich, who
wanted to possess themselves of Strathglass, and the
Chisholms, who succeeded in keeping possession of it to
this day.   The guests at first anxiously listened at the
drawing-room windows to the conversation which was
passing between The Chisholm and his clansmen, but they
soon made their way quietly down stairs and passed
through the back door and garden to the stable, where
they mounted their horses, galloped off helter-skelter,
followed by the shouts and derision of the assembled
tenantry across the river Glass, spurring their horses
and never looking behind them until they reached the
ridge of *Maoil Bhuidhe*, a hill between Strathglass and
Corriemony.   Here they looked back for the first time,
when they saw a procession being formed at Comar
House—pipers playing, and The Chisholm being carried
to Invercannich House on the brawny shoulders of his
tenantry.   Instead of this visit being a cause of sorrow,
it turned out the happiest day that ever dawned on Strathglass.   Chief and clansmen expressed mutual confidence
in each other, and renewed every ancient and modern
bond of fealty ever entered into by their forbears.   All

this extraordinary episode in the history of Strathglass
I heard related over and over again by some of the men
who took part in chasing the southrons out of the district." Mr. Chisholm adds that about forty-two years ago
he related to Mary Chisholm, then Mrs. James Gooden,
London, the Strathglass version of this incident, every
word of which that lady corroborated, at the same time
adding regarding her own actions later on—" When my
father died in 1793, I felt that the welfare of the tenantry
left in charge of my mother depended in a great measure
on myself. I was brought up among them, I used to
be the Gaelic interpreter between them and my mother,
and they had great confidence in me. However, it was
in after years, when old age began to impair my mother's
memory, that I had the greatest anxiety lest the agents
of The Chisholm should succeed in depriving her of the
tenantry. I had two objects in view. The first was to
keep the people comfortable, and the second to hand
them over as an able class of tenantry to my first cousin,
the young Chisholm, at the demise of my mother." This,
as has already been shown, she completely succeeded in
doing.

It will be remembered that Alexander, the twenty-second
chief, left his widow free to choose as her portion a
certain sum of money per annum, or alternately the rents
of so many township lands or joint farms and the grazings
attached to them, and that, fortunately for the tenants,
she made choice of the latter. These townships with
their grazings were: on the north side of the Cannich—
the davoch of Invercannich, Craskie, Lietry, Shalvanach,
Mulardich, east and west, Ardtaig, Culdoire, and Màm;
on the south side of the same river—Tombuie, Lub-
Ghiuthais, Cruim, Fraoch-Coire, Lub-na-Meann, Coire-
Buidhe, Coire-Dhomhain, and Frianach Mhor. On the
south side of the Glass, she had Balnahaun, Crannaich,
and Druineach, and the grazings of Pollanfearna.

But although the tenantry who were fortunate enough
to possess holdings in these townships—retained as her

portion by the Dowager Mrs. Chisholm until her death—were allowed to remain in comfortable circumstances on their farms, it was not so, as already stated, in the case of those who were tenants on the portion of the estate which came under the full control of The Chisholm himself. They were, as stated by Colin Chisholm, at one time or another evicted almost to a man, although they were all in good circumstances, were not a penny in arrears of rent, and quite able to take over from Lord Lovat a large and valuable stock on the farm of Glenstrathfarrar, when, after the Chisholm evictions, his lordship provided them with holdings on his own estate.

The first great clearance carried out in Strathglass was in 1801. William, the Chisholm of that day, was always in delicate health, and the management of the estates fell largely into the hands of his wife, whom the natives to this day blame for having cleared the whole clan out of their native glen, except those who were fortunate enough to have been tenants of the " Fair Lady," or, as she is still endearingly called by the people of the district, "A Bhantighearna Bhàn." The evicted tenants crossed the Atlantic in hundreds, most of them settling in Cape Breton ; in the county of Antigonish, Nova Scotia ; and in Glengarry, Upper Canada.

Among those who were evicted at this time was Domhnull Gobha, the local Gaelic bard already quoted. Donald was now very far advanced in years, and did not at all relish the idea of being forced to leave his native land for a foreign country at his time of life, though all his relatives and friends were among those whom he was to accompany across the Atlantic. He, however, with characteristic cheerfulness, resolved to be as happy as the circumstances admitted of ; and to lighten his own heart and cheer up his friends, he composed a poem in which, while bitterly complaining of the inhuman system which drove him out of the land of his forefathers in his old age, he encouraged his companions,

and drew a hopeful picture of the prospects before them
and of the fruitfulness and other advantages of the new
country to which they were going. But of his own chief,
William, the man who so heartlessly drove away his
clansmen to make room for sheep and south country
shepherds, the bard in the anguish of his heart very
truly said—

> An t-uachdaran a th'air nar ceann,
> Tha mi 'n duil gun chaill e dhaimh,
> 'S fearr leis caoirich 'chur ri gleann
> Na fir an camp le feileadh.

There was another great clearance in 1810. It is referred to in a letter from Bishop Æneas Chisholm,
addressed to " Mrs. Chisholm, Dowager of Chisholm,
Edinburgh," dated " Fasnakyle, 20th January, 1810," and
now in our possession. After referring to a previous correspondence and to an arrangement about their farms
which had been "amicably and cheerfully adjusted and
settled" between Mr. Murray, on behalf of Mrs. Chisholm, and her tenantry, the Bishop proceeds :—

Your tenants are now the object of envy to their surrounding
neighbours, as they may sleep sound, without so much as a change
of one individual, or dread of being scattered among the four winds
of heaven, or where chance may drive them, as the bulk of their
countrymen presently are.   Oh ! madam, you would really feel if
you only heard the pangs and saw the oozing tears by which I
am surrounded in this once happy but now devoted valley of Strathglass, looking out all anxiously for a home without forsaking their
dear valley ; but it will not do, they must emigrate.   You will
have double the population on your locality by the first term that
The Chisholm will have on his whole property, if the plans adopted
may be followed, as it is meant, with rigour.   I think your King
and country should thank you.   Poor Knockfin, in the bed of distress as he is, and no flattering appearance of his recovery, was
deprived of his extensive farm without asking him the question if
he would give more or not.   A Peebleshire gentleman was preferred.   Mrs. Chisholm of this place has retained her farm with
large additions ; she calls for your humble servant to share it with
her.   Perhaps it may be the case, as I cannot aspire at what I
had for nine years past.   Allan Chisholm and his brother Duncan
are driven from their place by a vile fellow, and sixteen good

fellows driven out of their places to make room for them. So much of the Corrimony plan.

Every one of the Dowager Mrs. Chisholm's tenants remained in their holdings undisturbed until the end of her life, notwithstanding the many efforts which had been made by the agents of The Chisholm to induce her to hand over her township lands and people to him, in return for which she was offered not only to be relieved of all trouble and responsibility in connection with them, but payment, without any expense of collection or manage-ment to herself, of a higher rent per annum than she was then receiving from her tenants. These offers were so tempting and so persistently urged that, when Mrs. Chis-holm became old and frail, there was much danger that she might yield to the wiles of those who pressed her, but the constant care and watchfulness of her daughter, even after Mary married and took up her residence in London, pro-tected her.

One of the most active agents employed by The Chis-holm for this purpose was William Mackenzie of Muirton, W.S., Edinburgh. He made himself so obnoxious to the Dowager and her daughter by his persistent efforts and liberal promises that Mary, then Mrs. James Gooden, on one occasion insisted upon his promising never again to speak to her mother on the subject of her Strath-glass tenants. However, forgetting or disregarding this promise, Mr. Mackenzie returned some time afterwards and renewed his former offers, determined to get the tenants and their holdings out of the Fair Lady's hands, and under the immediate control of the chief. He was ready to complete the transaction, with pen in hand and paper before him, when Mrs. Gooden entered her mother's room and peremptorily ordered him out. "Here you are again, William," she said, "quite regardless of your word of honour and your promise as a gentleman; the sooner you take yourself out of this house the better I shall be pleased; and if ever you come here again on your unwelcome errand, to disturb my mother in her frail old age, I shall make Edinburgh too hot for you." Cowed with shame and confusion, Mr. Mackenzie gathered up his papers, left the house, and never again returned to it during the life of the venerable lady, who under the advice and constant care of her daughter, did not allow a single tenant on her jointure lands to be disturbed during the thirty-three years she had possession of them, from the death of her husband in 1793 until her own in 1826.

But this she was not always able to do without annoyance and expense. Colonel James Chisholm, a military officer who had risen from the ranks to the position of Lieutenant-Colonel in the army, took a fancy to the farm of Tombuie, in Glencannich, for his brother Roderick, and he succeeded in getting a promise of it from the Dowager on the representation that Archibald Chisholm, the occupant, was willing to give it up. The farm was thus let over the head of the tenant in possession and without his knowledge. Some friend, however, wrote on his behalf to Mrs. Gooden, telling her that Archibald Chisholm, who had three grown up sons and three daughters, never once thought of giving up his farm, and calling her attention to the fact that he was one of the loyal band who volunteered to make up his company for her uncle William, when he obtained his first commission in the Glengarry Fencibles. Mrs. Gooden at once communicated with her mother and her agent, Mr. Murray, Tain, who was married to Mrs. Chisholm's sister, with the result that that gentleman, on the Dowager's behalf, refused to ratify the agreement to let the farm. The rejected tenant sent in a claim for damages, dated 1822, amounting to £641 3s. But Mrs. Gooden, with characteristic generosity and patriotism, consented to satisfy the unreasonable demands made upon her mother by Roderick Chisholm and his brother the Colonel rather than see a single one of her mother's tenants evicted during her life. The claim for damages is as follows—

State of claim by Roderick Chisholm, late farmer at Comar,

now at Crask; James Chisholm, his eldest son, residing there; and Ensign John Chisholm, R.A.C., also residing there, against Mrs. Elizabeth Chisholm of Chisholm, relict of the deceased Alexander Chisholm, Esq. :—

Rent payable to Aigas from Whitsunday to Martinmas, ...	£36 0 0
Do. to Alexander Sinclair, wood merchant, Isle of Aigas, for pasture, two months from Whitsunday, ...	7 10 0
Do. to Peter Maclaren, farmer at Comar, for sheep pasture from Whitsunday to 2nd September last, 120 sheep at 6d per head each month, 3 months nine days, ...	9 15 0
Damage sustained by the necessity of selling 120 sheep to Peter Maclaren at 12s each, 4s loss, valued by James Laidlaw and James Brydon at	24 0 0
Expense of removing and selling cattle, horses, furniture and crop, from Comar to Aigas, 15 miles distant	7 5 0
Do. once to Tain from Strathglass, 40 miles	2 5 0
Do. hire for three days at 5s each	0 15 0
Do. trips from Strathglass to Mr. Reach	13 13 0
Meliorations paid Aigas for houses	40 0 0
Damages in name of solatium for not getting possession ...	500 0 0
	£641 3 0

Is it any wonder that the memory of these ladies, the Dowager Mrs. Chisholm and her daughter, Mrs. Gooden, should still be green in Strathglass, and that their names should continue to be revered as benefactors of the native tenantry by every loyal member of the clan not only in their ancestral straths and glens but in every part of the world wherever a Chisholm resides? On the contrary, when the times in which they lived and the circumstances by which they were surrounded are taken into account, it would be a stain on the best side of human nature if such noble and entirely unselfish conduct as theirs were not endearingly remembered and commemorated; and we are not a little gratified at the part which has fallen to our lot in these pages to add a stone to the cairn of affectionate regard which the people of Strathglass have, in their hearts of hearts, raised to the memory of the Dowager Mrs. Chisholm and her ever watchful and devoted daughter.

Mary Chisholm married on the 12th of December, 1812, James Gooden, a wealthy London merchant, with issue—

JAMES CHISHOLM GOODEN CHISHOLM,

Born on the 26th of September, 1816, and now of Tavistock Square, London.   He is thus the grandson in direct lineal descent of Alexander, twenty-third chief, and great-grandson of Alexander, the twenty-second chief, who entailed the estates; and had not the late James Suther-land Chishlom and his son, Roderick Donald Matheson Chisholm, barred the entail in 1884, James Chisholm Gooden Chisholm would now be in possession of the Strathglass estates, in terms of the entail of 1777, and the charter of 1786.   The deed of entail, after mention-ing all the entailer's brothers and their heirs male, proceeds—

Whom failing, to Archibald Chisholm, eldest son of the deceast Alexander Chisholm of Muckerach and the heirs male of his body, whom failing, to Lieutenant John Chisholm, second son of the said Alexander Chisholm of Muckerach and the heirs male of his body, *whom all failing, to my nearest and lawful heirs whatso-ever the eldest heir female and the descendants of her body, excluding all others heirs portioners, and succeeding always with-out division through the whole course of female succession in all time coming,* heritably and irredeemably all and whole the lands and estate which formerly pertained to Roderick Chisholm, late o. Comar.

It has already been conclusively shown that the last male heir of all those whose names appear in the deed of entail became extinct in the person of Roderick Donald Matheson Chishclm, the twenty-eighth chief, who died unmarried in 1887, when the estates would un-doubtedly have reverted to James Chisholm Gooden Chisholm, London, as lawful and nearest heir whatso-ever, he being undoubtedly the eldest heir female of the entailer, had the entail not been barred.   But this is not all.   By the same deed he was not only entitled but bound to assume, retain, and bear the surname of the family and the arms and designation of Chisholm of Chisholm as his own proper arms, surname, and designation, in all time coming. And more imperative still, it is expressly laid down and provided in the deed of entail that it shall not be lawful for any of the entailer's heirs, male or female, to change the order of succession specified in the deed, or to do any act, directly or indirectly, whereby the succession may be altered, innovated, or changed. That there may be no mistake on this point we shall here quote the clause by which these distinct conditions regarding the family name and arms and against any change in the order of succession specified in the entail are expressly declared. It is in the following terms—

With this provision also that my said eldest son and his heirs substitutes and successors above mentioned, shall possess and enjoy the lands and others before disponed by virtue of these presents, and the charters and infeftments to follow hereon, and by no other title whatsoever, and likewise with this provision, that the said Duncan Chisholm, my eldest son, and his heirs substitutes and successors above mentioned, *as well male as female, and the descendants of their bodies who shall happen to succeed to the lands and others before disponed, and the husbands of such of the said heirs female (if any be) shall be holden and obliged to assume, and constantly retain, use, and bear the surname, arms and designation of Chisholm of Chisholm as their own proper arms, surname, and designation in all time thereafter, and farther, it is hereby expressly provided and declared that it shall not be leisome or lawful to my said eldest son or to any of the heirs substitutes or successors above mentioned to alter, innovate, or change the order of succession above specified, or to do any other act or deed directly or indirectly whereby the same may be anyways altered, innovated, or changed.*

The entailer then finally provides and declares regarding the succession, failing heirs male, to his nearest heir female as follows :—

And I hereby bind and oblige me and my heirs and successors to make due and lawful resignation of the lands and others before disponed in the hands of my immediate lawful superiors thereof,

in favours of and for new infeftments of the same to be made and
granted to myself, and after my decease to the said Duncan Chisholm my eldest son, and the heirs male of his body, whom failing
to my other heirs substitutes and successors above mentioned,
according to the order of the substitution and destination of succession above specified, *whom failing to my nearest and lawful
heirs and assignęes whatsoever, the eldest heir female and the descendants of her body, excluding all other heirs portioners, and
succeeding always without division through the whole course of
succession in all time coming*, and that with and under the express
conditions, provisions, burdens, restrictions, limitations, clauses,
irritant and faculties, above written allenarly, and no otherwise."

It may be said, no doubt, that all these conditions and
provisions were afterwards affected and liable to be changed
by the Act of 1848, and the amending Acts of 1875
and 1881 ; and so they were.   But it is a very glaring instance of the many cases of legalised robbery with which
the Highland people have been of late years becoming
familiar.   James Chisholm Gooden Chisholm was robbed
of his undoubted ancestral rights by an Act of Parliament
which the late James Sutherland Chisholm, with the con-
currence of his son, thought it just, in the circumstances
described, to give effect to.   Very good.   If the rightful
and legal owner of landed estate can in this way be justly
deprived of his family rights by Act of Parliament, why
not extend the principle ?   Why not, in the same way,
by other Acts of Parliament, restore all the landed estate
in the Highlands and elsewhere to their rightful owners,
the people ?   If it be just by an Act of the Legislature to
divert a valuable Highland property from its rightful and
legal owner, as in the case of Strathglass, to those who
have no other natural or moral right whatever to it than·
an Act of Parliament, how much more just and righteous
must it be, by similar means, to restore all the land in
the Highlands to its original and rightful owners, the
Highland people ?   We must leave this important aspect
of the case to the consideration of the landed classes
who are at present so plausibly and stoutly engaged in
maintaining that it would be a great moral wrong to

deprive any of them of their estates, under any conceivable circumstances, even by Act of Parliament.

James Chisholm Gooden Chisholm has for nearly half a century been widely and favourably known in London Scottish circles. Among his countrymen there, as well as throughout the whole north of Scotland, he has always been recognised, from his Celtic sympathies and patriotic sentiments, as one of our most genuine living Highlanders. He has ever been ready to befriend and assist young men and others from the Highlands, and to promote and support every object and movement which he considered conducive to the best interests of the Highland people. He has for more than forty years taken an active interest and prominent part in the management of the Highland Society of London, and has long been and still is one of its honorary Treasurers. He has been a constant and liberal supporter of the Royal Scottish Hospital and of the Royal Caledonian Schools, and is at present a life director of both these excellent institutions. He is a member of the Council of London University College, and one of the Governors of University College Hospital. For many years he has been a liberal patron of young artists of promise, his sympathies in this direction being no doubt largely prompted by the fact that he was himself no mean master of the brush in his early days. He married, in 1851, Anne Elizabeth, daughter of John Lambert of Banstead, Surrey, with issue—

1. Chisholm Gooden, born on the 27th of September, 1856.

2. John Lambert Chisholm Gooden, who was born on the 6th of February, 1858, and died unmarried on the 30th of September, 1884.

3. Roderick Chisholm Gooden, born on the 30th of January, 1864. He is an officer in the 3rd Battalion Seaforth Highlanders.

4. Katherine Mary Chisholm Gooden, who married, first, in 1871, Francis James Lindsay Blackwood, with issue—one child, who died in infancy. She married, secondly,

in 1879, Henry Valentine Corrie, a member of the Stock Exchange, without issue.

5. Annie Elizabeth Chisholm Gooden, who married, in 1877, Arnold Trinder, solicitor, London, with issue— Arnold James, William Valentine, Robert Ellet, who died in infancy ; Annie Sophia, and Alice Mary.

6. Hannah Lucy Gooden.

7. Henrietta Ellen, who, in 1886, married her third cousin, Robert Marshall Middleton, barrister, London, a cadet of the Middletons of Fettercairn, and great-grandson of a sister of the " Fair Lady " of Strathglass.

Mr. James Gooden had, by Mary Chisholm of Chisholm, a second son,

Alexander Chisholm, who was born on the 4th of April, 1818, and died on the 22nd of August, 1841, in the twenty-fourth year of his age.   He was a scholar of Trinity College, Cambridge ; head of the Classical Tripos at that University, and Chancellor's medallist in 1840, taking a second class degree in Mathematics in the same year.   He died suddenly of peritonitis at Bonn, while reading for the Fellowship of his College, unmarried.

It is thus clearly established, legally and genealogically, that, had not the late James Sutherland Chisholm and his son barred the entail of 1777, James Chisholm Gooden Chisholm would not only have succeeded to the Strathglass estates but would also have been obliged in terms of that entail, to assume, and constantly retain, use, and bear the surname, arms, and designation of Chisholm of Chisholm as his own proper arms, surname, and designation in all time coming, as heir of line and nearest heir female of the entailer.

When, in 1887, the estates went out of the entailer's family, on the death, unmarried, of the late Roderick Donald Matheson Chisholm, the last heir male, who left them to his mother—a lady who cannot be said to have the remotest claim to the property, either by right of descent or deed of entail, or on any other ground whatever, except that she· was the wife of one Chisholm

and the mother of another—it was only natural that James
Chisholm Gooden should claim his rights as heir of line
of Alexander Chisholm, the entailer, of which no action
on the part of the late Chisholm or of his father, or of
both combined, could ever deprive him. His claim was
not only natural, but it was his bounden duty, out of
respect to the intention and desire of his ancestors, and
what he owed to himself, to his family and posterity, to
take the necessary steps to give effect, so far as in his
power lay, to the conditions laid down by his great-grandfather and grandfather, the twenty-second and twenty-third
chiefs, both of whom entailed the estates on the heir of
line, failing heirs male, as they did fail in 1887 in the
person of the last male representatives of the Muckerach
family. He therefore applied to the Lord Lyon King-
at-Arms, to grant him *as the eldest heir female* and in
terms of the deed of entail, the full arms and insignia
of the family of Chisholm. It will be observed that while
he never made any claim to be the heir male or chief
of the clan, he has proved conclusively to the Lord
Lyon that there was now no heir male of Alexander, the
entailer, to whom the grant of arms was made in 1760,
in existence, and that he, as Alexander's heir of line and
eldest heir female, had not the entail been barred in
1887, would unquestionably have succeeded to the estates,
and not only be entitled to assume the family name and
arms, but would have been bound in terms of the deed
of entail to do so. To his application the Lord Lyon
King-at-Arms, replied on May the 17th, 1887, in the
following terms—

I have been carefully considering the question regarding supporters as put in your letter. In no circumstances, even had the
entail of 1777 still stood, would you have had, even by heraldic
rule, an absolute right to supporters, but your claim to them *ex
gratia* would have been very strong, *very much stronger than that
of the heir of line of the younger family.* But the possession of the
estates by the Muckerach branch brings their heir of line into such
a position that were an application made by him (or her) at a
future date it would be rather a strong measure to refuse it. *Her-
aldically, however, you are more entitled to the undifferenced Chis-*

holm coat than that representative could be, who, were he making application here, could I think only be allowed that coat with a mark of cadency, and, therefore, it does seem a little paradoxical that the undifferenced coat should be without supporters and the differenced coat with them. On full consideration, the result at which I have arrived—and that not without difficulty—is that though I would not be justified in allowing you the supporters exactly as recorded in our books in 1760 and 1812, the difficulty could be got over by an alteration in the attitude of the savages' clubs, making them in your case rest not on the shoulders but on the ground (as in the case of the supporters of the Earl of Morton and some other instances.) This would leave it open to the heir female of the younger branch to apply *ex gratia* at any future time for the supporters as recorded in 1760 and 1812.

Almost immediately afterwards it was officially announced that, in consequence of the late Chisholm, Roderick Donald Matheson Chisholm, having died unmarried, the Lord Lyon had granted *ex gratia* to James Chisholm Gooden, in virtue of his direct descent from Alexander the entailer, the arms of the Chisholm family with the supporters having their clubs reversed. He was also authorised to adopt and use the name of Chisholm, in addition to his own, to be borne in all time coming by himself, his family, and descendants. And he assumed the arms and adopted the name accordingly.

It is not a little curious to find that in the coat of arms engraved on the address presented by the Chisholms of Canada to Alexander William Chisholm in 1832, already given, the savages' clubs are reversed and resting on the ground instead of on the shoulders, exactly the same as in the arms granted to James Chisholm Gooden Chisholm by the Lord Lyon King-at-Arms in 1887. The Canadian savages, however, wear short kilts instead of the wreaths round the loins worn by the savages in the recorded Chisholm arms, which are described as follows:—

Arms—A boar's head couped or, on a shield gules. *Crest*—A dexter hand, couped at the wrist, holding a dagger erect proper, on which is transfixed a boar's head couped gules. *Supporters*—Two savages wreathed about the head and loins with laurel, and bearing knotted clubs over their shoulders proper. *Motto*—Feros ferio. Vi aut virtute.

THE CHISHOLMS OF KINNERIES AND LIETRY.

THIS family is descended from John Chisholm, XVI. of Comar, "son of Alexander and brother to Thomas," who was served heir to his father in the lands of Strathglass on the 19th of December, 1590. John married, as his second wife, the eldest daughter of Alexander Mackenzie of Coul (son of Colin Càm Mackenzie, XI. of Kintail, by Mary, eldest daughter of Roderick Mackenzie, II. of Davochmaluag), by his second wife, Christian, daughter of Hector Munro of Assynt. By Miss Mackenzie John Chisholm had issue—first, Alexander, his heir and successor; and second,

I. THOMAS CHISHOLM OF KINNERIES, called the "Tanaistear," and commonly known as "Tomas Mor Mac an t-Siosalaich." He married, about 1630, his cousin, Catherine, fourth daughter of Roderick Mor Mackenzie, I. of Redcastle, third son of Kenneth Mackenzie, X. of Kintail, by his wife, Lady Elizabeth Stewart, daughter of John, second Earl of Athol. Catherine, whose mother was Florence, daughter of Robert Munro, 15th Baron of Fowlis, married first, in 1605 (as his second wife), Kenneth Mackenzie, III. of Killichriosd, great-grandson of the redoubtable Kenneth a Bhlair, VII. of Kintail. From this, her first marriage, are descended the Mackenzies of Suddie and of Ord. To gratify the desire of his wife, who wished to be able to see her father's and her late husband's lands from her new residence, Thomas built his new house at Kinneries, on a rising ground above Eskadale. By her, who was advanced in years before their marriage, Thomas Mor had issue, an only son, Thomas Og. He married, secondly, a daughter of Fraser of Ballindown, with issue.

Thomas Mor died, according to the tombstone over his grave in the Chisholm portion of the Priory of Beauly, in January, 1670. On this stone, which is still in a fairly good state of preservation, notwithstanding its exposure to the elements for more than two hundred years, he is described as "ane honnest gentelman." He was succeeded by his only son, by the first marriage,

II. THOMAS OG CHISHOLM, who afterwards took the farm of Lower Knockfin, and the Ath-na-Muileach portion of Affric. Thomas was a celebrated sportsman in his day and district, his red gun, or "gunna dearg," never, according to local tradition, missing its deadly aim.

It is related that on one occasion he informed his gillies in the evening that he was to proceed next morning to a shealing in Affric, to which they were instructed to follow him about noon, and to look well about them on the way, as he would in all likelihood leave some evidence of his own prowess and the unerring accuracy of the "gunna dearg" on his track. Acting on these instructions, the gillies found, before reaching their destination, not less than nine roe deer which had been brought to earth by their master and his "gunna dearg." But, as if this were not enough for one day's sport, Thomas having, as they sat down to dinner, observed a herd of red deer on the sky line above Doire-Carnach, soon finished his repast, made for the hill, and within a very short time pulled down a magnificent stag from among the herd.

Those were the days of true sport and real deer-stalking and not ours, when the deer are driven like tame cattle to a narrow gorge and shot down in dozens as they pass along within a few yards by a "sportsman" sitting in an easy chair, while one attendant loads his rifles and another supplies him with liberal libations of brandy and soda to keep up his courage.

Thomas lived all his days and died at Lower Knockfin. He married a daughter of Fraser of Struy, with issue, an only son—

III. ARCHIBALD CHISHOLM, who succeeded him. He married a daughter of Colin Mackenzie, Contin, locally known as "Cailean Buidhe," with issue—

1. Colin, who succeeded his father.

2. John, who married and had a son, John Bàn Og, who died at Allangrange, and was the last of the family interred in the old family burying ground in the Priory of Beauly.

3. A daughter, who married Alexander Mackintosh, with issue. They afterwards, in 1801, emigrated to Nova Scotia.

Archibald was succeeded in Lower Knockfin by his eldest son,

IV. COLIN CHISHOLM, who fought both at Sheriff Muir and at Culloden. In after life he showed great attachment to the arms which he carried, and, from all accounts, very effectively used, on these occasions. When after the 'Forty-five the Disarming Act, which compelled the Highlanders to give up their arms, was passed, Colin succeeded in evading the law, and, by a ruse, to keep his highly treasured weapons. Before his death he enjoined upon his family to take the greatest care of his claymores in particular, an injunction which has been faithfully given effect to. That which he used at Sheriff Muir is in possession of one of his descendants in Nova Scotia, and the other, used at Culloden, a heavy weapon of Solingen manufacture, is carefully preserved by his great-grandson, Colin Chisholm, Namur Cottage, Inverness.

Colin gave up the farm of Lower Knockfin, and removed with his family to Lietry, in Glencannich.

He married, first, a daughter of Fraser of Ballindown, with issue—

1. Roderick, who married Anne, daughter of John Chisholm, "Ian MacAlastair," farmer, with issue—(1) Colin, who went to America and was lost sight of; (2)

Alexander, who married Mary, daughter of Alexander Macrae, farmer, Glencannich, with issue—(*a*) John, who married Isabel, daughter of John Mackenzie, Lietry, with issue—a large family now in Cape Breton, Dominion of Canada ; (*b*) William ; and (*c*) Roderick, both of whom went to Nova Scotia.   (3) Duncan, who married Margaret Bain, whose father was tenant of Carnach, Strathglass, with issue—a large family of sons and daughters, some of whom emigrated to Canada and the West Indies.   (4) William, an engineer, who went to Canada, and of whose descendants, if any, nothing is known.   (5) John, who married Janet Chisholm, widow of Christopher Macdonell, with issue—(*a*) John, who emigrated in early life and of whom nothing is known ; (*b*) William, who married Margaret Maclaren, with issue—among others, John, now in his father's and grandfather's farm in Breackachy ; (*c*) Roderick, who married Eliza, daughter of John Chisholm, Comar, with issue ; he emigrated to Australia where he is still alive ; (*d*) Archibald, who also went to Australia, where he resides, married, with issue ; (*e*) Alexander, who died in Strathglass unmarried.   (6) Archibald, who married Catherine, daughter of Colin Chisholm, with issue, the only one of whom anything is known being Roderick, a farmer in Aberdeenshire.   (7) Helen, who married Alexander Chisholm, farmer, Knockfin, with issue.   He emigrated to Nova Scotia in 1801. (8) Catherine, who married Duncan Macrae, farmer, Crasky, Glencannich, with issue—two sons and three daughters ; Finlay married without issue ; William, who died unmarried ; Margaret, who married John Chisholm, farmer, Balnahaun, with issue—William, farmer, Barnyards, who married Helen, daughter of Roderick Chisholm, farmer, Comar, with issue—several sons ; Finlay, who married Mary, daughter of Finlay Macrae, farmer, Strathconan, with issue—one son, the Rev. James Chisholm, priest at Castlebay, Barra, and several daughters ; John, who died unmarried ; Valentine, a priest, who died at Bridge of Allan ; Alexander, who married Flora, daughter of

William Mackenzie, farmer, Wester Croicheal, with issue—
several sons and daughters ; Duncan, who married Isabel,
daughter of Donald Macdonald, farmer, Dell, Stratherrick,
with issue—two sons, one of whom is the Rev. Donald
Chisholm, priest at Stratherrick, and several daughters ;
Ann, who died unmarried, and Helen, who married
Donald Chisholm, farmer, Crasky, with issue—one son,
Finlay, a farmer in Stratherrick, who married and died
there in 1889, leaving issue.

Colin married, secondly, Mary Macdonell, " Mairi
Nighean Ian Ruaidh," by whom he had issue—

2. Colin, who succeeded him in Lietry.

3. Mary, who married Hugh Macdonell, with issue,
from whom are descended the Rev. John Chisholm,
Heatherton, county of Antigonish, Nova Scotia, and his
brother, the Rev. Archibald Chisholm, Cape Breton.

4. Griadach, and

5. Helen, both of whom died young.

Colin was succeeded in Lietry by his eldest son by
the second marriage,

V. COLIN CHISHOLM, who married Eliza, daughter of
William Chisholm, Comar, and sister of Alexander Chisholm, Samalaman, proprietor of Lochans, Glenmoidart,
with issue—

1. Duncan, who died unmarried in New York.

2. Colin, who succeeded his father in the farm.

3. James, who died in infancy.

4. John, who married Catherine, daughter of John Chisholm, Comar, with issue — a son, Duncan, who died
unmarried, and a daughter Mary, who married James
Maclean, Midmain, with issue—four daughters. James
Maclean died in March, 1890, and was buried in Tom-
nahurich Cemetery, Inverness.

5. Archibald, a captain in the Royal African Corps.
While in command on the coast of Senegambia he dis-
tinguished himself by the capture of several slave dhows.
The following extract from a letter, dated " Goree, 22nd
April, 1814," and addressed to his superior in command,

Major (afterwards Colonel) James Chisholm, affords a good illustration of the dangerous work in which he was almost constantly engaged. Archibald writes :—

In compliance with your orders, I beg leave to submit for your information the following statement of the circumstance which occurred in the river Gambia on the 16th inst. Captain Mackenzie, with upwards of forty men, was on board of the schooner " Union ; " Ensign Walker and eighteen on board of the brig " Neptune ; " and I, with twenty-seven, on board of the sloop " Young Frederick." About eight o'clock in the morning we saw the Spanish brig laying at anchor about three miles up in a small branch of the Gambia, called Samel River. Without any loss of time we approached her and proceeded to enter the creek, but found that it was very difficult to get where she was but by high water ; we consequently anchored at the mouth of the creek, and sent a boat with a sergeant and six men to the Spaniard to acquaint him with our determination to attack him if he should not surrender his vessel. When our boat got near him he fired a round of grape shot at it, which luckily did no more harm than obliged it to return. He instantly followed it with his own boat for the purpose of getting a view of us, and when I saw that he was returning back to his vessel I directed a gun to be fired at him from the sloop which broke one of the oars in his boat, and, judging from his conduct towards our boat, and not coming to when we fired at him, that his intention was to make resistance or endeavour to run away, we immediately sailed up the river, but, unfortunately, the brig got aground as she was entering the creek. The Spanish captain, seeing that she could render us no assistance, made every attempt to set sail, from which we were obliged to proceed without him. The Spanish vessel was moored across the river, with all her guns on one side, in order to bear upon us. The " Union " having the lead, received the first broadside from her, which killed two men. She then unfortunately ran on shore at the same time, and only fired two shots at the Spaniard, nor was she able to give me the smallest assistance. I instantly went between them in order to board the Spaniard, but before I could effect that he fired two broadsides at the sloop, but at last I got in below his bowsprit and the brave soldiers kept up a constant firing at him. They in fact almost cleared the upper deck before we boarded him. Then the Spaniard opened his ports on the other side and tried to remove his guns to get them to bear on the sloop, which was fastened to his vessel by our anchor. However, he failed in that attempt, and all his men were immediately driven from their guns by the gallant soldiers' musketry and bayonets, which soon obliged them to leave the centre deck entirely and run to the hold.

But when the Spanish captain found himself overpowered, and seeing no chance of escaping, he set fire to one of his magazines, by which his own cabin and the greater part of the upper deck were blown up in the air, and set fire to the whole of his rigging, and which killed some of the soldiers, and left the rest of them in a very deplorable condition with their heads, hands, and feet bruised and burnt. In this distressed situation we were left. The Spaniards made a desperate attack to clear their own deck, and to board us, as they saw that the ammunition we had was expended. I, however, found a few rounds in a cask, and gave them to the men, who kept up a very brisk fire, and cleared the deck of the Spanish vessel a second time. We then got possession of a large basket of their ammunition, which enabled us to decide the affair in a very short time.

The Spanish captain and most of his crew were killed; the rest of them after being severely wounded jumped into the water. When I saw that, I ordered the soldiers to save them and to pick them up out of the water, which order was soon obeyed. After the action was over, I had but very little hope of saving the sloop or the lives of the remainder of the men under my command from the violent flames of the other vessel, by which she was consumed to ashes in less than three hours after we quitted her. Though the men were in a disabled state, their dexterity, and great exertions in cutting cable ropes, etc., were wonderful. I may say with truth, that were it not for the assistance afforded us by Mr. Wilson (late mate of the "Dores" Transport), who came to us at the close of the engagement with a boat from the "Neptune," as he knew we had none of our own, it was impossible for us to succeed in disentangling the two vessels.

The following letter was sent to Archibald's father, by his commanding officer, Colonel James Chisholm, intimating his early death :—

To
    Mr. COLIN CHISHOLM, senior,
        Lietry, Strathglass,
            By Inverness, N.B.

                  20 Suffolk Street, Charing Cross,
                    14th October, 1816.

My dear sir,—It is with the sincerest grief that I am obliged to convey to you the sorrowful tidings of your most worthy son, Lieutenant Archibald Chisholm's death. He departed this life on the 21st of July last, after eleven days' illness, of the yellow fever.

The only consolation I can offer you on this melancholy occasion is that your son died as he lived, a real good Christian, and that his death is greatly lamented by every person who had the pleasure of his acquaintance, and by none more so than myself. His conduct from the day he joined the regiment was such as will ever endear his memory to me, and as a mark of my regard for him it was my intention to have purchased a Company whenever it could be accomplished, and the very day I received information of his death I made application to that effect.

I think it right to acquaint you that I have £300 in my possession belonging to your late and much regretted son, which I shall be ready to deliver to you or any of his other friends as may be directed in his will, as I have every reason to believe, from the uniform regularity of his conduct, that he has left one, which will, of course, be found among his papers and sent home.

I have written to Lieutenant James Maclean on the subject, and when I receive his answer I shall write to you again. In the meantime, if you are in want of any money, you may draw on my agent (Angus Macdonald, Esq., of Pall Mall Court.)—I remain, my dear sir, with best wishes, very sincerely yours,

J. CHISHOLM, Lieutenant-Colonel.

Archibald died at St. Helena, unmarried, on the 21st of July, 1816.

6. Mary, who married Alexander Chisholm, farmer, Carrie, Glencannich, with issue. They all emigrated to Nova Scotia in 1803.

7. Anne, who married Angus, son of Alexander Macdonell, farmer, Invercannich, with issue—two daughters, who, with their mother, emigrated to Glengarry, Canada.

8. Helen, who died young.

Colin died on the 8th of February, 1833, his wife having predeceased him by many years on the 1st of May, 1795.

He was succeeded in Lietry by his eldest son,

VI. COLIN CHISHOLM, who married Mary, daughter of Alexander Macdonell, farmer, Invercannich, with issue—

1. Colin, afterwards of Her Majesty's Customs.

2. Æneas, now tacksman of Invercannich, who married, first, Christina, daughter of Angus Mackenzie, Inchmhuilt, by whom he had issue—two sons who died in infancy.

She died on the 15th of March, 1849. He married secondly, Flora, daughter of Duncan Macdonald, farmer, Kingillie, with issue—(1) Archibald Alexander, Procurator-Fiscal, Lochmaddy; (2) Duncan, Broadmoor, Colorado Springs, United States of America; (3) Jessie Christina, a Franciscan nun in Glasgow; (4) Mary. His second wife died on the 11th of December, 1863.

3. Archibald, a priest, who, on the 11th of December, 1869, died in Glasgow.

4. Alexander, tacksman, Glencarron, who married May, daughter of Angus Mackenzie, Inchmhuilt, with issue—(1) Colin; (2) Donald, drowned in Glencoe; (3) Katherine; (4) Mary.

5. Duncan Chisholm, coal merchant, Inverness, who, in 1886, married Christina, daughter of the late Duncan Chisholm, Culbo, descended from the first marriage of his own ancestor, Thomas Og Chisholm, of Lower Knockfin, without issue.

6. Theodore, who married Margaret, daughter of William Mackenzie, Gaick Forest, with issue—(1) Colin Aloysius, solicitor, Denver, Colorado, United States of America, who married Mary O'Connor. She died in 1887, without issue. (2) George Æneas, who died in infancy; (3) Archibald Alexander, Denver, Colorado; (4) George Æneas Hugh; (5) Mary Isabella; (6) Eliza Theresa, who, in 1885, married Louis Pallett, with issue—Margaret Mary Theodora; (7) Helen Matilda, a sister of Notre Dame, Battersea, London; and (8) Georgina Mary.

7. Hugh, Canon of St. Mirrens, Paisley.

8. Eliza, who married Alexander Chisholm, farmer, Raonbhraid, Strathglass, with issue—(1) Donald, who died young; (2) Duncan; (3) Colin, Inspector of Police, London, who married Anne, daughter of Hugh Maclachlan, Ross of Mull, with surviving issue—Colin Alexander, Margaret, and Elizabeth Emily; (4) Isabel, who married John Mackenzie, London, Ontario, Canada; (5) Margaret, who married Donald Chisholm, farmer, Breackachy, with issue—Alexander, Donald, Katherine, and Elizabeth; (6) Anne,

unmarried; and (7) Christina, who married Alexander Chisholm, Superintendent, Inverness-shire County Police, Inverness, with issue—Donald, Alexander Joseph, and Eliza Mary.

9. Helen, who married Peter Chisholm, farmer, Glencannich, cousin-german to the late James Sutherland Chisholm, who succeeded to the Strathglass estates in 1858, and died in 1885. He died on the 21st of February, 1875, having had issue—(1) Alexander; (2) Colin John; (3) Duncan, who died in Africa in 1872; (4) Archibald; (5) William, who died in Colorado in 1889; and (6) Eliza.

10. Isabel, who married John Fraser. They emigrated to Australia. She died on the passage out on the 4th of November, 1854.

11. Mary, who married the late Thomas Forbes, Cononbank, Kirkhill, with issue. She died on the 27th of December, 1860.

Colin died on the 29th of December, 1846 (his wife having died on the 29th of May, 1864) when he was succeeded as representative of the family by his eldest son,

VII. COLIN CHISHOLM, now of Namur Cottage, Inverness. Having secured an appointment in Her Majesty's Customs he proceeded to Liverpool in 1835, where he remained until 1842, when he was transferred to London. While in Liverpool he had under the same roof with him, and as one of his companions, Evan MacColl, the Bard of Lochfine, living and still singing sweetly as the mavis in his eighty-third year in Kingston, Canada. Another of Mr. Chisholm's acquaintances in Liverpool was the late John Mackenzie, of the *Beauties of Gaelic Poetry*, who made a prolonged stay there at the time, taking the names of subscribers for his famous collection of the works and lives of the Gaelic bards. On Mr. Chisholm's removal to London, he very soon became a central figure among the best and most patriotic Highlanders in the Metropolis. Having joined the Gaelic Society of London, in a few years he became one of its most active office-bearers, and ultimately its president, a position which he held from 1869 to 1876, when he left London for Inverness. There, though trammelled by the rules of the public service in which he was employed, he patriotically held aloft the Gaelic banner. He was about the first to advocate, in London, the principles which were, to a certain extent, afterwards given effect to, in 1886, in the Crofters Act. In season and out of season he opposed the deer-foresting mania, which has been the cause of so much distress and misery in the Highlands, and he has consistently, during the whole of his official life and since, advocated the abolition or very great curtailment of the system. In 1871 he retired from the public service, and in 1876 removed with his family to Inverness, where he soon became one of the most energetic and useful members of the Gaelic Society, whose annual volume of transactions he has so much enriched by many valuable contributions on the social condition, history, poetry, and traditions of the Highlands. His papers on "The Clearing of the Glens," first published in *The Transactions of the Gaelic Society of Inverness*, have been extensively quoted, and his "Traditions of Strathglass," which originally appeared in volumes VI. and VII. of the *Celtic Magazine*, have been considerably drawn upon in and much to the advantage of this work. Mr. Chisholm is a walking encyclopœdia of Highland traditions, Gaelic poetry and lore, and is in this respect, it is believed, without any living competitor among the present generation of Highlanders.

He married, in 1851, Anna, youngest daughter of William Suggate, Oulton, Suffolk, with issue—

1. Colin, who died in his sixth year.
2. Mary, who died in infancy.
3. Isabel, who also died in infancy.
4. Helena.
5. Emilie Monica.
6. Flora, who died in her seventeenth year, on the 1st of August, 1878.

Mrs. Chisholm died, in London, on the 2nd of December, 1868.

THE CHISHOLMS OF KNOCKFIN.

THE Chisholms of Knockfin are descended from Alexander Chisholm, XVII. of Strathglass, by his wife, a daughter of Alexander Mackenzie, V. of Gairloch. The first of the family was

I. COLIN CHISHOLM, son of Alexander, as above, and brother of Angus, the eighteenth chief, commonly called "An Siosal Càm," who died without issue, and of Alexander, the nineteenth chief, known in the district as "An Siosal Og," or the Young Chisholm. It is the common tradition in Strathglass that this Colin of Knockfin was among the earliest of the natives who began cattle-droving in the Highlands. He first bought the cattle of his neighbours and afterwards, extending his operations, purchased wherever he could find them for sale all over the North. That he was successful in making a great deal of money in this way is proved by the fact that he was able, in 1678, to advance to his brother Alexander, who succeeded to the estates and chiefship in 1677, the sum of twelve thousand merks for a wadset of Knockfin. The grant is docquetted, "Contract of proper wadset betwixt Alexander Chisholm of Comer and Colin Chisholm, whereby the former wadsets and impignorates to the latter and his heirs and assigns whatsomever the half davoch, town and lands, of Knockfin, commonly called Easter, Middle, and Wester Knockfin, with certain other grazings redeemable for 12,000 merks Scots, dated 19th August, 1678."

Colin is said to have been the leader at the local

battle of Glasbuidhe or Aridhuiean, an engagement which took place in his time on a hillside above Fasnakyle House between the Camerons and Macmillans of Lochaber on the one hand and the Chisholms of Strathglass on the other. The Lochaber men came, as they had done on many previous occasions, with the intention of "lifting" the cattle of the district, a practice in those days prevalent in many parts of the Highlands, and for which the people of Lochaber were notorious beyond all others.

The tradition is that Clann 'ic Gille-onaich and the Macmillans of Lochaber formed the idea that they could on this occasion, by uniting their forces, not only lift the cattle, but take possession of Strathglass itself. The Chisholms naturally failed to see the justice of all this. Such an attempt would be very galling to them at any time, but especially so, for various reasons, at this time, and their reply was an immediate declaration of war, expressing their readiness to abide by the arbitration of the sword, and to decide the merits of their contention on the moor of Baile-na-bruthach, between Clachan and Balnahaun. The raiders objected to that large level black moor as the battle field, saying that it was too much surrounded by club-farms, and that women and children from these townships might be killed unintentionally. Unfortunately for them it was ultimately decided by the leaders on both sides to fight the battle on the field of Aridhuiean, where, no doubt, it was an advantage for the Chisholms to fight on ground which they must have known much better than their opponents, especially as there are several little hillocks on Aridhuiean and a burn running through it. This enabled Colin of Knockfin, who led the Strathglass men, to place all the forces under his command in a favourable position.

It is stated that the Macmillans and their friends were dreadfully shattered by the first fire. Whether this was the result of the absence of proper discipline among them, or want of ability on the part of their leader, is not known.   But it has always been said that Knockfin disposed his men in such a masterly manner as to enable them to pour their bullets simultaneously into the front and flank of the invaders.   Decimated as their ranks were, the Lochaber men rallied and returned again and again to the charge, but without success.

In the afternoon, after the engagement was over, two of the enemy came forward under a flag of truce and obtained permission to bury their dead and to carry their wounded away.   On the following day no less than sixteen were removed for this purpose on improvised ambulances.   This mode of conveying the sick, wounded or dead, was called in Gaelic "cradh-leabaidh," a term, meaning literally in English, anguish or agony bed.

The defeated Lochaber men did not consider it safe to pass through Strathglass by the ordinary road, but decided to cross the River Affric with their melancholy procession at the rough fords east of Achagiad, called Na Damhanan.   In their flight, two or three of them observed an old woman trying to conceal a little boy from their view, but one of the party succeeded in getting hold of him.   The simple old nurse implored him not to hurt the child, pleading as her reason that he was the son of Chisholm of Knockin.   "No fear of him," said the raider, "keep quiet, I will take care of him, and he will probably take care of me, till I get out of the Strathglass woods."   So saying he raised the boy upon his shoulders, remarking in Gaelic, "'S e guailleachan as fhearr leam a gheibh mi gu h-oidhche," he is the safest tunic I can get until night.   The faithful nurse was naturally much alarmed, but she was told to follow quietly, and when the Lochaber men passed out of the wood above Guisachan, the boy was restored to her none the worse of his part in the retreat of the invaders.

One of the enemy was left lying mortally wounded on the field of battle, and crying piteously for some one for the love of God to give him a drink of water.   A Strath-

glass man who heard him said, "As you ask for it in
that Name you shall certainly have it," and so saying he
went to the burn which ran through the field, took off
his bonnet, filled it with water, and hastily returned to
the sufferer. Stooping down and holding the water
to the lips of the wounded man, the ungrateful wretch
whom he was thus assisting pulled from his pocket a
"madadh-achlais," or stilletto, and plunged it in the heart
of his benefactor.

During the skirmish another Strathglass man was killed
in a still more treacherous manner. He was attacked by
two of the enemy's swordsmen, both of whom he kept
at bay with his good blade for a considerable time, but
at last, being hard pressed, he placed his back against a
mud hut which stood near him. Here he successfully
parried every stroke and thrust aimed at him. Whether
the length of his sword or his own superiority in wielding
the weapon enabled him to defend himself against the
sanguinary efforts of his two deadly enemies it is now
impossible to say. It is, however, certain that they saw
no chance of vanquishing him by fair means, so one of
them conceived the idea of killing him in a most cowardly
way. To accomplish his object he slipped round, entered
the bothy quietly by the door, and by raising a sod made
an aperture from within, whereby he obtained a view of
the two swordsmen outside, eager as tigers for each other's
life blood. Finding the Strathglass man within reach of
his sword, he thrust it into his body, from behind, through
the aperture in the mud wall. Thus the gallant Strathglass man fell, without wound or scar, except the fatal
stab from his cowardly assassin.[*]

Some time after this skirmish, Colin of Knockfin paid
a visit to Lochiel in Lochaber. While on his way he
called on a native, in whose house he refreshed himself
and shaved his beard. Before leaving he discovered that
his host was the father of two fine young men whom he
had slain with his own hand in the conflict at Aridhuiean.

---

[*] Colin Chisholm's *Traditions of Strathglass.*

It was fortunate for him that he was not recognised, for he used to say afterwards that had he been so the probability was that he would have had his head as well as his beard cut off in the house of his entertainer.

Colin married on the 24th of June, 1662, Mary, second daughter of Patrick Grant, fourth of Glenmoriston, by his wife, a daughter of Fraser of Culbokie, with issue—

1. John, his heir and successor.

2. Archibald, of Fasnakyle, who married, first, a daughter of Kenneth Macrae, of Achtertyre, Lochalsh, with issue— (1) Kenneth, who succeeded his father in Fasnakyle, and who married Mary, daughter of George Mackenzie, II. of Allangrange, and sister of Margaret who, as his second wife, married Alexander Chisholm, XXII. of Strathglass. Kenneth, by Mary of Allangrange, had issue—an only child, Margaret, who married John Chisholm, tacksman of Comar, with issue, among others, Theodore Chisholm, Struy, now heir male of the house of Chisholm. (2) Alexander, who married a daughter of Fraser of Ballindown, brother of Captain Fraser of Eskadale; they emigrated to Carolina. (3) A daughter, who married Alexander Chisholm, I. of Muckerach, with issue, for which see the Muckerach family. Archibald, of Fasnakyle, married, secondly, a daughter of Fraser of Aigais, with issue—(4) another Kenneth whose descendants, if any, we are unable to trace; (5) a second Alexander, who married Miss Grant from Urquhart, with issue—two daughters; and (6) a daughter, who married Colin, IV. of Knockfin, with issue—John, who succeeded his father.

3. Alexander, of Buntait, who married a daughter of "Eachainn Maol" of Mald, with issue—Colin, commonly called, "Cailean na Craige." Colin, the eldest son, married Mary, daughter of Allan Macdonell, farmer, Acha-na-h'Eaglais, Guisachan, with issue—(1) Alexander who emigrated to Canada; (2) Allan Mor, farmer, Muckerach, Glencannich, who married Helen, daughter of Valentine Chisholm, Inchully, with issue—(a) Captain Valentine, of the 12th Regiment of Foot, and afterwards tacksman of

Lakefield, Glenurquhart. Captain Valentine married Anne,· daughter of Archibald Macrae, Ardintoul, by his wife, Janet, daughter of John Macleod, IX. of Raasay, with issue—the late John Chisholm, Charleston, near Inverness, who married Ellen Consitt, daughter of Alexander Stevenson, S.S.C., Edinburgh, with surviving issue—Charles John, commission agent, Montreal, who married Mary Robertson, of that city, without issue; Edward Consitt, Travancore, India, who married Arabella, daughter of Captain Windsor Cary-Elwes, of Blackmore Grange, Worcestershire; Francis Louden, Travancore, India; Minna, who married Andrew Macdonald, solicitor, Inverness, with issue—three sons and seven daughters; and Ellen Mary. Captain Valentine also had a daughter, Jessie, who, in 1880, died unmarried at Inverness. (*b*) Lieutenant Æneas Chisholm, who died, unmarried, at the Cape of Good Hope; (*c*) John Chisholm, farmer, Mid Crochell; (*d*) Alexander Chisholm, who went to Canada; (*e*) Mary, who married John Forbes, with issue; (*f*) Anne, who married John Mòr Chisholm, farmer, Balnahaun, who emigrated to Nova Scotia, where they had a large family. (3) Duncan Chisholm, farmer, Kerrow, who married Janet, daughter of Theodore Chisholm, tacksman of Comar, with issue—(*a*) Alexander, a captain in the Royal African Corps, afterwards M.P. for County Glengarry, Canada, and Colonel-Commandant of the 2nd Battalion Glengarry Militia. Alexander emigrated to Canada in 1817, and there married a Miss Macdonald, with issue—Colin Duncan Chisholm, now Clerk to the District Court in Alexandria, Glengarry, Canada, and several other sons and daughters. His father, Duncan, followed him to Glengarry in 1822. (*b*) John, who emigrated with his brother, Captain Alexander, in 1817. (*c*) Colin who also went to Canada in 1822, whither he was accompanied, in that year, by his father and mother and two younger brothers. (*d*) Roderick; (*e*) Theodore; (*f*) Mary, who married Peter Macdonald, farmer, Wester Crochell, with issue—several sons; and (*g*) Eliza, who died unmarried in Canada. Alexander of Buntait, third son of Colin, first of Knockfin, had a second son John Bàn Chisholm, tenant of a small holding at Lietry, who married Catherine, daughter of John Macrae, with issue—(1) Alexander, who died unmarried; (2) John, a Serjeant-Major in the army, who also died unmarried; (3) James, who enlisted as a private soldier, and by sheer merit, after distinguished service, rose to the rank of Lieutenant-Colonel in the army. He secured commissions for several of his own relatives, some of whom afterwards rendered excellent service to their country. He died, at a comparatively early age at Strathglass, and was buried at the Clachan of Comar, where the following inscription is recorded on his tomb :—

Here rest the remains of Lieutenant-Colonel James Chisholm, of the Royal African Corps. This most distinguished officer having served his King and country for a period of thirty-eight years in different parts of Europe, Asia, and Africa, returned to his native glen covered with wounds. He died on the 19th November, 1821, aged 56.

He married, on his deathbed, Mary, daughter of Captain John Chisholm, Fasnakyle, without issue. (4) Roderick, farmer, Comar, who married Isabell Macrae, with issue— two sons and six daughters—(a) James, who secured a commission in the army through the interest of his uncle, and who himself attained the rank of Colonel in one of the Colonial regiments. He raised a native regiment in Africa at his own expense, and was subsequently appointed Governor of the Gold Coast, in which responsible position he died unmarried at a comparatively early age. (b) John, who also received a commission through the good offices of his uncle, Colonel James, and was an Ensign in the army. He retired from the army on half-pay, and took a lease of the farm of Comar, Strathglass. He married Mary, daughter of Farquhar Macrae, Fadoch, Kintail, with issue—James, now tenant of Mid-Craggie, Daviot, who married a daughter of Finlay Macrae, farmer, Scardroy, Strathconan, with issue ; and two daughters. John had also two daughters, both married with issue.

He died on the 15th of February, 1831. Roderick's
six daughters were Margaret, Janet, Catherine, Christina,
Anne, and Helen, all married, with issue. (5) Archibald, who married Eliza Chisholm, without issue (6)
Duncan, a private soldier, killed in action in America.
He married a Miss Maclean, by whom he left issue—
one son, James, who followed his father's profession,
obtained a commission in the army and was killed,
unmarried, at Quatre Bras, where he served as Lieutenant. (7) Alexander, junior, of whom nothing is
known. John Bàn Chisholm had also five daughters,
one of whom, Catharine, married Donald Maclean, Carrie,
with issue—Roderick, a Captain in the army, who died,
unmarried, in the United States of America; James, a
Major in the army, who subsequently settled at Boulogne,
in France, where he died and where his daughter married
the Mayor of the city; Duncan, an Ensign in the army,
who died young, unmarried. These three officers also
obtained their commissions through the interest of their
maternal uncle, Colonel James Chisholm of the Royal
African Corps.

Colin was succeeded by his eldest son,

II. JOHN CHISHOLM of Knockfin, generally known as
"Ian Ruadh." He commanded about two hundred of
the clan at the battle of Sheriffmuir. Roderick the chief,
though present, was a minor and too young and inex-
perienced to assume the command himself. John was
one of those who, along with The Chisholm and several
other Highland chiefs and gentlemen signed an address,
couched in the most loyal terms, to George I. on his
accession to the British Crown in 1714, though they all
fought against him, under the Earl of Mar, at Sheriffmuir,
in 1715.

When Alexander Chisholm of Muckerach obtained possession of the Strathglass estates, after the forfeiture of
Roderick, the twenty-first chief, he, in 1727, redeemed
the wadset on Knockfin, but on the 3rd of May, 1728,
he gave John a new wadset of the same lands, and

another of the township and lands of Buntait, for a similar amount.   This contract is docquetted, "Contract of wadset 'twixt Alexander Chisholm of Muckerach and John Chisholm of Knockfin, of the davoch, town and lands, of Buntait, mill and pertinents—wadset to Knockfin for 12,000 merks."   On the 26th of May, 1721, a Bailie Court was held at Erchless for the whole lands belonging to Roderick Chisholm, the twenty-first chief, described as "late of Strathglass," by William Ross of Easter Fearn, who had been appointed Bailie by the Commissioners for forfeited estates.   The following minute was recorded :—

The said William Ross of Easter Fearn, factor aforesaid, insists and craves that John Chisholm of Knockfin make payment to him of the rents of the lands of Wester, Easter, and Middle Knockfin, the shealings and grasings of Collovie, and shealings and grasings of Arnamullach.

John of Knockfin, who was present,

Acknowledges possession of the lands and contends that he cannot be obliged to make payment of the rents of any part thereof in regard he possesses the same by virtue of a contract of wadset passed betwixt the deceased Alexander Chisholm of Comer, grandfather of the person attainted, and Colin Chisholm of Knockfin, his father, whereby the said lands and imprignorate and wadset to him for the sum of 12,000 merks Scots money, and redemption of the lands, he has good right to uplift the rents for his own use, for proving whereof he produces his father's sasine [dated the 24th of July, 1679] in the said lands, under the hand of Alexander Fraser, notary public, and registered at Chanonry the 15th August, 1679.

Thus the lands of Knockfin were saved from forfeiture, when the remainder of the Strathglass estates was lost in consequence of the part taken by the chief and clan at Sheriffmuir.   From this it would appear that the Government did not know that John of Knockfin commanded the Chisholms on that occasion ; for had they been aware of this fact it is certain that his lands would have been forfeited as well as those of his chief.

John married a daughter of Grant of Corriemony, with issue, two sons and five daughters—

1. Colin, his heir and successor.

2. A son, who cannot be traced.

3. Isabella, who married John, son of Theodore Chisholm, son of Alexander, XIX. of Chisholm, with issue.

4. Margaret, who married Captain Grant of Milton, an officer in the Chisholm contingent in 1745, who was killed at Culloden. He was the grandfather of Charles Grant, M.P. for Inverness-shire, great-grandfather of Lord Glenelg, and belonged to the Shewglie family, who were cadets of the Grants of Corriemony.

5. A daughter, who married one of the Macdonells of Ardnabee, from whom descended the late Bishop Macdonell of Glengarry, Canada.

6. A daughter, who married Fraser of Muily, generally described of Aigas.

7. A daughter, who is said to have married a Cameron, who went to France.

Colin was succeeded by his eldest son,

III. COLIN CHISHOLM of Knockfin who, in his younger days with his cousin, Fraser of Culbokie, and Coll Macdonell of Barrisdale, generally called "Colla Bàn," was a suitor for the hand of a lady of great beauty, the daughter of Macdonell of Ardnabee, a cadet of Glengarry. It is said that the lady herself favoured Colla Bàn, who was the handsomest of the three and one of the finest looking men in the North of Scotland. Her father, however, preferred Culbokie, who was by far the wealthiest, but the choice of the old family nurse fell upon Colin of Knockfin, who was a famous deer-stalker; and to attract the young lady's attention, she is said to have composed one of the best and sweetest songs in the Gaelic language, entitled "Crodh Chailein," in praise of her favourite Colin. The burden of the song is, that Knockfin had numerous herds of the most beautiful and graceful kind, the red deer of the mountain and corry.

To settle their differences at the point of their claymores, Colin and Barrisdale, each accompanied by a friend, met in the woods of Coogy, in the Braes of Strathglass, with what result has not come down to us, but certain it is that neither of them won the fair lady; for she soon afterwards married Fraser of Culbokie, by whom she had nine sons and five daughters.

Colin is said to have won his bride as follows :—He and Colla Bàn of Barrisdale, who had, like himself, been an unsuccessful suitor for the hand of Macdonell of Ardnabee's daughter, became rivals for the hand of Helen Grant of Glenmoriston. While both of them were one day on a visit at her father's house, a ride to the country was proposed. When about to start, and with the horses ready at the door, it was discovered that no chair had been brought out to enable Miss Helen to mount her steed; whereupon Barrisdale, with characteristic politeness, rushed into the house to bring one. Before, however, he could return, Colin of Knockfin lifted the not reluctant damsel in his arms, and placed her in the saddle. Glenmoriston, who was looking on, judging from this interesting incident the direction in which the feelings of his daughter ran, addressed Knockfin, saying, "Colin, the lass is yours;" and they were soon afterwards married.

He thus married Helen, daughter of John Grant "Ian A Chragain," sixth of Glenmoriston, by his second wife, Janet, fourth daughter of Sir Ewen Cameron Dubh of Lochiel, with issue—seven sons and one daughter.

1. Colin, his heir and successor.

2. and 3. went abroad, where they died.

4. 5. and 6. died young.

7. Valentine, who resided at Inchully, Strathglass, and lived to the great age of ninety-six years. Of this patriarch Colin Chisholm says, "I well remember the time when Ualan of Inchully attended the wedding of John Forbes—Ian Bàn Foirbeis—who married Mary, daughter of Allan Chisholm, Kerrow. Mary, the bride was a grand-daughter of Ualan. Nothing would please the young people at the wedding better than to see the

venerable patriarch on the floor. The old gentleman was at the time over ninety years of age, but to please his young friends he acceded to their wish, and stepped on the floor with a firm gait, offering his arm to the bride. 'Now, young people,' said he, 'let another couple of you come forward to dance the reel with the bride and myself.' 'Too glad of the chance,' responded Ian Mor Mac Alastair 'ic Ruairi, at the same moment giving his arm to his own grand-aunt, the bride's mother. This John Mor Chisholm was great-grandson of Ualan's. There were now four generations on the floor, when a fifth came on in the person of Alexander, one of John's sons, a great-great-grandson of Ualan, so that there were actually five generations of the same family of the name of Chisholm dancing the reel together."

Valentine married first Janet, daughter of Macdonell, farmer, Mid Crochell, with issue—(1) Bishop John Chisholm, born in February, 1752, and died on the 8th of July, 1814. He was buried in Killchiaran, Lismore; (2) Bishop Æneas Chisholm, who died in 1818, and was buried in the same place; (3) a son, who died in the West Indies; (4) a daughter, who married David, son of Fraser of Struy, one of whose descendants was the late Bishop William Fraser, of Halifax, Nova Scotia, and another the Rev. William Fraser, a priest at St. Raphaels, Glengarry, Canada; (5) Helen, who married Allan Mor Chisholm, son of "Cailean na Craige," with issue, several sons and daughters—(a) Captain Valentine Chisholm, of the 12th Regiment of Foot, who married Anne, daughter of Archibald Macrae, Ardintoul, with issue—the late John Chisholm, Charleston, near Inverness, and a daughter, Jessie, who died unmarried at Inverness, in 1880. (b) Lieutenant Æneas Chisholm, who died at the Cape of Good Hope. (c) John, farmer, Mid Crochell, who married Mary, daughter of John Macrae, farmer, Invercannich, with issue—Allan, who succeeded his father in the same farm. Allan, now at Mid Crochell, married Margaret, daughter of James Grant, farmer, Glencairn, and sister of

the late Right Rev. Colin Grant, Roman Catholic Bishop of
Aberdeen, with issue—two sons, James and John. John,
son of Allan Mor, had also a son, William, who died in
Glasgow; John, who married, with issue, and went to
Australia; Anne, who married Colin Mackenzie, with issue
—five sons, one of whom is the Rev. William Mackenzie,
priest in Laggan, Badenoch, and two daughters; Eliza;
Janet, who married Patrick Macdonald, with issue; Mary,
who married Donald Fraser, Inchmhuilt, with issue;
Margaret, who married James Macdonald, post-master, Invercannich, with issue; Lilias, who married Mr. Gardner,
Glasgow; and Helen, who married William Chisholm,
farmer, Barnyards. (d) Alexander, who went to Canada.
(e) Mary, who married John Forbes, with issue. (f) Anne,
who married John Mor Chisholm, farmer, Balnahaun, who
emigrated to Nova Scotia, where they had a large family.
Three other daughters, Janet, Catherine, and Helen, died
unmarried. (6) Mary, who married Alexander Macrae,
farmer, Carrie, Glencannich, with issue—(a) the Rev. Philip
Macrae, a priest in Strathglass. (b) Colin Macrae; and
(c) Angus Macrae. The two last named were Ensigns
in the Royal African Corps, and died unmarried in
Africa. (d) Valentine Macrae, farmer, Carnach, who
married Margaret, youngest daughter of Alexander Macdonell, farmer, Invercannich, with issue, two sons and
two daughters—Angus, who married, with issue, several
sons and daughters; Colin, unmarried; Eliza, who married
Roderick Macdonald, inn-keeper, White Bridge, Stratherrick, with surviving issue—Alexander Macdonald, now
of White Bridge Inn, and the Rev. Æneas Macdonald,
the present priest at Craigtown, Barra. Valentine Macrae's
second daughter was Mary, who married John Macdonald,
Millifiach, with issue. Alexander had also four daughters.
(e) Mary, who married Alexander Chisholm, farmer,
Kerrow, with issue. (f) Janet, who married William
Mackenzie, farmer, Lietry, with issue—seven sons, John,
Valentine, John, and Colin, who still survive, the Rev.
Angus, who was accidentally poisoned in Dingwall in

1856, and two others who died young. Janet had also three daughters, Flora, who married Alexander Chisholm, Boblanie, with issue, and two others, who died young. (g) Isabella, who married Finlay Macrae, farmer, Strathconon, with issue—several sons and daughters, one of whom, Mary, married Finlay Chisholm, farmer, Eskadale, with issue—the Rev. James Chisholm, now priest at Castlebay, Barra, and a daughter. Another of Isabella's daughters, Anne, married Alexander Macrae, farmer, Hughton, Eskadale, with issue—one of whom is the Rev. Angus Macrae, now priest at Iochdar, South Uist. (h) Anne, who married Ewen Macdonald, farmer, Glenconvinth, with issue—several sons and daughters.

Colin married, secondly, a daughter of Grant of Corriemony, without issue.

He was succeeded by his eldest son,

IV. COLIN CHISHOLM, "Cailean Og," of Knockfin, who, in 1749, married first, Margaret, daughter of Alexander Mackenzie, III. of Ballone, and widow of James Macrae, of Conchra, Lochalsh, only son of the Rev. John Macrae, minister of Dingwall. By her Colin had issue—

1. Colin "a b'Oige," born on the 1st of February, 1750. He died unmarried, before his father, having been killed at the siege of Quebec, on the 17th of January, 1781. At the time of his death he was paymaster of the 71st Regiment, or Fraser Highlanders.

2. Alexander, who was born on the 20th of September, 1752, and emigrated to America at the head of a large number of his fellow-countrymen from Strathglass, when the first Glengarry emigration, between 1780 and 1790, took place. If any male descendants of this Alexander remain one of them would now be the nearest male heir and head of the house of Knockfin.

3. Helen, born on the 20th of August, 1754. She married one of the Grants of Glenmoriston, with issue—(1) Colin, a priest who emigrated, and died in Nova Scotia. (2) Peter, a Lieutenant in the 68th Regiment, married, with issue. He died at Reraig, Lochalsh. (3)

Janet, who married Alexander Chisholm, grandson of Alexander Chisholm, first of Muckerach, with issue— Duncan, who, in 1858, claimed the estates of Strathglass, but died soon after, without male issue. Janet had also three daughters, two of whom were married in Nova Scotia.

Colin of Knockfin married, secondly, his cousin, a daughter of Archibald Chisholm, Fasnakyle, with issue—

4. John, who succeeded his father at Knockfin.

5. Archibald, born on the 15th of December, 1765. He was killed, unmarried, by the explosion of a powder magazine, while engaged as a volunteer in the American War.

Colin was succeeded at Knockfin by his eldest son by the second marriage,

V. JOHN CHISHOLM, who was born on the 2nd of January, 1762, and in 1792, married, first, Jane, daughter of William Fraser of Culbockie, with issue—

1. John, a colonel in the H.E.I.C.S., born on the 16th of August, 1793.

2. William, who was born on the 9th of November, 1794, and was killed, unmarried, on the 1st of January, 1818, at Corrygaum, in an action against the Peiswah's army, in the Deccan, East India, he being at the time serving as a Lieutenant in the Madras Artillery.

3. Colin, born on the 28th of December, 1795. He practised as a solicitor in Inverness, and married Margaret, third daughter of John Macdonald, XI. of Glenalladale. He died in 1877, having had issue—(1) John Archibald Chisholm, of the Holm Mills, Inverness, born in 1829, and died on the 27th of March, 1885. He married Christina Stewart Beattie, daughter of Andrew Macdonald, Sheriff-Substitute of Ross-shire at Stornoway, with issue —Archibald, who died young; Colin, born on the 22nd of September, 1870; John Archibald; Margaret; and Mary Stewart Beattie. (2) William, in Australia, unmarried. He was born in 1831. (3) Colin Chisholm, now of the Holm Mills, Inverness, born in 1835. He married Dora

Campbell, Milton, King's County, Ireland, with issue—
John; William, born in 1872; Mary Jane. (4) Æneas,
now a priest in Banff. (5) Jane, who died unmarried;
(6) Sarah, unmarried; and (7) Clementina, who died
young.

4. Archibald, born on the 15th of February, 1798.
He was a Major in the Madras army, and married Caroline Jones, a native of Northampton, the Mrs. Chisholm
of emigration fame, with issue—(1) Archibald, who died
unmarried; (2) William, who also died unmarried; (3)
John Henry, married in Australia, with issue; (4) Sydney,
married in Australia; (5) Caroline, who married the late
Edward Dwyer Gray, M.P., editor of the *Freeman's Journal*,
with issue—one son and two daughters; and (6) Harriet
Monica, who married Arthur Lloyd Gruggen. He farms
extensive lands of his own in Assiniboia, North-West
Territory of Canada.

John married, secondly, Hannah, daughter of Fraser of
Achnacloich, a cadet of the family of Struy, with issue—

5. Thomas, a priest in Strathglass, born on the 6th of
July, 1807, and died on the 22nd of February, 1872.

6. Alexander, who was born on the 19th of November,
1808. He emigrated to Australia, where he died, at
Sydney, in 1854.

John, who died in 1811, and was the last who occupied
Knockfin, was succeeded as representative of the family in
this country by his eldest son,

VI. COLONEL JOHN CHISHOLM, of the H.E.I.C.S., for
many years residing at Cheltenham. He married on the
12th of February, 1822, Eliza, second daughter of Hugh
Fraser of Eskadale, son of Thomas Fraser of Achnacloich,
with issue—

1. John, born on the 1st of November, 1825, at Madras.
He was a physician on the Madras establishment, and died
unmarried shortly after starting on the march to Lucknow
during the Mutiny in 1857.

2. Hugh Fraser, born at Fasnakyle on the 10th of
December, 1828. He died of measles at Edinburgh in

his eighteenth year, on the 23rd of January, 1846, while attending the University of that city.

3. William, born on the 3rd of April, 1836, at St. Thomas's Mount, Madras, Major in the 40th Regiment Madras Native Infantry. He is unmarried.

4. Thomas, born on the 4th of June, 1838, at Secunderabad, Nizam's Dominions, India. He was a Lieutenant in the 1st Madras European Fusiliers, and died unmarried on the march, near Lucknow, during the Mutiny.

5. Anne Jane, born at Bombay. She resides at Cheltenham, unmarried.

6. Juliana Charlotte, a nun at Swansea, South Wales.

Colonel John Chisholm, late of Cheltenham, was succeeded, as representative of the family, by his only surviving son,

VII. COLONEL WILLIAM CHISHOLM, late Major in 40th Regiment Madras Native Infantry, residing at Cheltenham, unmarried.

THEODORE CHISHOLM'S FAMILY.

I. THEODORE · CHISHOLM was the second son of Alexander Chisholm, XIX. of Chisholm, by his wife, the eldest daughter of Roderick Mackenzie, I. of Applecross. He lived and died at Balmore, Invercannich. He married Margaret, daughter of Fraser of Culbokie, with issue—one son,

II. JOHN CHISHOLM, who lived and died at Wester Knockfin. He married, Isabella, daughter of John, II. of Knockfin, with issue—one son,

III. THEODORE CHISHOLM, who lived and died at Comar. He married Mary, daughter of Alexander, second son of Archibald Chisholm, Fasnakyle, with issue—

1. John, who succeeded him in Comar.

2. Eliza, who married Alexander Macdonell, farmer, Invercannich, with issue—(*a*) Angus, who married Anne, daughter of Colin Chisholm, Lietry, with issue. (*b*) John who died unmarried ; (*c*) Theodore, who married Madeline, daughter of Hugh Fraser, farmer, Boblanie, with issue—three sons and two daughters. (*d*) Hugh, who married a daughter of Alexander Macrae, a native of Dornie, who, like himself, had emigrated to Canada, with issue ; and (*e*) Christopher Macdonell, who married Anne, daughter of Hugh Fraser, farmer, Deanny, Glenstrathfarrar, brother of the late Robert Fraser of Aigas, with issue—two sons and two daughters. (*f*) Mary, who married Colin Chisholm, Lietry, with issue. (*g*) Isabell, who married Colin Chisholm, Clachan, Strathglass, with issue—Archibald, Duncan, Hugh, Alexander, and Mary, who married John Bisset, Fanellan, with issue, among others, the Rev. Alexander Bisset, a priest, now at Stratherrick.

(*h*) Margaret, who married Valentine Macrae, Carnach, with issue.

3. Margaret, who married John Macrae, farmer, Inver-cannich, with issue—(*a*) Christopher, a Captain in the Royal African Corps. He died, unmarried, on the West Coast of Africa. (*b*) Alexander, farmer, Invercannich, who married Margaret, daughter of Hugh Fraser, of Deanny, with issue—several sons and daughters. All the sons went abroad. (*c*) Finlay, an Ensign in the Royal African Corps. He died in that service, unmarried. (*d*) Theodore, a Captain in the same corps. He married Christina, daughter of Allan Macdonald, Lochans, Moidart, with issue, among others, the Rev. Allan Macrae, now priest at Eskadale. Theodore died at Struy. (*e*) William, an Ensign in the Royal African Corps, who died, un-married, at Inverness. (*f*) Angus, who emigrated to Australia, and died there unmarried. (*g*) Isabell, who married William Chisholm, Inchully, with issue—several sons and daughters. (*h*) Mary, who married John Chis-holm, farmer, Mid Crochell, with issue—three sons and five daughters.

4. Janet, who married Duncan Chisholm, farmer, Ker-row, third son of "Cailean na Craige," son of Alexander Chisholm of Buntait, with issue, for which see the family of Knockfin.

5. Mary, who married, first, David Fraser, farmer, Crasky, of the family of Struy, with issue—(*a*) William, a priest in Glengarry, Canada. (*b*) Alexander, who died, unmarried, in Strathglass. She married, secondly, Roderick Macdonell, the hereditary standard-bearer of the Chis-holms, with issue—a daughter, Mary, who married Duncan Macpherson, schoolmaster, Glencannich. The whole family, along with the mother and her husband in their old age, emigrated to Glengarry, Canada.

6. Isabell, who married Duncan Macdonell, farmer, Carrie, Glencannich, with issue—(*a*) Hugh, who emigrated to Cape Breton, where he married Helen Cameron, with issue—several sons and daughters. (*b*) Colin, who went

to the same place, where he married a Miss Chisholm, whose father, William Chisholm, was originally from Knockfin, Strathglass, with issue.   (*c*) Theodore, who died, unmarried, at Judique, Cape Breton.   (*d*) Mary, who married a Chisholm in Cape Breton, with issue; and (*e*) Anne, who married another Chisholm, also in Cape Breton.

Theodore was succeeded, as representative of the family, by his only son,

IV. JOHN CHISHOLM, who resided most of his time at Comar, and died at Struy.   He married Margaret, daughter of Kenneth, eldest son of Archibald Chisholm, Fasnakyle, with issue—

1. Kenneth, who married Anne, daughter of John Fraser, farmer, Achblair, Guisachan, and died without issue.

2. Theodore, now heir male of the Chisholms of Strathglass, residing at Struy.

3. John, who emigrated to Australia, where he still lives, unmarried.

4. Alexander, who also emigrated to Australia, where he also resides, unmarried.

5. Catherine, who married John Chisholm, farmer, Lietry, with issue.

6. Mary, who died unmarried.

7. Margaret, who married John Maclaren, farmer, Comar, with issue—several sons and daughters, all of whom emigrated to Australia.

8. Eliza, who married Roderick, son of John Chisholm, farmer, Breackachy.   They emigrated to Australia, where they had a family of sons and daughters.

9. Lilias, who died unmarried.

John is succeeded as representative of the family by his eldest surviving son,

V. THEODORE CHISHOLM, residing at Struy.   Since the death of Roderick Donald Matheson Chisholm, XXVIII. of Chisholm, in 1887, Theodore, possessing not an inch of land, and without any visible means of subsistence, is heir male and chief of the ancient house of Chisholm. He is now about eighty-one years of age and unmarried.

THE CHISHOLMS OF MUCKERACH, NOW OF STRATHGLASS.

THE first of this family, the representative of which succeeded to the Strathglass estates and the chiefship of the
clan in 1858, was,

I. ALEXANDER CHISHOLM, of Muckerach, of whom so
much has already been said in connection with the forfeiture and restoration of the estates after Sheriffmuir.
He was second son of John Chisholm, XX. of Strathglass, commonly called "an Siosal Ruadh," and immediate
younger brother of Roderick, the twenty-first chief, in
whose person the estates had, after 1715, been forfeited
to the Crown. He married his cousin, a daughter of
Archibald Chisholm, of Fasnakyle, and grand-daughter
of Colin, I. of Knockfin, with issue—

1. Archibald, his heir.

2. Captain John Chisholm, of Fasnakyle, mentioned in
the entail of 1777. He married a daughter of Patrick
Fraser of Fingask, with issue—one son, Patrick, who died
in India, unmarried, and two daughters, one of whom
married Fraser of Kinmylies, and Mary, who married
Colonel James Chisholm of the Royal African Corps
withou! issue.

He was succeeded as representative of the family by
his eldest son,

II. ARCHIBALD CHISHOLM, of Muckerach, upon whom
Alexander, the twenty-third chief, in 1777, entailed the
estates, failing heirs male of his own body, and of his
five sons, and two brothers. He married Catherine, third

daughter of John Matheson, V. of Fernaig and Attadale, with issue—

1. Roderick, his heir.

2. Captain Donald Chisholm, of the 42nd Highlanders (Black Watch), and afterwards of the H.P. Royal Highlanders of Canada. He was twice married, with issue—two sons, the eldest of whom died unmarried in China while in the service of the well-known house of Matheson, Jardine, & Co. The other died while a student at Blairs College, Aberdeenshire.

3. Alexander, who married Janet, daughter of one of the Grants of Glenmoriston, and emigrated to Nova Scotia, where he settled, in the County of Antigonish. He had issue—one son, Duncan, who was a claimant to the Chisholm estates in 1858, and died unmarried; also two daughters.

4. Catherine, who married Alexander Chisholm, farmer, Craskie, with issue—(1) Roderick, who married Anne, daughter of John Chisholm, farmer, Balnahaun, with issue—one son and several daughters. (2) Peter, who married Helen, daughter of Colin Chisholm, farmer, Lietry, with issue. Alexander had also three daughters, Anne, Mary, and Catherine, the last of whom married William Chisholm, farmer, Craskie, with issue—several sons and daughters, one of whom is the Rev. Archibald Chisholm, priest at Nairn.

Archibald was succeeded, as representative of the family, by his eldest son,

III. RODERICK CHISHOLM, who emigrated to Canada and settled in the North-West Territory, where he was engaged on the staff of the Hudson Bay Company. There he married Miss Sutherland, with issue—

1. James Sutherland, his heir.

2. Jemima, who, on the 8th of January, 1840, married Mr. Milner, a Government contractor, in Kingston, Upper Canada.

He died of cholera in Montreal, in 1832, when he was succeeded, as representative of the family by his son,

IV. JAMES SUTHERLAND CHISHOLM, who, on the death of Duncan Macdonell Chisholm, XXVI. of Strathglass, unmarried, in 1858, succeeded to the estates of the family and chiefship of the clan.   He was at the time employed in a mercantile house in Montreal.   Having secured possession of the Chisholm estates, he returned to Canada, and there, on the 13th of November, 1861, married a relative of his own, Annie Cecilia, daughter of Angus Macdonell, a cadet of Glengarry, by whom he had issue—

1. Roderick Donald Matheson, his heir.
2. Mary Isabella, who died young.
3. Louisa Jane.
4. Annie Margaret.

He died at Erchless Castle, Strathglass, on the 28th of May, 1885, in his eightieth year, when he was succeeded in the estates and chiefship of the clan by his only son,

V. RODERICK DONALD MATHESON, who was born on the 20th of September, 1862, and was thus only in his twenty-third year when he entered into possession.   He died, unmarried, at March Hall, near Edinburgh, on the 24th of April, 1887, and was interred in the family burying-ground, near Erchless Castle.   His father, who was the last heir male mentioned in it, having barred the entail, Roderick was able to leave the estates, with a rental of £10,000 a year, by trust disposition to his mother, who is now in possession.

On the death of Roderick Donald Matheson Chisholm, unmarried, in 1887, the last male heir of the Muckerach family and the last male representative of all those mentioned in the entail of 1777 died in his person, when Theodore Chisholm, now residing in a small thatched house, at the roadside, near Struy, on Lord Lovat's estate, became male heir and chief of the ancient Clan Chisholm.   Theodore's family, and those of Knockfin and Kinneries, were excluded from the entail, but even if they had not, any rights they might have inherited would have been barred by the action of the late James Sutherland

Chisholm when he disentailed the estates. It is, however, doubtful if any rights of succession remained in these families as heirs male, even in the absence of the provision that the estates were to revert to the entailer's nearest heirs female when all the male heirs of the others mentioned in the deed had become extinct ; for they all broke off from the main stem prior to the forfeiture in the person of Roderick, the twenty-first chief, for the part he took in the Rising of 1715. It has therefore been maintained that any rights of succession which, in the absence of the forfeiture and the entail, would have accrued to Theodore or to any of the other remaining male representatives of the family are entirely barred, quite independently of the provision in favour of heirs female in the deed of 1777, and of the disentail by the late James Sutherland Chisholm.   This is, however, a question more for the lawyer than for the historian.

THE BORDER CHISHOLMES.

WE began our account of the Northern Chisholms by
giving at length the late James Logan's impossible deduction of that family from the Earls of Caithness and
Orkney. We shall begin our account of the Border
Chisholmes (who have always retained the final E in their
name) by the reproduction of a well-written, though not
quite accurate genealogy of the Southern Chisholmes, by
the late John Scott Chisholme of Stirches, the acknowledged head of that branch of the family. The following
is a criticism by Mr. Chisholme of a manuscript history
or genealogy of the Chisholms of Comar or Strathglass,
sent to him for his opinion in the form of notes, by
the late Augustus Colin Mackenzie of Findon, one of a
family the members of which have made for themselves
an enduring name in connection with Highland family
genealogy. It is not a little remarkable, when the lack
of authentic material is considered, how closely Mr. Chisholme's results agree, on almost every important point,
with and corroborates the conclusions arrived at from
other and independent sources in the beginning of this
work, on the earlier Chisholm chiefs. Mr. Scott Chisholme
says—

"I have looked over the Chisholm MS. which is a very
funny book, for open it where you will something amusing
turns up. I relish exceedingly the jest of the author
appropriating a dozen or so of my ancestors, with the
entire Cromlix branch directly descended from them. It
is rather unkind of him however to assert that I am not
my father's son, but merely the son of my great, great
grandfather. Thus handing me down to posterity in the

character of the wandering Jew. I promised to put notes on your copy of the MS., but it is so confused and disconnected that my doing so would not render it more intelligible.

"The author, whoever he is, proceeds on the plan of seizing upon every Chisholm in the records as prize to Comar—steel clad barons of the Border, mitred bishops, monks, abbots, and kilted Highlanders, a grim group, all marshalled regardless of chronology, genealogy, or any other ology, as ancestors of the Comar family. Having thus appropriated the whole race, it is not surprising that I am left a poor genealogical orphan. But is it surprising with such unlimited materials that he has so signally failed to make a plausible story.

"Had he left to me the Border barons and the bishops, I would have mode him welcome to prove, if he could, that the Comar family are descended from Harald Thane of Caithness, Orkney, and Shetland, who married the daughter of Mudac or Machead, Earl of Athol, the last male descendant of Donald Bàn, King of Scotland, but I decline the honour of having such Royal ancestry thrust upon me, either by him or the reveries of Sir Robert Gordon, specially because Boece and other historians affirm that William the Lion hanged Harald, put out the eyes of his only son, Torphin, after causing him to be cruelly mutilated, and emasculated every male of his race, a procedure on the part of that monarch so inimical to my existence from such a source that I prefer the more humble Norman origin in which I have been taught to believe substantiated as it is by indisputable written evidence.

"The object of the MS. is to show that the name Chisholm is of pure Celtic origin, that the race has existed in the Highlands as a clan from time immemorial, of which Chisholm of Comar is the chief.

"This assumption is at variance, not only with the recorded opinions of all the old etymologists, genealogists, antiquarians, and heralds, but with their own records.

The construction of the name De Cheseholme, as it is
written in all my early records, is so obviously Anglo-
Norman, that it is impracticable to find for it a Celtic
or even a Norse derivation. To assert that it is Celtic
and that the Chisholmes of that Ilk in the county of
Roxburgh sprung from it, and founded a family on the
Border prior to the reign of Alexander the 3rd is contrary to all family and national history, for there is not
a solitary instance on record of a Northern Celt acquiring
possessions among the Saxons and Anglo-Normans on
the Marches; on the contrary the Saxons and Anglo-
Normans early blended and gradually pressed back the
Celts north of the Forth. After the commencement of
the Succession Wars, the Anglo-Normans began slowly
to obtain a footing along the North-East coast of Scotland, and they gradually spread inland in increasing
numbers, until they had introduced their Norman names
and Norman customs into the remote regions of the
North. The best and most conclusive evidence of the
fact is derived from existing Highland families, the Gordons, the Frasers, the Chisholms, Huntlys, etc., etc., were
all Anglo-Normans who acquired lands in the North by
gift or marriage, about the same era. Gordon in Berwickshire was the original seat of the Gordons, Huntly that
of the Huntlys in the same county, Peebleshire of the
Frasers, and Chisholme in Roxburghshire that of the
Chisholmes.

"Skene, author of *Manners and Customs of the Highlanders* (one of the best authorities on Highland Genealogy), in writing of the Comar family, says—'Few families
have asserted their claim to be considered as a Gaelic
clan with greater vehemence than the Chisholms, notwithstanding that there are few whose Lowland origin is less
doubtful; hitherto no one has investigated their history,
but their early charters suffice to establish the real origin
of the family with great clearness. The name Chisholm
does not appear in Battle Abbey Roll, so there is no
distinct authority to prove that the name is actually Nor-

man, but their documents distinctly show that the name
was introduced from the low country into the Highlands.
Their original seat is in Roxourghshire, as we find the
only person of the name who signed Ragman's Rolls is
Richard de Chisholme, del Counte de Rokesburgh, and
in that county the family of Chisholme still remains.
Therefore their situation, with the character of the name
itself, seems with sufficient clearness to indicate a Norman
origin.'

"Smibert in his Clans professes the same opinion, and
now that the family history has been carefully investigated,
the Anglo-Norman origin of the family is proved beyond
disputation. The question, therefore, is not whether the
surname is Anglo-Norman or Celtic, but from which individual of the name is the Comar family descended?

"To enable us to trace this we must abandon the
fabulous legend about Harald, who was hanged, and all
his emasculated ràce, and keep in view that the only
place in Scotland of the name of Chisholme is the old
Barony in the county of Roxburgh, that its possesors
have borne the same name since the reign of Alexander
III., and for how long before is unknown, as no records
relating to the family are extant prior to that period.
Traditions there are, but as I belong to the strict sect
of genealogists, I put little confidence in mere oral tradition, and decline to accept any statement unless supported
by documentary evidence.

"FIRST, we have JOHN DE CHESEHOLME, or John of
Chesholme, named in a Bull of Pope Alexander IV., and
who, in the reign of Alexander III., had a charter granted
to him and to Emma de Vetereponte, his wife, by
William de Vetereponte, Lord of Bolton,of the lands of
Paxtoun and fishings of Brade in Tweed, with certain
pendicles in the village of Paxtoun, with the pertinents
and fishings belonging thereto.

"SECOND, RICHARD DE CHESEHOLME, his son and
successor, del Counte de Rokesburgh, who along with
his son, John de Cheseholme, del Counte de Berewyke,

did homage to Edward I., anno. 1296 (*Ragman Rolls*).

"THIRD, the above JOHN DE CHESEHOLME, afterwards Sir John, was forfeited by Edward II. for adherence to Robert Bruce. In the Mandate by Edward, addressed to his 'Beloved James de Broughton, Chamberlain of Scotland,' dated at York, 18th September, 1317, this John is styled, 'our Scottish enemy and rebel' (*Rot. Scot.* 2, Edw. 2). His brother Alexander de Cheseholme was also forfeited along with Adam de Paxtoun (*Rot. Scot.* 10, Edward 3).

"King Edward appears to have conferred a part of the estate on Ranulphus de Home, and the remainder on Robert de Manvers, but the whole was recovered and restored to John de Cheseholme, and confirmed to him and to his heir male by a charter of Robert the Bruce, dated in the 14th year of his reign (1320).

"Sir John de Cheseholme married Anne, daughter and heiress of Sir Robert Lauder of Quarrelwood, who was constable of Urquhart Castle, and had large possessions in the counties of Elgin and Nairn. The issue of this marriage, so far as is known, was Robert, afterwards Sir Robert and John, whose name appears in the *Rot Scot.*, in the years 1359-60 and 1363.

"FOURTH, ROBERT DE CHESEHOLME, who was knighted by David II. and taken prisoner with him in the battle of Durham, anno. 1346. (*Foedera* 20, Edward III). Sir Robert de Chesholme, on the death of his maternal grandfather, Sir Robert Lauder, succeeded to the whole of his estates in the counties of Elgin and Nairn, and was appointed, prior to 1357, Constable of Urquhart and Sheriff of Inverness. For "on the 8th April, 1359, Lord Robert de Chesholme, Sheriff of the county of Inverness gave in his accounts with all his expenses and receipts from Martinmas, 1357" (*Chamberlain's Rolls*, anno. 1359). There are many deeds still extant, public and private relating to this Sir Robert, but I shall only here refer to two. The first is a grant made by him of six acres of land within the old Castle lands of Inverness, for the weal of his soul and the souls of his ancestors and successors. It is dated at Inverness, the Feast of the Epiphany of the Holy Cross, 1362. In that deed he styles himself 'Robert de Chesholme, Knight and Lord of the same,' and as there is only one place in the Kingdom from which he could take his designation, viz., the Barony of Chisholme in the county of Roxburgh, the evidence that he was the Border Baron and head of his family is by it completely proved. He was also the Lord Cheseholme of Auld (Old), whose arms were emblazoned by Sir David Lindsay of the Mount in his MS. preserved in the Herald Office. 'Gules a boar's head, with the neck pendant, couped argent,' which we have borne from time immemorial, confirmed by patents. The other deed, which is now before me, is the marriage contract of his only daughter, Joneta de Chesholme, with Hugh Rose, fourth Baron of Kilravock. It is dated at the Church of Auldearn, 2nd January, 1364, and witnessed and sealed by the Bishop of Moray and Ross, and by William, Earl of Ross and Lord of Skye. In this contract Sir Robert de Chesholme is designated as the grandson of Sir Robert Lauder, which proves that it was his father, Sir John, who married the heiress of Quarrelwood, and not his son Sir Robert, as has been asserted, who only succeeded to the Lauder estates in Elgin and Nairn in right of his mother.

"I have thus explained the cause which led to the introduction of the Anglo-Norman name de Cheseholme into the North of Scotland ; and there is not one document, public or private, or even an adminicle of evidence, to show that the surname existed north of the Forth, prior to the reign of David II. Sir Robert de Chesholme died in 1384. He had issue, so far as is known, Robert, afterwards Sir Robert, who succeeded him. Alexander, the second son, who married Margaret de la Ard, styled Domina de Erchless, co-heiress of the Ard and Erchless in the county of Inverness, whose sister married William de Fenton, Lord of Bakey ; William, the third son, a churchman, and treasurer of Moray, whose name frequently appears in the Register of Moray between 1371 and 1399; and one daughter, Joneta, who married Hugh Rose, fourth Baron of Kilravock, in 1364. Other sons he may have had; if so, not the slightest trace of them is to be found.

"FIFTH, SIR ROBERT DE CHESHOLME succeeded his father, Sir Robert, in 1384. He married early in life Margaret, daughter of Halyburton of that Ilk, in the county of Berwick. In 1386 he voluntarily resigned the lands of Abereachy and others into the hands of the Bishop of Moray, which lands were granted and confirmed to Alexander, Lord of Badenoch, in feu ferm (*Reg. Great Seal*, p. 176, No. 39).

"In 1393, on the 30th August, he appended his seal to a mort ancestry award, finding that John Sibbald is rightful heir to the lands of Aldrochty, etc. He had two sons, John who succeeded him, and Robert who eventually succeeded his brother John.

"SIXTH, JOHN, the eldest son, styled by Sir George Mackenzie (King's Advocate for Scotland in the reign of Charles II., in his notice of this family), 'John Chesholme of that Ilk, in the Shyre of Roxburgh,' married Catherine, daughter of Bisset of that Ilk. He granted a charter to her relative, John Rose of Kilravock, of the lands of Cantrabundy and Little Cantray, dated 24th April, 1420 (*Kilravock Papers*). He died in 1436 without heirs male of his body, leaving an only daughter, Morella de Chesholme, who married Alexander Sutherland of Duffus, grandson of Nicholas Sutherland, second son of Kenneth, Earl of Sutherland, killed at the battle of Halidon, anno. 1333 (*Douglas' Peerage*, 2nd edition).

"Morella succeeded to the estates in Moray, Elgin, and Nairn, acquired by the marriage of her ancestor with the heiress of Sir Robert Lauder of Quarrelwood, but the Border estates being male fees, talzied on heirs male, she was excluded from them, and they devolved on Robert de Chesholme, her father's brother, who, as next heir, male, carried on the line of the family. Rose gives a very distinct account of this event in his history. He says, 'Alexander Sutherland of Duffus got Quarrelwood, Kinsterie, Brightmanie, etc., in the reign of James II., by marrying Morella de Chesholme, heretrix of them. The Chesholmes, her predecessors, had gotten the samen lands by marrying the daughter and heir of Sir Robert Lauder of Quarrelwood, and constable of Urquhart Castle, of whom our histories make honourable mention. Her father was Chesholme of that Ilk, being heritor of Chesholme in Teviotdale, and of Paxtoun. But it seems these have been talzied on heirs male, and thereupon she was secluded from them.' Shaw says, 'Morella de Chisholme married Alexander Sutherland of Duffus, and brought into that family a rich succession of lands which had been the heritage of the Lauders, and the heirs male of Chesholme enjoyed the proper estate of that family.

"SEVENTH, ROBERT DE CHESHOLME succeeded his brother, and was retoured, as his heir male, on a Brieve from the Chancery of James I., directed to the Sheriff of Teviotdale, 'To serve Robert of Chesholme, brother of John of Chesholme, in all lands, etc., in which the latter died vest, and seized at the King's faith and peace within his sheriffdom, dated 13th Sept., anno. reg. 30 (1436).' This Robert was a person of considerable note. He was one of the Lords who gave decree on the action raised by William Stirling of Cadar against Gilbert of Stirling, 21st January, 1442 (*Keir Papers*), in which he is styled Robert of Chesholme. He married Marion, daughter of Sir William Douglas of Drumlanrig, ancestor of the Duke of Queensberry, by whom he had four sons, John, the eldest, who succeeded him, Robert, the second son, William, the third, a churchman and eventually vicar of Pettin, and Edmund, the fourth son, who *founded the family of Cromlix and Dundorne*, in the county of Perth. Malcolm says, 'Edmund Chesholme was the first of Cromlex. He was a son of the Laird of Chesholme's House in Teviotdale. He married first Margaret Sinclair of Dryden, widow of Ramsay of Balmain, by whom he had two sons; secondly, he married Janet Drummond of Coldoch' (*Malcolm's History of Drummond and Chisholme*, p. 117). Keith, in his *Scottish Bishops*, p. 178, concurs with Malcolm as to the origin of this branch. The Cromlix family rapidly attained to wealth and power; they became hereditary bailies and justiciaries of the ecclesiastical lordship of Dunblane, made great alliances by marriage, produced several knights and churchmen, four of whom were bishops, but became extinct in the reign of Charles II.

"I have given you an outline of the descents of the Border family from the earliest period of its history, supported by documentary evidence. The cause of its connection with the North, to the time when that connection ceased by the North country estates passing with an *heiress* to the family of Duffus, after which its history is entirely associated with the Border. From the succession of Robert Chesholme, who was retoured as heir male to his brother John, the father of Morella, the descents to the present time from father to son are all established by charters and sasines. From the reign of James III. the French particle 'de,' previously in use before old surnames when the surname and title were the same, gradually fell into disuse, and the title 'of that Ilk' was substituted, which implies the head or chief of the name. In all their English deeds, this family are so styled 'viz., Chesholme of that Ilk,' and also by the old historians and genealogists, in the Parliamentary rolls, and in the roll of Border Barons, 1587, etc. In their Latin deeds their designation is generally in this form, which I give from a recorded sasine, dated 15th December, 1623, 'Walteri Chesholme nunc juniores de Eodem, fillii et heredis quondam Walteri Chesholme de Eodem sui patris.'

"I have also given the origin of the Cromlex branch, between whom and the parent stem a firm friendship existed, through the wars of the Reformation, and the reign of Mary.

"The other branches of this family were the Chisholmes of Parkhill in the county of Roxburgh, of Hayerhope in the county of Peebles, and of Selkirk in the county of Selkirk, etc., etc." Thus far Mr. Scott Chisholme.

It will be observed that he is in perfect agreement with us regarding the first three heads of the family—John, Richard, and Sir John de Chisholme. Mr. Chisholme, however, has no notice of Alexander de Chisholme, the fourth in our line of chiefs, though he is undoubtedly on record and described in an authentic document, dated 1335, as "Alexander de Chisholme of that Ilk." Mr. Scott Chisholme's fourth chief, Sir Robert de Chisholme, is our fifth, and his fifth, a second Sir Robert, whose very existence has been doubted by some authorities, is our sixth; while his John de Chisholme and sixth chief takes the place of our second Sir Robert and sixth chief. Our sixth chief and second Sir Robert, Mr. Chisholme adopts as his seventh chief, whereas we hold that the Robert who at that time (1436) came into possession of the Chisholme lands on the Border was not *Sir* Robert but another and later Robert, the third son of Sir Robert de Chisholme by his wife, Margaret, daughter of Haliburton of that Ilk, county of Berwick, and a younger brother of John and Alexander de Chisholme, both of whom unquestionably succeeded their father, Sir Robert de Chisholme, as chiefs of all the Chisholms, north and south. That this Robert was the brother of John and Alexander is clear from the service, which Mr. Scott Chisholme himself quotes, by the Sheriff of Teviotdale, who was directed to serve Robert of Chesholme, *brother* of John Chesholme, in all lands, etc., in which the latter died vest and seized at the King's faith and peace *within his sheriffdom*," dated 13th September, 1436. That is, within the sheriffdom of Teviotdale. He apparently succeeded to the Border portion of the family inheritance in terms of some agreement with his niece Morella Chisholme, who, on her marriage with Alexander Sutherland of Duffus, carried all the Border, as well as a great portion of the northern estates, to her husband.

That Morella inherited the lands of Chisholme in Teviotdale has been conclusively proved in the course of this
history. In a document dated the 20th of April, 1512,
it is stated that Morella's *daughter*, "the said Christian
Sutherland, Lady of Berriedale, *is heir of line to follow
and pursue the lands of Chisholme in Teviotdale, together
with the lands of Paxton and other lands of the which
she is very heir to*," and again, referring to Wiliam Sutherland, Alexander and Morella's son, and "now laird of
Duffus," the same document says that he "may never
have entry to the said lands of Chisholme nor to any
pertinents thereof, but so much as his grandame, Muriel
(Morella) of Chisholme, gave him in her widowhood *by
resignation*."* It is obvious that Morella could not have
had these lands to resign unless she had inherited them,
along with his other lands, from her father, who admittedly
died without male issue.

When John de Chisholme died, a family arrangement
seems to have been entered into by which his eldest
brother Alexander succeeded to a portion of the northern
lands, while Robert succeeded to the Border estates,
though they continued to be nominally claimed by his
niece and her husband, Alexander Sutherland of Duffus,
then and for some time afterwards—at least down to 1512—
by their descendants. Alexander having succeeded to very
extensive possessions in the Highlands on his marriage
with Margaret de la Aird and Lady of Erchless, would
naturally be disposed to leave his niece and brother
Robert to carry out the terms of this arrangement and
settle the succession to the Border estates of the family
among themselves. This is what he seems to have done,
and they finally fell, as was usually the case in those days
in similar circumstances, to the male competitor, who was
sure to have had the support of the vassals resident on
the property in such a dispute with a female member
of the family, who could not lead them to battle at a

* See pp. 25-27 for these documents at length.

time when it was necessary to have a leader of their own name in such a hotly-contested region as the Scottish Borders.

Mr. Scott Chisholme no doubt asserts that the Border estates of the family were then "male fees talzied on heirs male," but he produces no evidence in support of that contention except a statement by the Rev. Hew Rose, author of *The History of the Roses of Kilravock*, who says that "Her father (Morella Chisholme's) was Chesholme of that Ilk, being heritor of Chesholme in Teviotdale and of Paxtoune. But it *seems* these have been talzied to heirs male, and thereupon she was secluded from them." From this the natural inference is, that the Border estates were talzied on heirs male after the death of Morella's father, when she was "thereupon secluded" or excluded from them,* though, as it appears from the document already quoted, she and her descendants laid claim to them for some eighty years later, notwithstanding that one of the male heirs held actual possession. The point is, however, by no means quite clear, and it would be unwise to dogmatise too much in favour of either contention in the absence of more conclusive documentary evidence than is at present available.

We derive the Border family as follows. The first of whom we find any record is

I. JOHN DE CHISHOLME, who is mentioned in a Bull of Pope Alexander IV. in 1254. He married Emma de Vetereponte or Vipont, daughter of William de Vetereponte, Lord of Bolton, who as a marriage portion made him a grant of the lands and village of Paxton in the county of Berwick, and certain fishings in the Tweed. By this lady John had issue—

II. RICHARD DE CHESEHOLME, who in 1296 is described as "Del Counte de Rokesburgh." He was succeeded by his eldest son,

III. SIR JOHN DE CHESHOLME, who is designated

"Del Counte de Berwyke" in the same document in which his father is named "Del Counte de Rokesburgh." It will be seen that, as already stated, Mr. Scott Chisholme agrees with us regarding the foregoing as being the first three chiefs of the family on record. The next in our list is,

IV. ALEXANDER DE CHISHOLME. Mr. Chisholme has no notice of him. But that he succeeded and was head of the family between Sir John and Sir Robert is fully established. He is described as "Lord of Chisholme in Roxburgh and Paxtoun in Berwickshire," and also as "Alexander de Chisholme of that Ilk" in a disputed case about fishings in the Tweed in 1335. He was succeeded by his son,

V. SIR ROBERT DE CHISHOLME, one of the "Magnates of Scotland," who fought and was taken prisoner at the battle of Neville's Cross in October, 1346. He married Anne, daughter and heiress of Sir Robert Lauder of Quarrelwood in Morayshire, constable of Urquhart Castle, on Loch Ness, and the owner of extensive lands in that neighbourhood as well as in other parts of the county of Inverness, to which, in right of his wife, Sir Robert de Chisholme ultimately succeeded, and thus became the owner of a considerable Highland landed estate. By his wife he had issue—

1. Sir Robert, his heir and successor; and

2. William de Chisholm, Treasurer of Moray.

He was succeeded by his eldest son, also

VI. SIR ROBERT DE CHISHOLME, who is described as "Lord of Chisholme in Roxburghshire" and as "Constable of the Castle of Urquhart on Lochness." He was knighted by David II. in 1357, during his father's life. In 1359 he is described as "Lord Robert de Chisholme, Sheriff of the county of Inverness," and in 1362 he designates himself "Robert de Chisholme, Knight, and Lord of the same." In the same year he makes a grant of lands in the vicinity of Inverness to the poor of the parish. In a document dated the 25th of January, 1376, he describes himself as "Robert de Cheshelme, Lord of that Ilk, Justiciar of the said Regality of Moray." On the occasion of King Robert II.'s visit to Inverness in 1382 that monarch granted to his son, Alexander, Earl of Buchan, lands in Glenurquhart and Glenmoriston, which formerly "belonged to Robert de Chisholme, knight, and which the said Sir Robert gave up and resigned to the King." He is repeatedly on record in connection with the North, but for a more extended notice of him and his predecessors the reader is referred to the earlier part of this work—pp. 13 to 27. Sir Robert married Margaret, daughter of Haliburton of that Ilk, in the county of Berwick, with issue—

1. John de Chisholme, his heir and successor.

2. Alexander de Chisholme, who, on the death of his brother John, without male issue, succeeded to the chiefship and the Inverness-shire estates.

3. Robert, who ultimately, on the death of both his elder brothers, succeeded to the original family possessions in Roxburghshire, and became progenitor of the present Border Chisholmes.

4. Janet, who, in 1364, married Hugh Rose, IV. of Kilravock, with issue.

Sir Robert was succeeded in all the family inheritance, and as head of the House, by his eldest son,

VII. JOHN DE CHISHOLME, who married Catherine Bisset, daughter of Bisset of that Ilk, without male issue. On his death in 1436, his only child, Morella Chisholme, carried the lands of Quarrelwood, Clunie and Clova, in Moray; Paxtoun in Tweeddale, Kinsterrie in Nairnshire, and other extensive possessions, to her husband, Alexander Sutherland of Duffus. John's next brother, Alexander, succeeded to the chiefship and family possessions in the Highlands. His youngest brother,

VIII. ROBERT DE CHISHOLME, ultimately succeeded to the Roxburgh estates and became the head and progenitor of the Border branch of the family. That this Robert was not *Sir* Robert as claimed by Mr. Scott Chisholme, is clear from the Brieve quoted by himself;

for had he been Sir Robert he would have been so described in that document.   There is also the insuperable difficulty to be got over that even the second Sir Robert Chesholme is on record as early as 1358, or seventy-eight years earlier than 1436, the date at which, according to Mr. Scott Chisholme himself, this Robert succeeded to the Border estates of Chisholme; and this question of dates is much more conclusive than it at once appears.   When we first meet with the second Sir Robert in 1358 he is one of the Justices of the King, and must, therefore, have been not less than twenty-one years of age. The Robert who succeeded to the Border estates of Chisholme in 1436 must also have been of age before he was served heir to his brother John.   In this way twenty-one years' at least must be added to the seventy-eight which intervene between the date on which the second Sir Robert appears on record in 1358 and this Robert's succession in 1436, making the impossible gulf for one man to bridge over of more than a hundred years, even if he died immediately after succeeding to the Border estates. But, on the contrary, he certainly lived down to 1442, and probably much longer; for he was one of the Lords of Justiciary who, on the 21st of January in that year, gave judgment in an action raised by William Stirling against Gilbert of Stirling, in which connection he is styled "Robert of Cheshome."*   But if there was only one Sir Robert, as some authorities maintain, this impassable gulf would become wider still, for we find the first Sir Robert on record in the capacity of one of "the Magnates of Scotland" as early as 1346, a date at which, from what we know of his history, he must have been considerably advanced in years.   True Mr. Scott Chisholme introduces us to a John Chisholme after his second Sir Robert, but as he admits this John to have been the third Robert's brother, the difficulty as regards the dates cannot to any material extent be affected; for this John de Chisholme grants a charter to John

* *Keir Papers.*

Rose, VII. of Kilravock, as late as the 24th of April, 1420, and he is said to have lived down to 1436, the same year in which his brother Robert succeeded him in the Border estates of Chisholme. These dates we think must be held as conclusive, not only in this particular case but as regards all the preceding heads of the House.

The Robert Chisholme who succeeded to the Border estates of the family in 1436, must have been, in these circumstances, the younger son of the second Sir Robert; and from him we now proceed to show, as clearly as possible, with the slender materials at our disposal, the descent of the present Border family.

Robert married Marion, daughter of Sir William Douglas of Drumlanrig, Hawick, and Selkirk, all three Baronies of which he received a charter of confirmation, dated the 30th November, 1412, from James I., written on vellum in the King's own hand. Sir William was an illegitimate son of James, Earl of Douglas and Mar, killed at Otterburn on the 19th of August, 1388. By Marion Douglas, whose mother was Elizabeth, daughter of Sir Robert Stewart of Durisdeer, Robert Chisholme had issue, four sons—

1. John, his heir and successor.

2. Robert, whose descendants, if any, we have not been able to trace.

3. William, who was bred to the church, and became vicar of Pettin.

4. Edmund, progenitor of the Chisholms of Cromlix, and of whom separately.

He was succeeded by his eldest son,

IX. JOHN CHISHOLME, who married, with issue—

X. ROBERT CHISHOLME, who married, with issue, several sons, all of whom apparently predeceased their father, except

XI. GEORGE CHISHOLME, the youngest, who succeeded. He engaged, with Scott of Buccleuch and other Border chiefs, to relieve James V. of Scotland, at his own instigation, from the control and tutelage of the Earl of Angus. They were defeated at the battle of Melrose in 1526, when Chisholme and the other principal leaders were forfeited. On the accession of James, however, in 1528, the Border chieftains received remission for their past offences, and George Chisholme received a charter, dated at Edinburgh on the 12th of November, 1531, of the lands of Chisholme, Chisholme Middon, Mouslie, Woodburn, Merrynier, and other lands in the South of Scotland. He married, with issue, four sons and two daughters. He was succeeded by his eldest son,

XII. WALTER CHISHOLME, who was infeft in his father's lands on the 13th of March, 1538. He supported Queen Mary during her unfortunate rule in Scotland, and was actively engaged in her cause during all the civil wars of her reign. In 1564 William Cranston of that Ilk is mentioned as "Breder" of this Walter Chisholme—a half-brother of course, by the same mother. He married, with issue, and on his death, in 1588, was succeeded by his eldest son,

XIII. WALTER CHISHOLME, who was infeft in his father's lands on the 17th of February, 1589. He married Margaret, daughter of John Graham of Wark. He died in 1618, leaving issue—an only son,

XIV. WALTER CHISHOLME, who was infeft in the estates on the 15th of December, 1623. During the civil war of the period he was a staunch Royalist, and served in the King's army. He was taken prisoner at the battle of Preston in 1648. He married and had issue—

1. Walter, who succeeded him.

2. William, who settled in the North of England.

He died at Breda in 1652, when he was succeeded by his eldest son,

XV. WALTER CHISHOLME, who acquired the property and became the first Chisholme of Stirches. He married Margaret, only daughter of James Balderstone, with issue—

1. William, his heir and successor.

2. Robert, born on the 3rd of July, 1653. He was bred to the legal profession, and was afterwards appointed

Sheriff-Clerk of Selkirkshire. He was the first of the Chisholmes of Selkirk. One of his descendants, a great-grandson, made a fortune in Jamaica, and on his return home in 1874, he purchased the Chisholme estate, the original possession of the family in Scotland, from Sir James Stewart of Coltness. The late Gilbert Chisholme of Stirches, writing to a friend in April. 1826, says, "I knew his" (the then proprietor of the old Barony of Chisholme's) "grandfather very well. He was ever after he became a man a surgeon in Selkirk; he educated and brought up his eldest son to his own profession, and sent him to Jamaica to some friends there, where he made a good deal of money. He was the father of this young man." This purchaser, whose name was William Chisholme, married, with issue male—an only son, who succeeded his father, and died without issue in 182—, when the property devolved on his cousin, Scott of Coldhouse, in the county of Roxburgh, in right of his mother, Margaret Chisholme, who was a sister of William who bought the estate. On the accession of Scott of Coldhouse he assumed the name of Chisholme. The estate has since been sold out of the family.

Walter Chisholme died in 1681, when he was succeeded by his eldest son,

XVI. WILLIAM CHISHOLME, who was born on the 11th of January, 1652. He and his son John are on record in 1698. He married Mary, only daughter of James Brotherstone of Glencairn, with issue—

1. John, his heir and successor.

2. Mary, who was born on the 9th of August, 1684, and married on the 25th of October, 1708, William Oliver of Dinlebyre, with issue—a son, John, and a daughter, Mary, who married John Scott of Synton.

He was succeeded by his only son,

XVII. JOHN CHISHOLME, who was born on the 11th of September, 1682, and married on the 4th of February, 1708, Mary, second daughter of John Oliver of Dinlebyre, Roxburghshire, with issue—a son,

XVIII. John Chisholme, who, on the death of his father on the 17th of July, 1755, succeeded to the estates. On the 5th of August, 1736, he married Margaret, eldest daughter of Alexander Scott of Synton, county of Roxburgh, by his wife, Magdalene, daughter of Sir William Eliott of Stobs, and aunt of the celebrated General Augustus Eliott, created Lord Heathfield on the 16th of July, 1717, for his gallant defence of Gibraltar in 1782. By this lady John Chisholme had issue, several sons, two of whom predeceased him. On his death, in 1784, he was succeeded by his third but eldest surviving son,

XIX. Gilbert Chisholme, who married, first, on the 21st of July, 1768, Christina, second daughter of Michael Anderson of Tushilaw, county of Selkirk, by his wife Janet, daughter of Sir James Nasmyth, baronet of Posso. She died in 1800, without issue. He married, secondly, on the 17th of August, 1802, Elizabeth, second daughter of John Scott of Whitehaugh, county of Roxburgh, by Margaret, eldest daughter of co-heiress of Walter Scott of Newton Chamberlain, in the same county, with issue—

1. John, his heir and successor.

2. Gilbert, who died unmarried in 1820.

3. Margaret Scott, who died unmarried in 1854.

4. Christian Anderson.

He died on the 5th of December, 1826, and was succeeded by his eldest son,

XX. John Scott Chisholme, who married Margaret, eldest daughter and co-heir of Robert Walker of Mumrills, county of Stirling, by his wife Christian Tytler, daughter of John Borthwick of Newton. John Chisholme, in 1852, succeeded to the estate of his maternal uncle, James Scott of Whitehaugh, when, in terms of the will of that gentleman, he assumed the surname of Scott in addition to his own. By his wife, who still survives, he had issue—

1. John James, his heir and successor.

2. Christina, who, in 1869, married Robert Pringle, M.D., son of William Pringle of the family of Whitebank.

3. Elizabeth Scott.

He died on the 15th of January, 1868, when he was succeeded by his only son,

XXI. JOHN JAMES SCOTT CHISHOLME, now of Stirches, an officer in the 5th Lancers, on active service in India.

THE CHISHOLMS OF CROMLIX AND DUNDORNE.

THE heads of this Perthshire family were styled of Cromlix, and sometimes of Dundorne. Cromlix is situated on the south-west borders of the county and in the temporalty of Dunblane. The founder of the House of Cromlix was

I. SIR EDMUND CHISHOLM, who was the fourth son of Robert Chisholme, VII. of Chisholme, in Roxburghshire. This Robert was himself the third son of Sir Robert Chisholme, VI. of Chisholme, and brother of John and Alexander de Chisholme, VII. and VIII. of Chisholme, both of whom succeeded their father, Sir Robert de Chisholme, as heads of the family, north and south. Sir Edmund came to Cromlix early in the fifteenth century and was soon afterwards knighted. His mother was Marion, daughter of Sir William Douglas of Drumlanrig, ancestor of the Duke of Queensberry. He married first, Margaret Sinclair, a lady of the House of Dryden, and widow of Ramsay of Balmain, with issue—

1. James, his heir and successor.

2. A son, of whom nothing is known, unless the following refers to him. In the reign of Henry VIII. the Bishop of Dunkeld, writing to Thomas Magnus, the English Ambassador, requests him to send Patrick Sinclair or Sir John Chisholm to confer respecting some matters of importance then under consideration. It has been suggested that this Sir John was Edmund's second son, and that the *Sir* in his case was simply the ecclesiastical *dominus*, as indeed it was in many other instances where

the parties are supposed to have been knights, but where they were only a higher grade of priest. A *John* Chisholm was Archdeacon of Dunblane in 1541. He died in 1542.

He married, secondly, Janet, daughter of James Drummond of Coldoch, a younger brother of John, first Lord Drummond, with issue—

3. William, who afterwards succeeded his eldest brother in the Bishopric of Dunblane, and of whom presently.

4. A son of whom no record can be found beyond the fact that he existed.

By this lady he had also three daughters, one of whom was

5. Janet, who married Sir Alexander Napier of Merchiston, ancestor of the present Lord Napier and Ettrick, K.T. He fell at Flodden on the 1st September, 1513, and left issue, an only son—Alexander Napier, who succeeded his father and carried on the representation of the family. She was thus the great-grandmother of John Napier, the inventor of Logarithms, who himself became united with the same family by marrying, as his second wife, Agnes, daughter of James Chisholm of Cromlix,* by whom he had five sons, who founded families of their own, and five daughters, all of whom were respectably married. Janet Chisholm married, secondly, Sir Ninian Seton of Touch and Tillibody, by whom she had issue—Sir Walter Seton, who succeeded his father and carried on the representation of that ancient House.† The Cromlix family rose rapidly in power and influence. Its head was made hereditary Bailie and Justiciar of the ecclesiastical lordship of Dunblane, but whether this office was first conferred on Sir Edmund or on his successor is not clear. He was succeeded by his eldest son by the first marriage—

* "He (Sir Alexander Napier) married Janet, the eldest daughter of Edmund Chisholme of Cromlix, the same family from which his great-grandson, the philosopher, took his second wife."—*Life of Napier of Merchiston*, p. 40.

† *Douglas's Baronage*, p. 168.

II. Sir James Chisholm of Cromlix, a man of great learning. He entered into holy orders and was made chaplain to James III. He, however, must have been married, and have had issue at least two sons. In 1486 Sir James was dispatched on a royal mission to Rome, when he made such an impression upon Pope Innocent VIII. that he appointed him to the See of Dunblane, which was then vacant, and in the following year he was duly consecrated Bishop of that diocese, a position which he occupied until he was compelled by old age in 1527 to resign, in favour of his half-brother William, the more laborious duties of the office. He, however, retained the administration of the fruits of his benefice in his own hands until 1534, when he died, leaving a high character for probity and justice. He was a careful administrator and in all respects a good bishop.

We shall now revert to Bishop William, Sir Edmund's eldest son by his second wife. He was appointed, in 1527, by Pope Clement VII., and was consecrated at Stirling on the 14th of April, 1527, by Gavin Dunbar, Archbishop of Glasgow, Chancellor of Scotland; George Crichton, Bishop of Dunkeld, and his own brother James Chisholm, Bishop of Dunblane. William had the title of "Administrator General" until the death of Bishop James in 1534, when the whole duties of the See devolved upon him. In 1554, he was appointed one of the Lords of the College of Justice, now known as the Court of Session. It was he who excommunicated the famous Wishart. He is described in Rankin's *Church of Scotland*, pp. 334 and 336, as "an ecclesiastic of the worst possible type for fornication, Church robbery, and persecution of the so-called heretics," as "a robber bishop," and "as a shameless wretch who wasted the See by fraudulent tacks to his three bastards and his nephew, and who burned men for heresy." He had a natural son, known as James Chisholm of Gassengal, on whom he bestowed a large portion of the property of his diocese. Being a stout upholder of the Roman Catholic Church, and an opponent of the Reformation, he expected no favours under the new system, the establishment of which he foresaw had become inevitable. It was then he began to alienate the property of the Church to his nephew of Cromlix, who got the largest share of it, and to his own bastard son and two daughters. These ladies carried the property to their respective husbands. One of them, Jean, whose mother was a lady of the Montrose family, married Sir James Stirling of Keir, with issue. The other, about 1555, married, as his second wife, John Buchanan, eighteenth laird of that Ilk, with issue—an only daughter, who married Thomas Buchanan of Hert, Lord Privy Seal.*

Writing of this period and of the part this licentious prelate played in it, the Rev. Dr. James Rankin says— "The first element of the dispersion (of Church property) consisted in this, that for two or three decades previous to 1560 there went on a deliberate and unprincipled system of what was called *dilapidation* of Church property of all kinds. Bishops, deans, provosts, preceptors, abbots, and priors, forseeing danger to the Church, put their houses in order by giving leases to relatives and favourites on terms that amounted to robbery and breach of trust, called more politely dilapidation. Two of the most flagrant offenders were Bishop Patrick Hepburn of Moray, already mentioned with his thirteen concubines, seven of whom were other men's wives,† and Bishop William Chisholm of Dunblane, who enriched his three bastard children and his nephew, Sir James Chisholm of Cromlix, at the expense of the See. This knave compounded for his dishonesty by a double portion of zeal against heresy. In 1539 he and Beaton condemned five men to the flames at Edinburgh."‡

Tytler, under date of 1538-39, informs us that certain converts to the principles of the Reformation belonging

---

* *History of the Surname of Buchanan*, p. 28.

† Letters of Legitimation under the Great Seal of State were passed for no less than ten of this "holy" villain's children.

‡ *The Church of Scotland*, pp. 426-427.

to the inferior orders of the Catholic clergy, and whose names he gives, "were summoned to appear before a Council held by Cardinal Beaton and William Chisholme, the bishop of Dunblane. It gives us," he says, "a low opinion of the purity of the ecclesiastical judges before whom these early disciples of the Reformation were called, when we find the bench filled by Beaton and Chisholme, the first notorious for his gallantry and licentiousness, the second commemorated by Keith as the father of three natural children, for whom he provided portions by alienating the patrimony of his bishopric.*

William lived until 1564, but tired of the troubles which had arisen, he resigned the Episcopal chair to his nephew, another William, in 1561, as colleague and successor, which act was confirmed by a Papal Brief, dated the 2nd of June in the same year, and was nominated by Queen Mary in 1564.

Bishop William the second had previously officiated as coadjutor of his uncle, and following his example dilapidated the remaining patrimony of the See. His principles got him into high favour with Mary Queen of Scots, by whom he was much employed in public affairs. Among other offices, he was appointed one of the Commissioners who procured and decreed the divorce of Bothwell and Lady Jean Gordon. The affairs of the Church kept him constantly employed in exciting work, for like all members of the Cromlix family, he was an active supporter of the Catholic party.† It was this prelate who had been sent to Rome to procure a dispensation from the Pope for the marriage of Queen Mary to Darnley. Under date of 1565, Tytler writes—"It was now the end of July, and Chisholm, Bishop of Dunblane, having arrived from Rome with a dispensation for the marriage, it was intimated to the people, by a public proclamation, that the Queen had resolved to take to her husband an illustrious prince, Henry, Duke of Albany, for which reason she commanded

---

* *History of Scotland.*   † *Keith's Catalogue of the Scottish Bishops.*

her subjects to give him the title of King." Bishop
Chisholm was ultimately forfeited, upon which he retired
to France, where he was appointed Bishop of Vaison, in
Normandy. He, however, continued to take an active
part in the affairs of the Scottish Catholics. In his latter
years he seems to have become weary of the ceaseless
intrigues of his former life, and resigning his French
diocese to a nephew, a third Bishop William Chisholm
out of the Cromlix family, he became a Carthusian friar
of Grenoble, and died very advanced in years at Rome,
in 1593. He was the last Roman Catholic Bishop of
Dunblane.

Regarding these bishops, Dr. William Marshall, in his
Historic Scenes in Perthshire, pp. 343-344, says—"Three
bishops of Dunblane were Chisholms of the Cromlix
family. They held the bishopric successively for the
eighty years immediately preceding the Reformation.
The second of the three was William. He was passion-
ately fond of song and music, and above all of the air
called 'Clout the Caldron,' so much so that he used to
say, that if condemned to die, he would go contented to
the gallows, provided that his ears were regaled with that,
his favourite spring. Discerning the signs of the times,
he prepared for the coming overthrow of his Church by
giving most of the revenues of his See to his nephew,
Sir James Chisholm of Cromlix, and to a son and two
daughters of his own, whom he, though a celibate, con-
trived to have. Spottiswood says that he utterly 'wracked'
the benefice. He was succeeded by his nephew, also
William, who followed in his uncle's footsteps, and still
further alienated what remained of the Church's patrimony."

Sir James married, with issue, at least two sons—

1. Sir James, his heir and successor ; and

2. William, who succeeded his uncle in the See of
Dunblane in 1564, afterwards became Bishop of Vaison,
in France, and died a Carthusian friar of Grenoble, at
Rome, in 1593, as already stated.

Sir James, the first bishop and second Chisholm laird

of Cromlix, who died in 1534, was succeeded by his eldest son,

III. SIR JAMES CHISHOLM of Cromlix, the nephew to whom his uncle, the first Bishop William, alienated a large portion of the Church lands of his diocese, shortly before the Scottish Reformation. On the 30th of November, 1571, he is "delaited" for remaining "fra the Raid of Leith." He was, however, discharged by the Treasurer.* In January, 1575-76, Sir James Chisholm, along with the Earl of Eglington, Lords Elphinstone and Livingstone, became cautioner that Sir Adam Gordon of Auchindown, brother of the Earl of Huntly, should enter and keep within ten miles of the burgh of Kirkcudbright, and that he should behave himself dutifully, and refrain from any treasonable practices against the King, the realm, and the lieges, under a penalty of 10,000 merks Scots. He married and had issue—

1. James, his heir and successor.

2. William, who succeeded his uncle William as the second Bishop Chisholm of Vaison.

3. John Chisholm, who, in 1572, was by his party sent to France for a sum of money, "the quhilk he obteinit," but on his return, arriving in the Firth of Forth, in July of the same year, the Regent ordered the vessels to be boarded and to have the passengers captured. John Chisholm, however, "beforehand was landit with a great sowme of gold, and had delyverit the same to the Abbot of St. Colomb's Inche in keaping. The Lord Lyndesay was directit to searche (for) him on the land side, and he was quicklie apprehendit. There was fundin among his writtis a minute of the gold delyverit to John Chisholm, and the said John being examinat, and this minute shawn to confront him, he was boisted with torture unles he sould tell whare it was; so that for feir, he declarit and thus was the gold quicklie gotten and delyverit to the Regent."†

* *Pitcairn's Criminal Trials*, part II., p. 28.

† *Pitcairn's Criminal Trials*, and *The History of King James the Sixth*, Bannatyne Club edition.

There is a fragment in the Cotton Collection of manuscripts in the British Museum, dated 1587, which is described as "The Bishop of Dunblane his embassy into Scotland from Philip of Spain and Pope Sixtus V." There is nothing in the document of any importance, but it explains the Bishop's mission to Scotland at this particular date and in the following year, when he is referred to in a letter to Archbishop Beaton. In 1588 a communication is addressed to Beaton in which the writer laments that "the langsumness of Monsr. Cheisholm's tary ther hes doin evil money wayis and hes henderit you in particular greatly, for haid we either gottin the procuratioun or the obligatiouns, na doubt we had put maiteris to sum stand and certainly we haid retirit ane pairt of the dettis." Then he says that the creditors would wait "quhil we sie quhat directioun ze pleas to send haime to us be Monsr. Cheisholme, whom we lang very meikle for." The writer proceeds—"The Bishop of Dunblane has almais bein continually seik sinss his in Scotland, and now being sumthing convalescit I think wald give his umest claith to be in the Charterous of Grenoble! Suirly he is estemit ane verie honnest and discreit prelat, and is zour maist affectionate friend and weil willar quhomsoever they speak their pleasuir of him here in the cuntraith. He hes him very hairtily commendit unto zou and wald maist gladly be quhar ze ar. Sa wald I myself, as God judge me! and wald give thryss the pryce of my voyage to heav ane dayis conference with you."†

The same writer in the same year in a letter "to his very assurit friend, the guidman of Casseingie," the first Bishop William Chisholm's natural son, says—"I wryt not Monsr. Cheisholme, expressly luiking for his awin comming haim hourly. God send him weil hither for he hes been lang luikit for."

John Chisholm's mission does not appear to have turned out of very great benefit to his friends. Sir

William Maitland of Lethington, writing to Archbishop Beaton, on the 28th of August, alludes to "the interception of Johne Chisholme" who had brought money to the Queen's party of which only "a small portion was put asyde and savit, quhan he and the rest was taken." Tytler says that in 1588-89, Bruce, a noted Jesuit, harboured in Scotland, informed the Duke of Parma "of the seasonable arrival of John Chisholm, their agent, with the large sum entrusted to him," and of their having secured Bothwell, who, though still professing the Protestant faith, had been bribed to embrace their party. On the 24th of May, 1589, this John Chisholm, described as "son to umquhile James Chisholm of Cromlix," was indicted with Lords Huntly, Bothwell, Crawford, and others for intercommuning with Jesuits, receiving money, and raising soldiers.*

Sir James has a process of slaughter raised against him three years after this date, for we find that, after long resistance, the Commendator of Inchaffray, and Lindsay of Kinfauns, on the 15th of January, 1592, became cautioners for "Schir James Cheisholme of Dundorne, knt., as principall, for himself and takand burdin far his haill kin, friends and surname," that they should observe the contents of Letters of Slains, dated the 25th of November, 1587, granted "to the chieff kinsmen and friends of umquhile Mungo Edmonstone," who had been killed at Stirling in 1585. On the 15th of February in the same year (1592-93), Cromlix was denounced a rebel for not appearing to answer an accusation "tuiching his practizing and trafficquing in sundrie tressonnable matteris agains the trew religion."† Sir James was deeply implicated in the plans of the Catholic Lords, as they were called, and was exposed to prosecution along with them. For having offered to carry the "Blanks" to Spain, the Earls of Huntly, Errol, and Angus were accused of treason, on which occasion, in the same connection, Sir James

---

* *Pitcairn's Trials.*   † *Pitcairn's Trials*, p. 283.

had to give a bond for his good behaviour in £10,000, and was allowed to remain in Scotland. He had cleared himself of the charge of having carried the letters to Spain, but as he did not reveal his knowledge of what the others were doing, and of their whole design he became subject to dittay of treason.* The lords and he were further pursued by the clergy of the Kirk, and were compelled to make an offer of sufficient security that they should give present obedience, and would hear any ministers appointed by the King, so that "efter ressoning they were throuchly resolvit" to adhere to the Kirk of Scotland; if not they agreed to "depairt furth of the cuntrie, thair to remane during his Majestie's plessour." They, however, did not give the necessary satisfaction. The Synod of Fife met in September, 1593, when they took into consideration " the impunity of that most monstrous, ungodly, and unnatural treason," of which Sir James and his friends were guilty by their attitude towards the Kirk. "The pride, boldness, malice, busyness, and going forward of these enemies in their most pernicious purpose" are severely condemned, arising, as it was said, "out of the said impunity and bearing with the King, so that now they not only have no doubt, as they speak plainly, to obtain liberty of conscience, but also brag to make us fain to come to their cursed idolatry, before they come to the truth." The Lords and Sir James were afterwards solemnly excommunicated, "quhilk," says the Rev. James Melville, "was done by my mouthe, Moderator for the time, and the quhilk God sa blessed that the haill Kirk of Scotland approvit the same, and the quhilk the Lord maid to be a speciall mean of preventing extreame danger of wrack of 'the Kirk and Commonweill of Scotland, and bringing of the enemies to forfaltrie and excyll."†

On the 12th of October in the same year the King was riding to Lauder when the three Earls and Sir James Chisholm met him. They "cam on the hie way

* Acts of Parliament, III., IV., Moyse, etc.   † *Melville's Diary*, p. 207.

at sik place and tyme as he bruikit not for," and upon
their kneeling down, His Majesty "usit sum few words
unto thaym," but would allow them no other favour than
a fair trial.   He, however, issued a proclamation that, as
they were to be tried, it should not be criminal to reset
and entertain them, as it had for some time been, but
the clergy would not relax their excommunication.   In
November, 1595, they were discharged by proclamation
from the penalties of their defaults, provided they embraced "the trew religion," kept a minister, and gave
security, the earls in £40,000 each and Cromlix in
£10,000.   They were allowed until February, 1596, to
answer, and if they did not accept the terms offered
to them, they were peremptorily charged to surrender.
They did neither the one nor the other; they were
finally forfeited, and their "armories were riven in the
Justice place in face of Parliament, and thereafter cassin
out at a wyndo by the Heralds."   Sir James Chisholm
is not mentioned as having undergone this final degradation; for he had in the meantime made his peace
with the Kirk.

On the 24th of June, 1595, during the eighth session
of that august body, he submitted himself to the General
Assembly at Montrose, where, according to Calderwood,
Sir James "compeared in presence of the whole brethren,
confessed with humility his apostacy from religion, for
which he craved God's mercy; declared he professed
with us the true religion, renounced the Anti-Christ and
all his errors, and craved from his heart to be received
into the bosom of the Kirk.   The Assembly concluded
he should be relaxed, and thereafter the form of his
satisfaction to be set down.   So in the ninth session he
was relaxed from the process of excommunication led
against him, he humbling himself upon his knees and
acknowledging his offence."   Curiously enough, notwithstanding all these troubles, he was Master of the Household to King James VI., with whom he was personally
an acknowledged favourite.

In his *Life of John Napier of Merchiston*, the late Mark Napier gives a most interesting account of this period and of the part taken in its affairs by his own ancestor, who occupied a prominent position on the Protestant side, and by Sir James Chisholm of Cromlix (whose daughter, Agnes, John Napier of Merchiston had married as his second wife) on the Catholic side. Having described the loss of the Spanish Armada and the tranquil state of the Kingdom in 1590, after the King's marriage, our author proceeds :—" The loss of the Invincible Armada had not entirely discouraged the King of Spain in his attempts against Britain ; and he met with secret countenance and aid from a few of the most distinguished persons in Scotland. In the very year after the destruction of the Spanish fleet, it appears that the Prince of Parma, Phillip's General commanding in the Low Countries, was in direct communication with a desperate faction in Scotland, of whom two of the most active and determined agents were Sir James Chisholm of Cromlix and his brother John Chisholm—the father and uncle of the lady to whom Napier was now united. His first wife, Elizabeth Stirling, died about the end of the year 1579, leaving him one son Archibald, the first Lord Napier, and one daughter, Jane. From among his own relatives, but from a family deeply dyed in scarlet, he took a second spouse in Agnes Chisholm, whom he married a few years after the death of his first. The ancient family of Cromlix, to which he was united by double ties, had shot forth a succession of Catholic bishops like stars from a Roman candle. The numerous progeny which he had by this lady were already considerably advanced, when a crisis arrived which must have been very appalling to the family at Merchiston. The Parliament of June, 1592, had solemnly ratified the liberties of the Church, and the freedom of its jurisdictions ; but the Scotch clergy, like other successful sects, evinced a spirit of persecution which had not the effect of overawing their opponents, and even rendered some of them more desperate. It was insisted that as the Reformed Religion had been constitutionally established, all who professed the Roman Catholic faith should be compelled either to embrace the Protestant doctrines, or suffer the pains of rigorous excommunication ; and that, after such delinquents had continued for the space of a whole year thus cast off from Christian society, their property should be forfeited to the Crown. This policy had been adopted against various individuals, and, in particular, George Kerr, a brother of the philosopher's class-fellow, Lord Newbottle, having refused to conform upon the requisition of the Presbytery of Haddington, was excommunicated. David Graham of Fintry, and Barclay of Ladyland suffered the same sentence.

" At this time Sir James Chisholm, who was the King's Master of Household, had fallen under no persecution, and was not even suspected. Yet since at least the close of the year 1589, he had become deeply involved in a treasonable plot to aid Spain against Britain ; and various members of his family were amongst the most active plotters. His uncle, William Chisholm, the ex-Bishop of Dunblane, and now of Vàison in France, where he had been driven for his adherence to the Catholic cause and the fortunes of Queen Mary, was of great account among the Jesuits, and seems to have been the person through whom Sir James was seduced. The bishop's other nephew, John, was the party employed to carry money from Spain to aid the cause in Scotland. This appears from the terms of a letter which fell into the hands of the Protestants after the plot was discovered. It is addressed by one Bruce, a Papist, to the Duke of Parma, written in French cypher, and dated from Edinburgh, 24th January, 1589. According to the translation made of it upon disclosure, it commences by informing the Duke that 'Monsieur Chesholme' had arrived in Scotland after a voyage of five days : that he instantly proceeded to the Earl of Huntly, and delivered letters from the Duke to that nobleman in

his own house in Dunfermline on the 13th of October:
the letter then acknowledges receipt by the hand of John
Chisholm of 'sax thousand twa hundreth thre scoir twelve
crounis of the sum, and thre thousand sevin hundreth
Spanish pistolets' from the Duke of Parma.   The writer
proceeds to detail the plans and resources of the Spanish
party in Scotland, and adds, 'likewise I sall help myself
by the prudence of Schir James Chesholme, eldest brother
to the said John quha brocht the money from your hienes,
for he is a man confident, wise, ane on our pairt, and
very little suspect.'   It appears, however, that some suspicion
had arisen against the family at this time, for the same
letter mentions, that one Thomas Tyrie had reported to
King James that Bishop William had spoken with the
Duke of Parma, very much to His Majesty's disadvantage,
and that John Chisholm was also in close communication
with his uncle the bishop.

   "Thus the celebrated plot of 'the Spanish Blanks' was
organised; and when nearly ripe, the person selected to
fire the train, by carrying the treasonable papers abroad,
was John Napier's father-in-law—the grandfather of his
numerous second family.   Probably that prudence which
might have added success to the scheme had Sir James
followed out the first plan saved him from so perilous a
part in the conspiracy.   George Kerr, finding it impossible to live in comfort or safety in Scotland under his
sentence of excommunication, was on the eve of quitting
the country, and it was finally arranged that the commission should be transferred to him.   While he was waiting
for further instructions, near the island of Cumray, Andrew
Knox, the minister of Paisley, acquired secret intelligence
of the plot, and with a spirit and determination worthy
the name he bore, proceeded with some armed men,
and several Protestant gentlemen, on board of the vessel
where Kerr was, and instantly seized him.   Various treasonable letters and papers were discovered in the coat
sleeve of one of the mariners.   Graham of Fintry and
Barclay of Ladyland were apprehended about the same

time.   This important intelligence reached Edinburgh
upon a Sunday during divine service.   The sensation
was so great that the clergymen brought their sermons
to a speedy conclusion, and exhorted the people to arm
themselves immediately in order to insure the safe custody of the prisoners   These unfortunate individuals,
escorted by a sort of national guard hastily got up
among the townsmen, were lodged in the Tolbooth of
Edinburgh.   Meetings and solemn conventions of the
ministers and well-affected barons followed, which at once
alarmed and enraged the monarch, who 'was haistit from
his pastyme sonar nor he thoght to have been.'   His
presence was the more necessary, that three earls, Huntly,
Angus, and Errol, were deeply implicated—their signatures having been found to certain suspicious blanks among
the papers; and before the King's arrival in Edinburgh,
the Earl of Angus had been carried a prisoner to the
Castle.

"A most disgraceful scene, not generally noticed by
our historians, now occurred before the Privy Council.
George Kerr would make no confessions; and it was
proposed to put him in the *bootikins*, an infernal instrument of torture, worthy of the most savage age of
heathen persecution.   The Justice Clerk, Sir Lewis Bell-
enden, alarmed at the menaces of Kerr's friends, refused
to comply; but the monarch himself ordered the torture
to proceed.   The nature of it was to lacerate and crush
the limb of the sufferer, by driving iron wedges between
the shin bone and the iron boot, the interrogations being
repeated at each successive stroke of the hammer.   Kerr's
fortitude was proof against the dreadful preparatives, and
the first blow; but upon the application of a second, he
cried out for mercy, and said he would confess all.   The
substance of his deposition taken on the 13th February,
1592-3, was—that in June, 1592, Sir James Chisholm had
obtained from the Earls of Angus and Errol, in their
own lodgings in Edinburgh, their respective signatures in
French, as if addressed to the King of Spain, but with

blanks above, to be filled up by one Mr. William Crichton, a Jesuit, as he pleased—that the other blanks produced, with their respective signatures, had been procured about the same time, and that Sir James Chisholm held secret conferences on the subject with David Graham of Fintry and the witness Kerr—that at first the noblemen implicated had agreed that Sir James, 'quha wes then ane of His Majestie's Maister Houshaldis, suld have gone to Spain with this commission, in respect he wes utherwise bounit towardis his uncle, Maister William Chesholme, callit Bischop of Dumblane, for Schir James had the first credeit of this erand with the nobillman,' etc; but not being ready in time, and 'Maister George Kerr being bounit off the countrie, it wes thocht best that the same commission suld be gevin to him,' and 'he wes employed in that errand the rather because baith his gud-dames were Creichtouns.' The result contemplated was, that 30,000 men should land out of Spain on the West Coast of Scotland, march to Carlisle, and invade England, leaving 5000 Spaniards with the noblemen in Scotland to proclaim liberty of conscience. David Graham deponed to the same effect. On the 15th of February, the Earl of Angus made his escape from the Castle; and upon the 16th, Fintry, more dead than alive, and certainly the least guilty of all concerned, was beheaded at the Cross. But Kerr's life was spared, and he was sent to the Castle of Edinburgh, from which he too made his escape on the 20th of June following.

"The most vigilant synod in the Kingdom, that of Fife, was summoned at St. Andrews on the 25th of September, 1593. Great excitement prevailed at this assembly, when it was determined that commissioners should be appointed from the separate estates of barons, boroughs, and clergy, 'to declare freely to His Majesty the mind and resolution of all his godly and faithful subjects within the province, that they are ready to give their lives rather than suffer the same to be polluted with idolatry, and overrun with bloody Papists.' The Assembly then solemnly de-

clared, 'that the principal and chief enemies, the Earls of
Huntly, Angus, and Errol, Laird of Auchindoun, and Sir
James Chisholm, have, by their idolatry, heresy, blas-
phemy, apostacy, perjury, and professed enmity against
the Kirk and true religion of Jesus Christ within this
realm, *ipso facto* cut off themselves from Christ and His
Kirk, and so become most worthy to be declared excommunicated, and cut off from the fellowship of Christ and
His Kirk, and to be given over to the hands of Satan,
whose slaves they are, that they may learn, if it so please
God, not to blaspheme Christ or his Gospel,' etc. It is
further added that 'the said Sir James Chisholm being
one of the principal complices and devisers of their most
malicious plots, the said Synod found that they had good
interest and occasion to excommunicate and cut him
off,' etc."

On the 11th of October following, a meeting of delegates was held in Glasgow which was convened "according
to the bond made by our sovereign lord and his estates
for maintenment of true religion." At this meeting "the
noblemen, barons, gentlemen, and ministers of the various
shires" present appointed commissioners, of which John
Napier of Merchiston, Sir James Chisholm's son-in-law,
was one, to meet at Edinburgh with commissioners from
the other provinces of the Kingdom. They met there
on the 17th of October, 1593. But "as Sir James Chisholm was not subject to the jurisdiction of the province
in which he had received sentence of excommunication,
the first act of these commissioners was to ratify all that
had passed, and then to ordain a proclaimation to that
effect from the pulpit of all the Parish Churches on the
following Sunday, which was the 21st. Our philosopher
must have been particularly conspicuous at this convention,
which confirmed the excommunication of his father-in-
law; and his family, if they attended their Parish Church
on the day appointed, heard their grandfather doomed
to exclusion from the social comforts of life, and the
blessings of the Church. The King was strongly opposed

to these measures, and used his utmost endeavours with the Protestant barons and clergy in advance to prevent effect being given to them.   His efforts, however, proved unavailing, the result, on the contrary, being that a select conĩmittee was appointed by the Convention to watch himself, follow him wherever he went, and to lay before him, "in a personal interview, certain well-digested instructions for the rebels, the safety of the Church, and the quieting of the public mind."   This committee, composed of six members, including John Napier, at once sought an interview with His Majesty, but, on the 12th of October, justfive days before the convention that appointed them, James, "harrassed by his clergy and haunted by witches, now dreading the King of Spain, and now in terror for the wild Earl of Bothwell, to whose harlequin treasons he was most unwillingly compelled to play pantaloon, was trotting at the head of his retinue to the Borders, with the temper of a goaded ox.   Suddenly a most unwelcome apparition arrested his progress at Fala.   The Earls of Angus, Huntly, and Errol, and Sir James Chisholm, had been hiding themselves among the mountains.   Aware of the royal progress, they determined to extort some favourable expressions from the King himself, and started up in his path on the highroad at the foot of Sontra Hill. Falling on their knees before him, they earnestly implored a fair trial, and that they should not be condemned unheard.   The King, though favourable to the Popish earls, was very much alarmed for the interpretation that might be put on this audience, and refused to treat with them ; but, instead of ordering them into custody, he dismissed them without committing himself, and immediately sent a report of the whole matter, by the Master of Glammis and the Abbot of Lindores, to Queen Elizabeth's ambassador and the clergy in Edinburgh." The select committee overtook His Majesty at Jedburgh. His reply to their representations was a violent attack on the Synod of Fife for having presumed to excom-

municate Sir James Chisholm, he being beyond the
bounds of its jurisdiction.   They, however, persisted in
making their statement.   The King refused to acknowledge the Edinburgh convention, which was constituted
without his authority, nor the commissioners appointed
by it.   But after a lengthened discussion he agreed to
receive and listen to them as subjects of the realm.   He
excused his reception of the three earls and Sir James
Chisholm at Fala on the ground that they came upon
him by surprise, and under circumstances in which the
meanest of his subjects would, in such an humble attitude,
on the highway, be entitled to secure attention from him.
The conspirators were ultimately brought to trial.   Our
author says—"With increased dislike to his clergy, and
a corresponding growth of favour towards the Popish
conspirators, James brought them to a collusive trial,
which had no other result than the well-known 'Act of
Abolition.'   This was in fact an acquittal under securities
which, in those lawless times, were of very little value.
They were absolved from all the consequences of the
'Spanish Blanks,' upon condition that they were not to
repeat such malpractices; that those of them who embraced the Protestant faith and discipline might remain
in the country within certain appointed bounds; that
they should purge their households of Jesuits, and if
they preferred a voluntary exile, were to become bound
not to plot or practice against their country; that the
Popish earls should find security each in forty thousand
pounds, and Sir James Chisholm and Gordon of Auchindoun each in ten thousand."   He adds in a foot-note—
"The battle of Glenlivet brought this matter to a crisis.
Upon the 8th of June, 1594, the Earls of Angus, Huntly,
Errol, and Auchindoun (who was Huntly's uncle), were
forfeited in Parliament.   Upon the 3rd of October following, Huntly and Errol defeated Argyle and his Highlanders, but Gordon of Auchindoun was slain, and the
Popish earls could make no head against the King himself, who immediately took the field against them.   I can

find no farther trace of Napier's father-in-law (Sir James Chisholm) after the Act of Abolition in which he is mentioned. He is not included in the Act of Forfeiture and sentence of treason passed against the .rest, nor does he appear to have been at the battle of Glenlivet. Probably the philosopher had persuaded him to accept the conditions of the Act of Abolition. His remains lie in a niche in the west wall, inside the nave of the church of Dunblane. His tombstone, executed in low relief, and exhibiting in a mutilated state the family arms, has an inscription in relief, of which the following words are legible :—*Hic jacet honorabilis vir Jacobus Chisholme eques auratus de Dundorn.*"*

Sir James married the daughter and heiress of Drummond of Innerpeffray, in the county of Perth, and by her obtained the lands and barony of that name. By this lady he had issue—

1. Sir James, his heir and successor.

2. Agnes, who, as his second wife, married the celebrated John Napier of Merchistoun, the inventor of Logarithms, with issue—five sons, all of whom founded respectable families, and five daughters, who were all well married. "She was a great-granddaughter of James IV., her grandmother being the daughter of that monarch and his celebrated and ill-fated love, Margaret Drummond. Agnes Chisholm was the second cousin of the philosopher's (John Napier) first wife, Sir James Stirling of Keir having married a daughter of the prelatic concubinage betwixt the Bishop of Dunblane and the Lady Jean Graham, daughter of the Earl of Montrose. She was also the second cousin of his father, whose grandmother was Janet Chisholm of Cromlix."†

Sir James, who died before 1598, was succeeded by his eldest son,

V. SIR JAMES CHISHOLM of Cromlix, of whom little is known, except an interesting account of his courtship

---

* *Memoirs of John Napier of Merchiston,* by Mark Napier.
† *Life of Napier of Merchiston,* Foot-Note p. 157.

and marriage. The Rev. William Marshall, D.D., in his *Historic Scenes in Perthshire* informs us that the fair lady who became Sir James' wife under the most extraordinary circumstances was "the beautiful and lovely daughter of William Stirling, brother of the laird of Ardoch," and that she is known in the local and traditional history of the district as "Fair Helen of Ardoch." "She and Sir James Chisholm, the fifth of Cromlix, were much together in their childhood; loved one another in their teens; and pledged their troth to take one another as husband and wife, as soon as circumstances would permit their union. To complete his education, or for some other purpose, the young knight was in the meantime sent for years to France. Before leaving he arranged for a regular correspondence with his love, without which even the temporary separation would have been intolerable to them. A friend, a young gentleman in the district, was, for certain prudential reasons, to receive the letters of both, which were to be enclosed to him, and was to forward them to their respective destinations. The arrangement wrought well enough for a season. By and bye Sir James' letters became less frequent. At length they ceased altogether. Helen's perplexity and distress can be easily imagined. She wrote him, complaining of his silence, but had no response. The confidant pretended to write him also to the same effect, but had no better success. He was not dead. No misfortune had befallen him. Helen learned that the family in Cromlix were constantly hearing from him, and had the best news of his health, and of his rising honour in France. What could she think in the jealousy of her love but that his heart had changed towards her, and that he was forgetting and forsaking her? The confidant confirmed her worst suspicions and fears, alleging that he had good information from France that the young knight had fallen deeply in love with a noble French lady, whom he was about to lead to the altar.

"Having thus prepared for it, the scoundrel now pro-

posed to Helen. Fortune had lately smiled on him. By
the death of a relative he had come into the possession
of a rich estate in lands and money. The friends in
Ardoch were urgent that he should be accepted; and,
after much delay, and with great reluctance, Helen yielded
to them. The marriage day came. The fair Helen,
arrayed in her bridal attire, was pale as a corpse; and
the sighs she heaved, and the tears that stole down her
cheeks, bespoke the anguish of her spirit. The nuptial
knot was tied; but a scene followed which baffles description. The gay party had no sooner entered the
banquetting hall than the bride, turning to the bride-
groom, denounced him as the basest of villains. As if
the dark plot, of which she had been made the victim,
had been set before her in an instant in the light of
noonday, he had, she cried out, betrayed the sacred
confidence reposed in him. He had kept back her
lover's letters. He had fabricated the story of his seeking
the heart and hand of another. He had in like manner
kept back her letters to her lover; and had written him
that separation had extinguished her affection for him,
and that she wished him to think of her no more.
Cromlix would yet appear to prove his constancy, to
vindicate his honour, and to avenge the wrong that
had been done to him and her. And as for herself,
on no consideration would she for the present quit
the protection of her father's roof. The company were
astounded. Confusion covered the guilty man. He was
speechless; shook like an aspen leaf; and slunk away
with his party, an object of unutterable loathing and horror.
All that Helen said in her impassioned exclamations
was soon verified. Cromlix, indeed, had already landed
in Scotland; he was hastening to Ardoch; and not many
days hence, they embraced with an ecstacy high in proportion to the depth of the misery which both had
suffered. The unconsummated marriage with the villain
confidant was dissolved. As soon as was practicable, her
faithful lover and the fair Helen of Ardoch were united

in the bonds of holy wedlock; and they were the parents
of the James and John whom we have mentioned as the
last Chisholm lairds of Cromlix."

A more extended version of the story is given in
Heroines of Scotland, by Robert Scott Fittis, who says
that "some secret whisper seemed to have reached the
bride's ear" of her lover's arrival in Scotland, as she
stood before the altar. "Young Cromlix had indeed
landed in Scotland, the victim of sorrow and despair. He
had been grossly deceived and slandered. He declared
that after a short period of constant correspondence, he
had written again and again, but no answer from Helen
was returned, and the confidant on being applied to informed him that she had changed her affections, and
desired that he should think of her no more. Smitten by
Helen's charms, this man had suppressed the letters that
he might cause a breach and supplant the favoured lover.
On the homeward voyage Cromlix sought relief for his
lacerated feelings by pouring forth his grief in a simple
melody, which has survived for nearly three centuries, as
a monologue of hopeless love," in the following terms:—

CROMLET'S LILT.

Since all thy vows, false maid,
    Are flown to air,
And my poor heart betrayed
    To sad despair,
Into some wilderness
My grief I will express,
And thy hard heartedness,
    O cruel fair !

Have I not graven our lives
    On every tree
In yonder spreading groves
    Though false thou be?
Was not a solemn oath
Plighted betwixt us both,
Thou thy faith, I my troth,
    Constant to be?

Some gloomy place I'll find,
  Some doleful shade,
Where neither sun nor wind
  E'er entrance had :
Into that hollow cave,
There will I sigh and rave,
Because thou did'st behave
  So faithlessly.

Wild fruit shall be my meat,
  I'll drink the spring ;
Cold earth shall be my seat :
  For covering
I'll have the starry sky
My head to canopy,
Until my soul on high
  Shall spread its wing.

I'll have no funeral fire
  Nor tears for me :
No grave do I desire,
  Nor obsequies :
The courteous redbreast he
With leaves shall cover me,
And sing my elegy,
  With doleful voice.

And when a ghost I am,
  I'll visit thee,
O thou obdured dame,
  Whose cruelty
Hath killed the kindest heart
E'er pierced by Cupid's dart :
No grief my soul shall part
  From loving thee.

Sir James, as we have seen, married Helen, daughter of William Stirling, brother of Stirling of Ardoch. Ardoch's wife and Helen's mother was Margaret, daughter of Murray of Strewan, one of the seventeen sons of Sir William Murray of Tullibardine. In 1617, prior to which she was left a widow, James VI. paid Ardoch a visit while on his way from Perth to Stirling.   The lady met his Majesty on the lawn, surrounded by all her family, dressed up, to receive the King with becoming honour.   His Majesty was struck with the number of children by which the Lady of Ardoch was accompanied, and he asked her —"Madame, how many are there of them ?" "Sire," she replied, "I only want one more to make out the twa chalders." As a chalder contains sixteen bolls, she meant the King to understand that her children numbered thirty-one.   It is said that James enjoyed the lady's remark ex-ceedingly, and that he afterwards paid her the honour of sitting down on a stone close by and eating a collop with her.

By Fair Helen James Chisholm had issue—

1. James, his heir and successor.

2. John, who succeeded his brother James.

3. Jane, who married her cousin, the Honourable James Drummond, second son of David second Lord Drummond. Her husband, the Honourable James Drum-mond, was raised to the Scottish Peerage on the 31st of January, 1609, by the title of Baron Maderty, and to him she carried back the lands of Innerpeffray, which were her mother's portion as daughter and heiress of Drummond of Innerpeffray. It was through this marriage of Jane Chisholm, her mother's sole heiress, that her grandson, General William Drummond, Major-General of the Forces in Scotland and Lord of the Treasury to Charles II., and afterwards, on the 6th of September, 1686, created Viscount Strathallan and Lord Drummond of Cromlix, inherited the Cromlix lands.

Sir James married secondly, about 1612, Margaret, third daughter of William, eighth Earl of Glencairn, with issue —a daughter, who, about 1631, married the Earl of Lothian.†

Anna Chisholm, "a daughter of the familie of Cromlix," married John Rose of Bredley, fourth son of William

† *Douglas's Peerage.*

Rose, XI. of Kilravock, and by him had issue—John Rose, who succeeded him in the lands of Bredley; James Rose, who was a captain in the Earl of Irwin's regiment, and died in France in 1643, after the battle of Rockroy; Captain William Rose of Meft, and afterwards Provost of Nairn, who died on the 25th of November, 1678; Hugh Rose of Newton, who died in December, 1682; Alexander Rose, who had the sole trust of the Earl of Caithness' affairs about the year 1661; and Harry Rose, who was alive in 1683-84. She had also by John Rose several daughters—Anna, who married Alexander Dunbar of Boath; Marie, who married John Dallas of Budzet, Dean of Ross; and Jean, who married James, a son of Mackenzie of Inverlael, and sub-Dean of Ross. Anna Chisholm died on the 31st of May, 1658.*

Sir James was succeeded by his eldest son,

VI. JAMES CHISHOLM of Cromlix, who appears to have been married to a daughter of Sir Ludovick Houston of that Ilk, and to have had issue—one son; for we find a petition to Parliament, on the 5th of August, 1641, from "Ludowick Chisholme onlie lawful son and appearand aer of umquhile James Chisholme of Cromlix," who, being a captain of foot in Lord Drummond's regiment, died at Kelso; and the prayer of the petition is, that ward and marriage may be granted without composition in the name of Sir Ludovick Houston of that Ilk, his gud-sire, and tutor testamentar. Ludovick seems to have died almost immediately after the presenting of this petition, for on the 22nd of September following we find John Chisholm, who describes himself as heir apparent of James, making a similar application.† On the 30th of January, 1647, an Act of Parliament was passed, referred to as the "Act, Laird of Cromlix," but we have not ascertained its purport.

James was succeeded by his brother,

VII. JOHN CHISHOLM, who, in 1661, was one of the

---

* *Kilravock Papers*, pp. 82-83.   † Acts of Parliament for 1641.

commissioners for uplifting £40,000, a portion of which
was ordered to be applied to the liquidation of a debt
owing to Lord Eglington on account of a fine laid on
Chisholm of Cromlix several years before. In 1663 he
was a Justice of the Peace. He appears to have been
twice married, without issue, the second time, in 1661,
to the Lady Creich in Fife, whose "marriage feast was
held at Dunbough," on the 8th of August in that year.*
He must have died before 1669, for in that year William
Drummond, one of the Lords of the Articles, is designated
"of Cromlix."

This gentleman, better known as General Sir William
Drummond, first Viscount Strathallan and Lord Drummond of Cromlix, inherited the Cromlix estates, as already
stated, through his mother, Jane Chisholm. Thomas Hay,
Earl of Dupplin, the sixth Earl of Kinnoul, who was a
Commissioner for the Treaty of Union between England
and Scotland, married Elizabeth, daughter of William,
first Viscount Strathallan, and Lord Drummond of Cromlix, who carried the Chisholm lands of Cromlix to her
husband.

In 1855, Captain Arthur Hay-Drummond, R.N., third
son of the tenth Earl, on the death of his elder brother,
Captain Robert of the Coldstream Guards, from wounds
received in the trenches before Sebastopol, succeeded to
the property, and "assumed the surname and arms of
Drummond of Cromlix and Innerpeffray," these estates
having always been the "appanage of the second son of
the Earls of Kinnoul," since the marriage of Elizabeth, General William Drummond, Viscount Strathallan's
daughter, to the sixth Earl of Kinnoul.

From the marriage of Jane, daughter of Sir James
Chisholm of Cromlix, to the Hon. James Drummond
are descended, not only the Earls of Kinnoul and the
Earls of Strathallan, but also the famous Drummond
bankers of London, who have founded county families of

* *Lamont's Diary.*

their own, and whose descendants formed marriage alliances with many of the leading aristocratic houses of England and Scotland. These now represent the Chisholms of Cromlix and Dundorne in the female line, but it is no part of our present plan to carry the genealogy further.

APPENDIX.

THE following are a few unpublished MS. notes referring to the Clan Chisholm, by the late Mr. James Logan, author of the *Scottish Gael*, supplemented, where indicated, by Mr. Colin Chisholm, Inverness :—

ARMORIAL BEARINGS.

The Chisholm carries, on a shield gules, a boar's head couped, or. *Crest*—A dexter hand, couped at the wrist, holding a dagger proper, on which is transfixed a boar's head of the second. *Supporters*—Two savages wreathed about the head and loins, and bearing knotted clubs, proper. *Motto*—above the arms, "Feros ferio," I smite the fierce animal. Feros, however, is more particularly applied to a wild boar. Underneath is "Vi aut virtute," by strength or by worth.

When Sutherland of Duffus married Morella, sole heiress of The Chisholm, about 1400, azure boar's head erased were added to the armorial bearings.

Cromlix being acquired by the Strathallan family, the boar's head was introduced in the arms, but it has been dropped by the Earls of Kinnoul. [The arms of Cromlix and Drummond of Innerpeffray were since, in 1855, assumed by Captain Arthur Hay-Drummond, R.N., second son of the tenth Earl of Kinnoul, on succeeding at the death of his brother, Robert, "to those estates, the appanage of the second son of the Earls of Kinnoul."]

Hairhope carries, in chief a boar's head erased, and in base two crescents. *Crest*—A boar's head erased.

Chisholm of North Shields, the same crest and motto as Chisholm of London; but the shield is azure, a boar's head erased, argent.

THE BADGE.

The Badge of the Chisholms has been said to be alder. This is not an evergreen, and consequently inappropriate. A better authenticated account assigns them the Rainneach or Fern, as their Suaicheantas.

THE BREACAN OR PLAID.

The Breacan or Plaid is classed among the red tartans, and shows a pretty arrangement of colours.

THE BRATACH OR CLAN BANNER.

The "Fear na Bratach," or standard-bearer of one clan, was by Celtic usage selected from another, or bore a different name, as with the Macgregors whose banner-men were Macphersons. That of the Chisholms was Ian na Bratach, who had carried it at Culloden, and survived long after the "affair of the '45." [His name was Macdonald. He afterwards emigrated to Canada.]

THE CHISHOLM PIOBAIREACHD.

The Piobaireachd or Gathering of the Clan is called Failte Siosalach Straghlais, being a Welcome or Salute. There is a traditional story applied to its origin which has also been applied to Macneil's March, and is allusive to the hospitality of the chief, who kept a table always spread for the entertainment of visitors. The pipers of the Chisholms were originally Camerons. There is a curious relic preserved from time immemorial at Erchless Castle. The story of this relic is told at pp. 73-74. The Chisholms were accounted excellent musicians, and the chiefs had often both fiddler and piper in their establishment, and two of these being contemporaries were remarkable for having each 'had five wives!

ORIGINAL CLAN LANDS IN MORAYSHIRE.

Of the lands in Morayshire which formerly belonged to The Chisholm, but have been carried off by intermarriages, are Quarrelwood, Clova, Clunie, Cantra, Kinstarie, Brightmonie, the Grieshop, Geddes, and several other lands in Strathnairn. Urquhart was in 1497, by decreet arbitral, adjudged to Rose of Kilravock, after a litigation with Mackintosh, and it is presumed the right was acquired through the marriage of Janet, heiress of Sir Robert Lauder, constable of the Castle of Urquhart, in 1354. Paxton in Tweeddale, which appears to have been in their possession before 1400, was carried to the Sutherlands of Duffus by the marriage of Morella.

PRESENT POSSESSIONS IN THE COUNTY OF INVERNESS.

The estates in Rhindoun and Strathglass are the present possessions of the family, with a portion of the Dabhach of Buntait in Gleann Urchadan.

The country of the Chisholms is remarkably picturesque, of a truly Highland character. The woods have suffered much, and the district, which must have exhibited extensive remains of the Caledonian Forest, is comparatively denuded.

The fir used by Cromwell in the construction of the Citadel at Inverness was entirely the product of the pine woods of Strathglass and Glenstrathfarrar. The great wood of Afrig is now much denuded, but there are still considerable cuttings; its former magnitude must have been nearly 20 miles in length and of proportionable breadth.

A CLAN BATTLE.

There is a prevalent tradition of a battle in which the clan were engaged, but the exact period at which it took place does not appear. A laird of Chisholm having carried off a daughter of Lord Lovat, he concealed her in an islet in Loch Bruiach, where she was discovered by her father, who had come to the rescue. A severe conflict ensued, but the issue is not recorded. Numerous tumuli attest the sanguinary event, and a plaintive Gaelic song deplores the catastrophe, which was deepened by the death of the young lady, who was accidentally slain by her own brother in the confusion of pursuit.

LIBERATING A CRIMINAL.

One of the clansmen having been put in the black hole at Beauly for theft, and condemned to death for some depredation by Lord Lovat, the Chisholms, determined to prevent a disgrace which would attach to the clan from a public execution of one of the tribe, went in a body and liberated their kinsman, carrying him off without detection. His grandson was accustomed, probably as an acknowledgment of the debt of gratitude owing by his family, to carry to Erchless a portion of prepared barley, for which he never would accept the smallest remuneration.

HUGH CHISHOLM (MACLEA), PROTECTOR OF PRINCE CHARLES.

When the unfortunate Prince Charles was wandering in the

mountains with a reward of £30,000 for his apprehension, his con-
cealment and his actual preservation depended on three poor
Highlanders who knew his retreat, and, eluding the vigilance of
the military, carried to his cave the few necessaries they could
procure. These three were the last that parted with him when he
left Arisaig, and one of them Hugh Siosal (Maclea), after shaking
the right hand of his Prince would never more give his own to
any man. Finlay Macmillan and Kennedy were the other two and
their names deserve to be recorded with the most magnanimous
and high minded of mankind.

[Mr Colin Chisholm informs us, on the lady's own authority,
that "as an act of great condescension he (Hugh Chisholm) gave
his right hand to Mary, the only child of his chief, The Chisholm.
At the same time he took special care to explain to Miss Chisholm
(afterwards Mrs James Gooden, of Tavistock Square, London,) that
she was the first and would certainly be the last to shake hands
with him after Prince Charles." The same gentleman says that
" Kennedy, who fought in the battle of Culloden, was afterwards
hanged in Inverness for stealing a cow! Yet this unfortunate
Highlander could have secured £30,000 for betraying his Prince."]

DISTINGUISHED CLANSMEN.

There lived in the year 1567 a gentleman named Chisholm who
was noted for his architectural knowledge. Queen Mary, anno
1567, ratifies and approves a charter of infeftment to her "lovit
servitoure Johne Chisholme, his aires and assignais."

Among those members of the clan who have distinguished themselves with credit may be mentioned one who is celebrated as assisting to improve the Wedgewood manufacture.

In 1808 Mr Chisholm, an architect, died at Carlisle. He was
a native of Aberdeen, and his biographer observes, "never did the
grave close upon a man more useful, or more entitled to the esteem
and reverence of his survivors."—*Gentleman's Magazine.*

THE CHISHOLM'S FOOL.

As was customary of old, with chiefs, and great lairds, every family
retained a fool or jester. One of the Chisholms was afflicted with
bad legs so much that he was deprived of the power of walking
and had to be carried about. When, one fine summer evening, he
was carried to a couch placed for him in the garden, seeing his
fool there he called him, in order to remain with him, for the purpose of keeping the flies off his legs. The fool carried a large
stick in his hand, and seeing a swarm of flies resting on his

master's leg, he suddenly aimed a blow at them, but to his astonishment, instead of destroying the flies, he nearly broke the chief's legs, and threw him into a swoon. Thinking that he had killed his master, the fool ran away as fast as he could to the neighbouring wood. When the servants returned to the garden to take their master home, they were much alarmed to find him in such a pitiable condition. On coming to himself, he told them what the fool, who was nowhere to be seen, had done. A search was made, but when they were on the point of giving it up as fruitless, the fool, from the top of a thickly branched tree, bawled out—"Ye needna sirs, for myself has just got myself." Having decoyed him down, and expostulated with him on the injury he had done to his master, he said, "It was the flies that did it, not me." But in the end it turned out, as the story goes, that The Chisholm's jester was the best physician his master ever had; for the decease in his legs disappeared altogether shortly after the sound slashes given them by Donald, the fool.—*Colin Chisholm.*

MARRIAGE OF BISHOP WILLIAM CHISHOLM'S ILLEGITIMATE DAUGHTER TO SIR JAMES STIRLING OF KEIR.

In a contract of marriage, dated the 23rd of February, 1571-72, the following reference to the marriage of Bishop William Chisholm's daughter, Jane, to Sir James Stirling of Keir. mentioned at page 195 of this work, occurs :—" Till all and sindry. . . . . Archibald Naper of Edinbillie, Knycht, that albeit the Rycht Honorabill Sir James Striveling of Keir, Knycht, with consent and assent of *Jane Cheisholime, his spouse,* for fulfilling of ane contract of mairage maid betwix thame and Elizabeth Striveling ; thair dochter, on the ane part, ánd ane reverend fader in God, Adam, Bishop of Orknay, Commendator of Halyrudehouse, me the said Archibald and Johne Naper my sone and apperand air, on the uther part, for mairage to be maid and solmnized betwix the saidis Elizabeth and Johne Naper."—*Memoirs of John Napier of Merchiston,* p. 130.

INDEX.

www.ingramcontent.com/pod-product-compliance
Lightning Source LLC
Chambersburg PA
CBHW020100030726

47498CB00006B/1873

* 9 7 8 3 3 3 7 3 2 2 1 0 6 *